Discovering Inverness-shire

q13 -

This book is to be returned on or before
the last date stamped below.

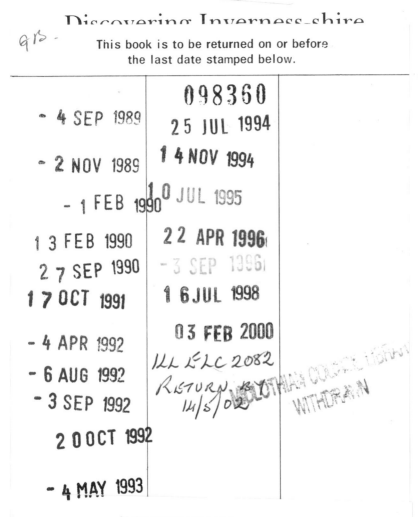

Discovering
Inverness-shire

LORAINE MACLEAN OF DOCHGARROCH

JOHN DONALD PUBLISHERS LTD
EDINBURGH

ISBN 0 85976 228 9

Thanks go to the following for permission to reproduce illustrations in the book: K.M. Andrew Esq; Colin Graham-Stewart Esq; the Highlands and Islands Development Board; Inverness District Council; J.A. McCook, Photographers, Nethy Bridge; the National Trust for Scotland; John Paul, Photographer, Inverness; and D.C. Thomson & Co. Ltd.

Phototypesetting by Newtext Composition Ltd., Glasgow.
Printed in Great Britain by Bell & Bain Ltd., Glasgow.

Before We Set Out

In reverting to the traditional stories fondly listened to in early life, the generality of men are apt to see them through the mists of memory magnified in proportion as they are imperfectly beheld — hence amid an ardent race like the Highlanders of the North, whose medium of communication from generation to generation has in a great degree been tradition, a variety of clannish anecdotes, originally of small account, even when founded in fact, have been occasionally magnified into local importance by their Bards and followers, the descendants of former rival clans.

But it is to a long succession of Southern Travellers who have assiduously sought, and sedulously listened to, the nightly rehearsal of the old men and women of the Glens, conversant with their weaknesses and wishes, that we chiefly owe those hordes of printed Highland anecdotes, which, like a rolling snowball, have been magnified wonderfully as they have passed from the earlier to the more recent Tourists' volumes, insomuch that the true Highlanders, even when most flattered by their exaggeration, have marvelled at, and pitied, their simplicity and folly.

So wrote Lieutenant General Sir Alan Cameron of Erracht, K.C.B. in 1827, and I feel that I am being rather rash in adding another Volume, even if it is not aimed particularly at the Tourists, but I hope that he will forgive me and that the Gentle Reader will enjoy the Stories about his beloved Highlanders of the North and of his County.

Contents

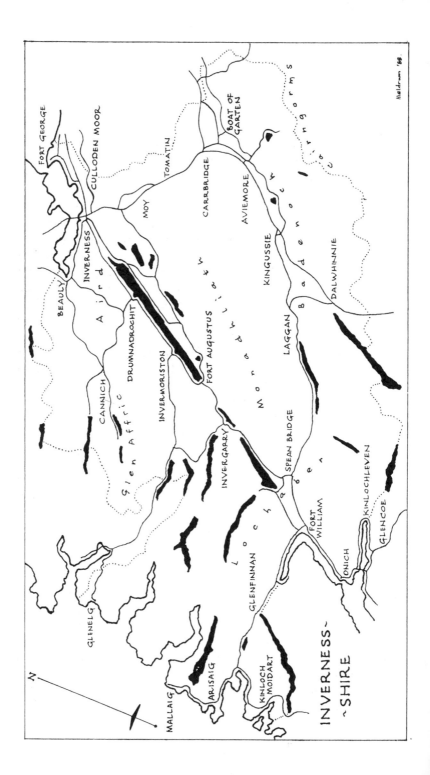

INVERNESS-
^SHIRE

Meldrum '66.

Introduction

When Dundee's army camped in Glen Spean in 1689 the weary men were convinced that they had come to the edge of the world. Waking the next day, they found that they were still in Inverness-shire, and that there were people living 'beyond the edge of the world'. The Lochaber people had been there for a very long time then, as they told the visitors, saying that they had once lived in the trees and then came down to the ground. For centuries they had lived on the ground as animals before they stood up and became men. They were a peaceful and easy-going lot until King Fergus heard of them and came to see what they were like. He had a large net constructed, and then drove the Lochaber people up into Glen Nevis, closing the entrance with the net. Having caught the whole population, the king released them and taught them Christianity and the Arts of War, in that order. From then on they were good Christians and doughty warriors, supporting the monarchy. Dundee's Standard-bearer, James Philip of Almericlose, listened to this story, took notes and put it into his account of the campaign, which he called *The Grameid* and wrote in Latin couplets. Perhaps Charles Darwin read it before he thought of his Theory of Evolution, but more likely, he did not.

This is a personal journey, Discovering Inverness-shire, so it is biased. Tom Anderson, from the Northern Isles, was quoted in *The Scotsman* in May, 1987. He said, 'Knowledge is not yours to keep. It's only on loan from whichever source it comes, and, if you don't pass it on, that's it finished'. The Scottish Women's Rural Institutes say, 'If you know a good thing, pass it on'.

There will be a list of books for further reading, which should be available through any good library, even if they are not on the shelves. Much of the information here comes from books, and much from good friends, many of whom are 'Rural' members, that is, they belong to the Scottish Women's Rural Institutes and so are knowledgeable about their own part of the world. My thanks to all and every one who provided stories and facts — one is the same as the other as often as not — and to those who have provided the illustrations.

This book covers only the mainland part of the country, with part of Appin in Argyll which is now in the Highland Region. It is written for those who travel the roads, by foot, bicycle, bus or car, or even in the imagination. It supposes an ability to read a map. The places are identified by map references, since some people think in miles and some in kilometres. It is not difficult to learn how to find a map reference; instructions are found on the margin of the recommended maps. These are the Ordnance Survey Landranger series, 1:50,000 (1¼ ins to 1 mile, 2 cm to 1 km) numbers 25, 26, 27, 33, 34, 35, 36, 40, 41, 42.

So far, so good. Unfortunately, Inverness-shire is not found on any of these maps, for since 1975 it has been swallowed up in the large Highland Region. The modern maps do not show the parish boundaries, either, which makes them useless for those tracing their ancestors. The useful 1 inch maps, which showed these details, are now out of print.

Inverness-shire therefore needs to be discovered.

There are seven main roads that leave the Royal Burgh of Inverness to go any distance. Six of them will be followed in due course, and the side roads, too, but the seventh, the A9 on its way north over the Kessock Bridge into Ross-shire, is so short as not to be considered, although the views from the bridge, which has pavements for walking or bicycling across, can be very fine, with splendid sunsets for photographers and probably equally good sunrises. The others, in a clockwise direction from the Kessock Bridge, are as follows:

The A96, the Aberdeen road. '
The B9006, the Culloden road.
The A9, the Perth and Edinburgh road.
The B862, the Dores, Whitebridge and Fort Augustus road.
The A82, the Drumnadrochit, Fort William and Glasgow road.
The A862, the Beauly and Dingwall road.

There are also roads that lead from these six, and they are described as they are met along the way.

When driving in the Highlands the usual Rules of the Road apply, speed limits and so on, but there are some other points to be noticed:

On 6 August, 1982, the Queen Mother unveiled the plaque that marks the opening of the Kessock Bridge. The Bridge carries the A9 northward over the sea and joins Inverness-shire to Ross and Cromarty.

1) Although there are a few miles of dual carriageway on the A9, there are so few anywhere else that they are not worth looking for.

2) Most roads are now double track, but there are still a good many that are SINGLE TRACK. These need special care.

a) There are Passing Places, usually marked by a white diamond on a pole. Use these to allow oncoming vehicles to pass, either by slipping into the nearest one on the left side of the road, or by stopping opposite the nearest one on the other side. If the oncoming vehicle is very large, it is sometimes better to cross the road and go into the Passing Place, but this is unusual. Use them ALSO to allow cars to OVERTAKE. The car behind could be a doctor on his way to a patient.

b) When near a passing place, look ahead to see if another vehicle is coming. This may save having to back to a passing place.

c) NEVER PARK IN A PASSING PLACE.

3) If towing a caravan or a trailer of any sort, or if just enjoying the view, or slightly apprehensive about the steepness of the road, and the rear-view mirror shows that there are vehicles behind, it is best to pull in to the next available space on the left side of the road and let them pass. If no more than three or four are held up, the delay will be less than a minute.

4) If another driver gives way, a lifted hand in thanks costs nothing, but courtesy eases the blood pressure on both sides.

5) When in a long queue of traffic, stay far enough back from the car in front to allow any idiot, who will overtake when he cannot see, space to get safely to his proper side of the road.

6) Any queue is usually the fault of the second car in the line, unless the leader is not allowing the second to pass (see 3 above). It is not so difficult to overtake one car, but to overtake more is often dangerous. Incidentally, if traffic is held up by a driver not letting his car be overtaken, he can be charged by the Police for Not Driving with Due Care and Attention.

7) Any LAMB, and they can be quite a size by the summer, will appear from nowhere and dash across the road to join its mother. They make a horrid mess of the car that hits them and the driver has to go and report it to the police.

8) ALWAYS REMEMBER THAN ANOTHER DRIVER MAY BE AS BIG A FOOL AS YOU ARE.

> I like to live by the side of the road,
> Where the race of men go by.
> The men that are good and the men that are bad,
> As good and as bad as I.

All that having been said, Inverness-shire is there, waiting for the explorers.

The county stretches 'from sea to shining sea'. The westernmost point lies far out beyond the Outer Isles at Rockall, best known as one of the areas mentioned in the shipping forecasts, which is 180 miles beyond St Kilda, and St Kilda is forty miles west of North Uist, which is one of the Outer Isles, most of which were in the old county of Inverness, but this book does not cover them. Fort George, the most northerly point of the county on the mainland, twelve miles

Pipe Sergeant Paul Mackillop in 1890. 'We raise our hats to the Old Brigade ... men who spent their lives with the colours. The Pipe Major was one of the figures in the town.' He joined the 74th Highlanders (the Highland Light Infantry) when he was 18, and served for 21 years in the West Indies and America, and then another 25 years in the Inverness Militia. His presentation stick is in the Regimental Museum in Fort George.

east of Inverness, lies approximately on a line that passes between Leningrad and Moscow, through the middle of Kamschatka, across the Pacific Ocean to a landfall at about Admiralty Island in Alaska, over the Belcher Islands in Hudson's Bay and so home, south of Lochmaddy to Fort

George. West of Rockall the nearest land is south of Cape
Mugford on the coast of Labrador.

Inverness-shire has the highest mountain in Britain, Ben
Nevis, 4406 feet, and, with the Glencoe area covered in this
book, 187 of the 276 'Munros' (hills over 3000 feet, 914.4m) in
Scotland. If Skye is included in the county, another 22 Munros
come into the total. The county has the deepest loch, Loch
Morar, 1080 feet (180 fathoms), and the biggest geological
fault, the Great Glen, which splits the county from north-east
to south-west in a way that makes geological maps most
unusual, the matching pieces of rock are so far apart. Whether
or not as a result of this, the county is also the home of the
Loch Ness Monster, and her cousin Morag who lives in Loch
Morar.

The Royal Burgh of Inverness was given the title *The Hub of
the Highlands* when the Inverness Field Club published its
Centenary Volume in 1975, and so it is, but it is by no means the
centre of Inverness-shire. Indeed, it lies only twelve miles west
of the county boundary with Nairn; its industrial area runs to
the southern end of the Kessock Bridge, which, soaring over
the sea, joins the counties of Inverness and Ross; while
Drumochter Pass, the boundary with Perthshire, is some sixty
miles south of the Royal Burgh. It is a little west of Plymouth
on the south coast of England. The weather map on the
television set is not set correctly.

Since Inverness lies so far north, it might be supposed that
the winters are hard and long, but this is not so. 'I have often
thought that the climate of Inverness might be used to more
purpose in advertising the town as a holiday resort. Our
rainfall is among the lowest in Scotland; our temperature,
especially in winter, is high, while our freedom from
thunderstorms is remarkable'. So wrote a nineteenth century
inhabitant of Inverness. The Gulf Stream sends a warm
current down both sides of Scotland, with a finger into the
Inverness Firth, so that the difference in temperature in the
winter between the town and a place even a few miles inland
can be considerable. In exceptionally hard winters the Beauly
Firth has been known to freeze, as it did in 1895, but Loch
Ness, because of its depth, keeps a consistent temperature of
42°F so that in winter it steams gently if the air is colder than

Competitors in the Women's Sword Dance at the Newtonmore
Highland Games. The piper stands behind them, but the dancers are
raised on a platform for the convenience of the judges and to give the
competitors a good surface for dancing. Meanwhile the other
competitions, hammer-throwing, racing, putting the weight and so on,
are taking place in other parts of the playing field.

that, but it does not freeze over. The average rainfall in Glen
Urquhart is thirty inches a year, about the same as
Bournemouth on the south coast of England.

The headquarters of almost everything are found in the
Royal Burgh, including the Regional Headquarters, the
Highlands and Islands Development Board, the Northern
Police and, of course, the hospitals, whether for bodies or
minds. The Regimental Headquarters of the Queen's Own
Highlanders (Seaforth and Camerons) is at the Cameron
Barracks, though their Museum is at Fort George. The
Inverness, Loch Ness and Nairn Tourist Information Centre
is in Church Street. There are others in Aviemore, Kingussie,
Fort Augustus and Fort William. Unfortunately, the burgh
fathers over the years have been prone to demolish what
buildings they thought would be better down, so few ancient

buildings have survived either their propensities or the frequent fires of earlier days.

When driving round the glens, the outlines of walls of houses and steadings can often be seen, and it is frequently said that they were much higher once but were demolished 'in the Clearances' or 'to build newer houses', and this can well be true, but the country houses (not 'The Country Houses', though some of them were not much better) were generally very primitive affairs, with stone footings that kept the bottom dry, but above that the walls were made of turfs cut from the hills. The fire, of wood or peat, which seldom went out, was for long in the middle and the smoke made its way as best it could through a hole in the roof, but tended to curl about before it found its way out, depositing a layer of soot on the 'ceiling'. Every few years the roof was taken off and used to fertilise the fields and replaced by a new one above the couples (wooden supports) which had their bases above the mud floor in spaces in the stone footings and carried the not inconsiderable weight of the roof. This was of turf or heather or, if in an agricultural area, straw thatch. When, for whatever reason, the roof was left off, the turf walls soon tumbled into a muddy mess over the stones, to be washed away entirely by the weather. Sometimes the walls above the footings would be of wood and the houses were often lined with wooden walls which were considered to be 'very snug'. But when Sir Allan Maclean of Duart, the chief of his clan, entertained Boswell and Johnson in his house on Inchkenneth in 1773 the good doctor found the floor muddy.

Many of the stories that survive are of 'battle, murder and sudden death', not because they were everyday occurrences, but because they were not. It has been calculated that the total of deaths in all the affrays and skirmishes between the clans comes nowhere near the deaths caused in England by the Wars of the Roses alone.

The Clan Maps that can be bought all over Scotland, showing the whole country neatly divided into colourful patches named Fraser, Cameron, Murray, and so on, are very misleading. The so-called Clan System is not of long standing: according to one learned paper the phrase is first found towards the end of the nineteenth century! To take one family, the Macleans, whose base is in Mull: the Macleans of Ardgour on Loch Linnhe have been there since about 1432 and Macleans have been settled in and around Glen Urquhart and Inverness since Tearlach arrived as Constable of Urquhart Castle for the Lord of the Isles in 1392. For obvious reasons they were rather cut off from their cousins, the nearest being at Ardgour, so they joined forces with Mackintosh and Macpherson and others in the Clan Chattan Federation and were among those who later signed the Clan Chattan Bond in 1609. Fortunately there has been no conflict between Duart and Mackintosh since then! Frasers were to be found on both sides of Loch Ness. Grants were brought from Strathspey to put out the northern Macleans. And so on.

The same rather goes for Tartan. The Highlanders are fond of cheerful colours but the gaudy setts of today would not have been of practical use to a man stalking his dinner, or raiding cattle further from home. The Gaelic for Tartan is Breachan, the root of which is Breac, meaning spotted, speckled, chequered, piebald. Remember Allan Breck Stewart in Stevenson's *Kidnapped*? He had had small-pox. Breac is a trout. When Martin Martin wrote about the Highlands and Islands in 1703, he expressly said that the tartans were used to distinguish the inhabitants of different districts, not different families. Born in Skye, he knew what he was talking about. Since the wool was dyed with whatever plants were available to the weaver, the colours were limited by the local flora. It was because no one could tell from his tartan on what side any man was, even as late as 1745, that the Jacobite army wore a white cockade in their bonnets and the Highlanders fighting on the side of the Government wore a black one.

The first regimental tartan was that of the 42nd, the Royal Highland Regiment, better known from their dark tartan as The Black Watch. The tartan is by no means black. Most of the other Highland regiments wore versions of this sett. The odd one out was the 79th Regiment, the Queen's Own Cameron Highlanders, which was considered later to be the county regiment of Inverness. Its tartan was designed by Marsaili Maclean of Drimnin, the mother of their founder, Sir Alan Cameron of Erracht. It is now worn by members of the Queen's Own Highlanders (Seaforth and Camerons) who also wear the so-called Mackenzie tartan of the Seaforth

Highlanders. Here the clan took over the regimental tartan for
their own use.

The bravery of the Highland regiments in the French and
Napoleonic Wars recommended tartan to the rest of the world,
particularly and oddly, to the French. The visit of George IV to
Edinburgh in 1823 and the 'Balmorality' that swept Society
when Queen Victoria spent her holidays in the Highlands kept
the fashion going, so that now families whose forebears would
sooner have died than be seen even wearing a kilt, let alone a
tartan one, can be seen all over the August society papers fairly
dripping with it. It is not considered right to wear a regimental
tartan unless the wearer once belonged to that regiment, but
although the other tartans are free to all, wearing a Campbell
kilt when among Campbells without any connection with that
clan is liable to be somewhat embarassing, as would be a
Cameron kilt among Camerons. There is nothing to prevent
anyone from designing a new tartan. One attractive new one is
the 'Hunting Cameron' which was designed by a man who
descended from a well-known Cameron, An Taillear Dubh, the
Black Tailor, but whose surname had developed as Taylor
rather than Cameron and who felt that it was not for him to
wear the ordinary Cameron tartan. Lochiel has since accepted
it as the Hunting Cameron. But females should avoid wearing
a kilt: their figures are not the right shape. A well-cut skirt
looks much better.

A word about Gaelic. It is probably no more difficult to learn
than any other language, but the written words do look odd
and the arrangement of the sentences is not the same as in
English – and no more is a German sentence. In Gaelic the
verb comes first, as a general rule, and the adjective usually
follows the noun that it modifies. There is no word for 'a', so
Tha Domhnall An Taillear Dubh is 'Donald is the Black
Tailor', but Tha Domhnall taillear math is 'Donald is a good
tailor'. The verbs conjugate and the nouns decline as in Latin,
which is why words alter. The spelling is, despite the look of
the words, regular and the words can be pronounced from
their letters. The principal rule is 'Broad to broad and Slender
to slender' – the broad vowels are a, o and u, the slender vowels
being e and i. The word *vowel* could not be written in Gaelic, o
being broad and e slender: it would have to be *vowal*. BH and

MH are pronounced as V, so in old Episcopalian prayer books Ar Ban-righ BHICTORIA is found, and h modifies the consonant it follows, so that THA is pronounced HA. The general rule is that the emphasis in a word is on the first important syllable, *Mall*aig, Mac*don*ald. Through this book some place names are translated, but not all.

The principal games played are golf, bowls and football, but in the country the ancient game of shinty has its own leagues and competitions. It is not unlike hockey, but to say that is to say that American baseball is not unlike rounders, and just about as popular. Once the autumn term has started in August small boys and their seniors can be seen carrying curved sticks. These are the camans with which the game is played on a large pitch. It is worth stopping to watch a game, if the chance arises.

So here is Inverness-shire, waiting to be visited. Ceud mile failte do siorrachd Inbhirnis – a hundred thousand welcomes to Inverness-shire!

CHAPTER 1

The Royal Burgh of Inverness

Inverness is an ancient place. Recent excavations in and around the town have produced evidence of our early predecessors. Some were living near Stoneyfield on a site (687456) now destroyed by the A9, as far back as the early Mesolithic period, about 5000 B.C., while a long bank of oyster shells at Muirtown, west of the Canal, shows that Stone Age people were there. In Castle Street itself, just to the north of Raining's Stairs, more Mesolithic finds showed occupation about 4000 B.C. Compared with this, the burned remains of houses dating from the thirteenth to fifteenth centuries on the same site are

The Camanachd Cup Final, the greatest moment in the Shinty year. From August to June the clubs battle against each other to reach this moment. Kingussie and Newtonmore are famous rivals, but occasionally an unexpected finalist arrives, as happened in 1988, when Glen Urquhart reached the final for the first time in 103 years, to be beaten but not disgraced, the score being 4-2 in favour of Kingussie.

12

as yesterday's buildings. A new shopping complex has just been built on this site.

Inverness exists because it stands at the lowest crossing of the River Ness. The river, only six miles long from the loch to the sea, flows with an unpolluted stream for its whole length, giving a setting of great beauty to the centre of the town, even with the present ugly modern buildings on its east bank. In few towns of any size can one lean on the parapet of the main bridge and watch seals playing, people fishing for salmon and others swimming – though not all at the same time. The proposed fish farms in Loch Ness are likely to deter the wild salmon from venturing up the river and may pollute it.

Although there was a settlement here so long ago, its original name is unknown. Inverness, meaning the mouth of the River Ness, is a Gaelic word. The Pictish language, apart from its King Lists, has been lost, for the Picts do not seem to have known writing although they were perhaps the most artistic race ever to have inhabited these islands. They used a curious, but sensible, method of inheritance. They were ruled by kings, but the king was not succeeded by his son, but by a relative through the female line: the king's sister's son, or the king's mother's sister's son. It is fairly certain who a man's mother is, but the father's identity can be rather more doubtful.

Brude was king of the Northern Picts, his rule stretching from Shetland to Perthshire, in the second half of the sixth century. St Columba visited him (and had a few words with a monster in the river) in 565 A.D. It is not known for certain where Brude lived. Some say that it was the vitrified fort on the top of Craig Phadrig, from which a splendid view can be had, but there is no apparent water supply there, and Auldcastle Hill may well have been the place. Bede describes Brude as 'a powerful monarch who, a few years after he commenced his reign, attacked the Dalriads and drove them back to their original seat in Kintyre, slaying their King Gabran'. St Columba was anxious about his Scottish kin, the Scots being an Irish tribe that settled in the part of Argyll known as Dalriada. It was basically a political visit, though no doubt he confronted Brude's priests. The earliest Christian missionaries had been in the neighbourhood a couple of hundred years before Columba came. Their roots were in the south at Candida Casa, St

Ninian's foundation at Whithorn in Galloway; they left their names, some known sites and some legends, but no records.

Inverness was the headquarters of the Province of Moray, one of the most powerful in Scotland. The best known of all the Mormaers, or Rulers, of Moray is also the best-known of all the Scottish kings, and the most maligned, Maelbeatha, better known as Macbeth. He had a good claim to the kingdom, only partly through his wife, Gruoch, and when Duncan, who was about thirty years old, was killed in a battle for the crown, Macbeth succeeded him in 1040 and reigned for seventeen years, though he moved his power-base from Inverness to Scone in Perthshire, on the southern edge of the old Northern Pictish kingdom. He made a treaty with Thorfinn of Orkney which kept the Norsemen from attacking the country. He is said to have gone on pilgrimage to Rome, which implies a stable state of affairs in Scotland, and he was on good terms with the Dukes of Normandy (who were to conquer and occupy England in 1066). Macbeth was killed at Lumphanan in Mar in 1057 in action against an army led by Malcolm III, Canmore (Big Head), Duncan's son, who had been raised at, and was backed by, the English court.

Although people had been living by the river crossing for so long, Inverness did not become a Royal Burgh until David I founded it as such between 1153 and 1165. It was then a 'new town', laid out to a standard plan, as were others at that time. At Inverness the Castle was built at the south end of the town, commanding the crossing. A street, now Castle Wynd and Church Street, joined the Castle to the Parish Church, and ran on to the harbour. To the north of the Castle, at the Cross, which stood at the place where the streets met, later called The Exchange, Bridge Gait (now Bridge Street) ran down to the Bridge and points west. East Gait, now the High Street, came in from the east; what is now Eastgate was Petty Street. The road from the south, Over Gait, or Deemsdale, now Castle Street, completed the skeleton of the burgh. King William the Lion, in 1180, in the town's first known charter, required the burgesses to build a timber palisade inside a fosse, which the king had had constructed. Inverness seems never to have had a stone defensive wall, but there was a ring of small motte castles around it.

Inverness Silver. Although silver objects have been made in Inverness for centuries, silver marked with the Inverness Assay Mark is hard to find, but this napkin ring shows the marks for 1977. The Queen's Head is there because this was the year of her Silver Jubilee.

Not only was the town new, it was 'planted' with Lowland Scots, and perhaps even English. They were craftsmen and merchants who traded in the produce of the hinterland, but the numbers were small, sheltered between the river and the walls, and did not really spread beyond them until the eighteenth century. There were linking vennels and, as more settled times arrived, courtyard houses developed. The houses in Church Street had gardens and orchards running down to the river at the end of the eighteenth century and the town, though small, was full of open spaces, though the Foul Pool still lay along what is now Academy Street and earned its name, for 'from the effluent from the Tan-pits behind Kirk Street came the Foul Pool'.

Fortunately for Inverness, after the Wars of Independence most of the more stirring events in Scottish history took place elsewhere. When troubles came, the people must have feared for their lives and property. Wooden houses and thatched roofs were easily burned when the Castle was besieged, taken and relieved. In 1410 the Lord of the Isles, annoyed by a rather cool reception, burned the Bridge, 'the famousest and finest off Oak in Brittain'.

The early Castle was probably on Auldcastle Hill and the first fortified place on the present site was built by King David. This would have been a motte-and-bailey with wooden buildings until Alexander of Mar, the Justiciar of the North, became Governor in 1412. He put up stone fortifications. The Castle was later held for the Crown by the Earl of Huntly and in 1508 he was ordered to build a strong stone tower 'upon vaults of stone . . . 100 feet by 30 feet by 30 feet high, covered with slate, with a kitchen in the hall and a chapel of competent length beside it'. He did nothing, but the buildings were probably completed by 1540.

Alexander Gordon was commanding in 1562 when Mary, Queen of Scots, not unreasonably demanded admittance to her own Castle. He refused her request and she slept in a house at the north-west end of Bridge Street, which was demolished in 1969, by order of the Secretary of State, despite objections from the people of Inverness and elsewhere. The barrel-vaulted cellars have been turned through a right-angle and rebuilt inside the entrance to the offices of the Highlands and Islands Development Board on Bank Street, where anyone may walk in and see them. To return to Mary: with the help of the Mackintoshes and Frasers, she took the Castle and Alexander Gordon was duly hanged.

In 1726 General George Wade set up his headquarters here and enlarged the Castle, turning it into a barracks for his troops and calling it Fort George, after his king rather than himself. The Castle was finally destroyed when one of Prince Charles Edward Stuart's French engineers blew it up, killing himself in the explosion and blowing his dog across the river. The dog lost its tail, but survived the blast.

The present buildings date from 1833-6, when the southern end was built in the 'English Gothick Castellated' style and it is now the Sheriff Court House. The northern end, built as the Gaol, was added in 1848. All that survives of the old Castle is the well, nearly fifty feet deep, and a part of the walling at the top of Castle Wynd.

Despite the distant origins of the Royal Burgh, modern Inverness is a railway town. It has a small centre, though it has

A 4-6-0 Jones Goods Locomotive, fitted with a snow plough, standing outside the Loch Gorm Works at Inverness c. 1905. This is now known as the Scotrail diesel depot. Even today, the railways can be cleared of snow more easily than the roads, and often are the only lifeline to the north when blizzards come.

spread widely round its edges during the last twenty years, so it is not difficult to walk round and see what has been left of the older buildings. The old centre lies more or less at sea level, but the Escarpment, an ancient sea-beach, rises up behind the High Street and Castle Street and runs out to the east. The red sandstone Castle has now been watching over the town for about a century and a half. By walking round it, two of the fine views to the north and south can be enjoyed. To the north, the scene includes the river, the Firth, the Black Isle and Ben Wyvis, often snow-capped in the autumn and usually in the winter. To the south of the Castle, Flora Macdonald and her dog (rare in a statue, though Sir Walter Scott has Maida with him in Princes Street in Edinburgh) gaze up the Great Glen to see whether Prince Charles is coming back to Inverness.

Across the river is the Episcopal Cathedral of St Andrew, dedicated in 1869 and consecrated (being free of debt) in 1874.

The original design, by Dr Alexander Ross, shows that the towers should have had twin spires, but these were never built. This must be one of the few cathedrals of which the architect has lived to be present at its Jubilee, in 1924. So many churches did Dr Ross build in the Highlands that it was jokingly said that the Diocese of Moray and Ross was named for him!

Castle Street used to have houses on both sides. The Overgait Port, or Gate, was where the Baptist church is now. Look at the roofs of the houses where snow-boards, which protect the passers-by from sudden falls of slush when a thaw comes, can be seen. As in most towns, the shops at street level are all much of a muchness to look at, but when the higher storeys are examined, they prove to be very different. The houses in Castle Street have largely been rebuilt, but some eighteenth-century houses can be recognised, such as 33-37, which has corbie-steps on the gable and a skewputt dated 1744. In the small close behind 43-53, known as Inshes Court, is a carved stone panel inscribed 'Feir God – Dvt Not' (Doubt Not) and 'H.A. Robertson A.R.' The Robertsons of Inshes had property in this street from about 1450 to 1700.

Further downhill, opposite the Town House car park, is Raining's Stairs, which lead up to Ardconnel Street. The old name for this part was the Barn Hill, and a cattle market used to be held here, which accounts for one of the names of another flight of stairs from here down to the High Street, which is sometimes known as Market Brae, and sometimes as Post Office Brae, from the time when the Post Office was at the bottom of it. The many small planned streets up here were largely built between 1860 and 1900. What is now the car park on the left at the top of the Stairs was the site until 1976 of Raining's School. The school was run by the Society for the Propagation of Christian Knowledge, who were given a legacy by John Raining of Norwich. It was a pleasant Georgian house, built in 1757; possibly John Adam was the architect.

Down the slope northwards from the Castle, the Museum and Art Gallery are on the left in the modern buildings. These may be ugly, but inside is an exhibition of life in the Highlands from the beginning. Upstairs is a collection of costume, silverware and Pictish stones. The original collection was made by the members of the Northern Institute, early in the nineteenth century. Later the 'Remains' came to the Inverness Field Club, which started in 1875, and it would seem that the Club, having nowhere to put them, handed them over to the Town Council, who shoved them into their cellars, so that little now remains of the original collection. Visiting exhibitions come to the Art Gallery. There are often lunchtime lectures on Thursdays.

On the right is the Victorian Town House, built between 1878 and 1882. It is open to visitors and has some fine portraits, including one of Provost Mackintosh of Aberarder by Raeburn and one of Dr Alexander Ross, 'The Christopher Wren of the North', and some quite appalling stained glass in the Town Hall, which is upstairs. On the stairs are two panels from the old Tolbooth, showing the Burgh and Royal Arms. In the Council Chamber in 1921 the then Prime Minister, David Lloyd George, held a Cabinet Meeting to discuss the Irish Problem. The signatures of all those present are in a frame on the wall. Do not miss the fine portrait of James Fraser of Castle Leather at the foot of the stairs, painted about 1714. It is easy to see why, when setting out for France to bring back Lord Lovat in 1714, he walked out of his house leaving his wife and children 'spralling on the ground in tears'.

Outside the Town House is all that is left of the Merkat Cross. It was mentioned in 1456, but destroyed in a scuffle about 1600. Probably it had a crucifix on it – most did – and the arms of Inverness were 'Gules a Crucifix proper supported by a camel and an elephant also proper,' which can be seen high on the front of the Town House. The remains of the old cross were later set into a new cross which stood in the middle of the street, in the area known as The Exchange, and all the proclamations were made from its steps. It is doubtful whether the shaft is that of 1689, or even that drawn by Burt in 1730. It reached its present site in 1900, and now has the palladium of the town set at its foot.

This is the Clachnacuddain (stone of the tubs). Some say that people used to rest their tubs of water on it as they came up from the river. Dwelly's Gaelic Dictionary says that it is *the rocking stone of Inverness*. Possibly it was once a standing stone with some religious significance to the people in early Inverness. It is said that as long as the stone is safe, the burgh will flourish, and that when Donald of the Isles burned the town in 1411, the stone was unharmed.

Over the years it has needed its defenders. In 1791 'an extraordinary uproar and sensation were produced by an intended transmigration of the Stone, by which the Magistrates of the day got into exceeding ill odour with the community'. In 1837 the stone was lowered to the level of the pavement, but the people 'looked upon this as an evil omen, derogatory to the dignity of the burgh'. The Town Council said that this was nothing to do with *them* but, according to *The Inverness Courier* of 6 September, 1837, 'The exhumation was accomplished on Saturday last . . . A considerable number of citizens assembled on the occasion, and when the stone was fairly excavated and placed in its 'fair proportions' before the public view, the work was greeted with three hearty cheers – William Fraser, better known by the name of 'Bill Duxy', standing up with his hat off like a prophet in drink, and giving the time with appropriate action and energy. A bottle of wine was also broken over the stone and a blessing pronounced'.

The last time that the Riot Act was read in Inverness, during the 1914-18 war, the sheriff stood on the Clachnacuddain to read it.

In the eighteenth century the magistrates, who were, it must be admitted, a very corrupt lot, much given to nepotism, were also much given to public entertainments. They owned the *town carpet* and the *town table* and the latter was frequently called out into the street at the Exchange or to the Islands. Even at the cross, they were liable to have a bonfire, but the picnics at the Islands were more rural affairs, though 'a hogshead to make punch in' makes it sound as though they were not very formal. After the battle of Culloden, the Provost, Mr Hossack, was kicked down the steps of the Town House by Cumberland. The carpet and table would not have been brought out on that day, though the town was by no means inclined to Jacobitism.

Since the 'improvements' of the 1960s, Bridge Street no longer has any interesting buildings standing except the old Court House and the Steeple. The first is on the site of the Tolbooth from 1436, when the Magistrates acquired the land, which has belonged to the burgh ever since. It was finally altered to make a new Court House and Gaol between 1787 and 1789, and although shops now occupy the street level, the fine Georgian upper storey remains, though the attractive balustrade at the top has been replaced by solid masonry.

The Steeple dates from 1791. It was damaged in the earthquake of 1816, when 'the beautiful spire attached to the Jail was at the distance of several feet from the top completely rent and twisted several inches round in the direction from the east to the north-west'. Hugh Miller, of Cromarty, the writer of many books, was one of the stonemasons who worked on its repairs in 1828. It is said that the larger of the gilt balls below the weathercock is filled with whisky from the Millburn Distillery. There are three bells in the belfry, the oldest dated 1658.

On the other corner of Church Street is another Georgian building, once known as The Athenaeum because it was a 'literary institute' from 1815 to 1823. Dating from a later occupation, the curious texts were carved on the walls. Next to it is what is now the Bank of Scotland, but it was built as the headquarters of the Caledonian Bank and opened on 10 February, 1838. The figures on the pediment represent the river Ness and all the good that flows from her.

Going down Church Street, there is a crossroads a few yards along it. To the left is Bank lane, where the National Bank had its office. At the foot of this street is the office of *The Inverness Courier*, which comes out twice a week. It was founded in 1817 and continues on the same site, despite all efforts by 'them' to demolish it when the offices of the Highlands and Islands Development Board were built in the 1960s.

On the other side of the crossroads is a narrow road which runs parallel to the High Street. Now known as Baron Taylor's Street, its old name was the Back Vennel. Further along it, where there is a camera shop, is the place where Boswell and Johnson went to church in 1773. It was not a church, for the Penal Laws lay heavily on the Highlands, and the numbers of Episcopalians who could meet for worship were strictly limited. Sometimes the building was adapted, so that the priest could celebrate in the middle, with the lawful number in view, but others were concealed by walls which did not reach the ceiling, so that they could at least hear the service. It is not known whether this happened here.

Abertarff House, built in 1593 on the west side of Church Street, is the oldest surviving house in Inverness. It was once the town house of the Frasers of Abertarff, and is now the Northern Head Quarters of the National Trust for Scotland and may be visited. The spiral staircase is contained in the circular projection.

The Caledonian Hotel is on the site of a Masonic Lodge, which was destroyed in 1746. The Masons claimed for damages and built a hotel in 1766. There has been so much alteration since that nothing from this date survives. Further along, numbers 43-7 are on the site of Lady Duff of Drummuir's house. Here she and her daughter, Lady Mackintosh, entertained in succession both Prince Charles and his cousin, the Duke of Cumberland. Lady Mackintosh, who had had most of the trouble of the visits, said: 'I have had two King's bairns living with me in my time, and I wish I may never have another'.

Abertarff House, on the west side of the road, is the oldest surviving house in Inverness. It is a fine example of Scots Domestic architecture and dates from 1593. It was hidden for many years by other houses between it and the street. It is now the northern headquarters of the National Trust for Scotland, but its interior has suffered from the time when it was ruinous.

Further on is the entrance to the Old High Church, the Parish Church of Inverness. Given its position on its mound, which is sometimes called St Michael's Mount, a name that often hides an ancient religious place, it is likely that it occupies an ancient holy site. In 1693 Sir Robert Sibbald wrote that there were 'two churches, the one for the English, the other for the Irish' language (Irish was what Gaelic was often called). Only the base of the tower survives from the mediaeval period. It is not hard to see where the eighteenth-century parapet and spire join the older base. It was ruinous for a time, but rebuilt in 1770 with galleries round three sides and an apse added later on the south side. Because no Gaelic was used in the services, it was known as the English Church. The 1660 mausoleum of the Robertsons of Inshes is just inside the graveyard, up the steps and close to the Gaelic Church, 1792, which is now the Greyfriars Free Church.

On the other side of the road is Dunbar's Hospital, built in 1668 by Provost Alexander Dunbar who gave it to the burgh. It has been put to many uses: a hospital, a school (where James Wolfe came to improve his arithmetic after Culloden), a library – even the fire engine was stored here. It has recently been restored.

Across School Lane from Dunbar's Hospital is Bow Court, which was restored in the 1970s. About 1729 it replaced an earlier building and was built by the same Katherine Duff, Lady Drummuir, who later entertained Prince Charles. Look at the plaque on the School Lane end of Bow Court. Bow Court is a U-shaped building, with the entrance from a pend to a house on either side. Now there are flats above the shops below.

The telephone exchange blocks the end of Church Street, but behind it is all that remains of the Dominican Friary which was founded by Alexander II. It was sufficiently important for some of the friars to go as ambassadors to King Haakon of Norway in 1263. The Dominicans are the Black Friars, who were teachers as well as preachers and had a school in the town, but for some unknown reason, Inverness decided long ago that they were Grey Friars (Franciscans) and cannot be persuaded otherwise. They are mentioned in a charter of Alexander II dated 1210 as 'our devout mendicant preaching Friars of our Burgh of Inverness'. All that survives from Alexander's foundation and the subsequent burnings and destruction at the Reformation and final stealing of stones for Cromwell's fort is one battered column. But, in what is now a small burying ground, there are some interesting stones to local families: the Mackintoshes of Borlum, the Macleans of Dochgarroch and the Baillies of Dunain lie here. A monument on the south wall may well be the figure of Alexander Stewart, Earl of Mar, who died in 1435.

To the right of the telephone exchange, and across the road, is the Chapel Yard, given to the town by a Cuthbert of Castlehill. 'There are a great many ancient and curious tombs and gravestones in this abode of the dead, but our limits will not admit of a description of them,' said an anonymous writer on the burgh in 1847. When the cholera struck in 1849, the victims were buried under the present paths.

Until recently, the land was a barrier, but the sea and lochs were open roads. With the narrow entrance from the east formed by Chanonry Point and Fort George breaking the worst of the storms at sea, the sheltered Inverness Firth, about seven miles long, is an invitation to ships to bring their loads to a safe harbour. Some would need repairs, and shipbuilding was important to Inverness for centuries. We cannot tell how many of the 150 ships of the Pictish navy that were wrecked in 729 further along the Moray coast were built on the banks of the Ness, but there is evidence that the Count of St Pol in Flanders came here to get a good ship to carry him to the Crusades in 1249, and someone must have recommended the Inverness shipbuilders to him.

The harbour lies further on to the north with the industrial area to its south.

When Cromwell ruled, he had a Citadel built near the harbour, large enough to hold a thousand men. 'Founded in May, 1652 and now [1655] finished – a most stately scene.' It is said that the soldiers used the stones from Beauly Priory, the Dominican Friary in Inverness and from Fortrose Cathedral, just across the water in the Black Isle. The Highland Chiefs and the Town Council pushed out the Government troops as soon as the Restoration was known, and the Citadel was largely demolished, its stones being used to build houses in the town. Today the site is mostly covered by fuel tanks, but by going round the large roundabout at the end of Friars' Bridge, and along the waterfront to the second turning, Lotland Place, though the sign that is visible when approaching from the town or bridge says Lorry Park, and turning right there, one of the original five ravelins can be seen today, a grassy triangular bank, close to an early aircraft hangar. A little further on, the so-called Clock Tower was originally an eighteenth-century windmill. Its attractive slate roof and clock date from the last century.

Cumberland's troops had a garrison at Inverlochy and, to supply it with the least trouble, they carried a bark, driven upon rollers, to the Loch end of Ness, and there enlarged it into a stately frigate, to sail with provisions from one end of the Loch to the other.'

The merchants and sailors of Inverness loaded their ships with what was available at any time, skins, fish, timber and so on, and timber can still be seen stacked on the quay near the new Harbour Offices which were opened by Queen Elizabeth in August, 1985. They sailed, not only to the Scottish islands, but to such ports as Dantzig (Gdansk), Bordeaux and Lisbon, as well as to some in the Mediterranean, remembering, long after the Reformation, that salmon are welcome Lenten fare in those countries that keep the fast. They returned with flax, iron, glass and wine, and later with tea, sugar and olive oil. Their ships were built on slipways on the banks of the river and this continued until about the 1870s, when wooden ships went out of fashion. In the 1930s there was shipbuilding, of a sort, at the Thornbush Quay, of battle practice targets, and up to three 'Landing Ships, Tank' could be hauled up and repaired there during the 1939-45 war, but today shipbuilding has gone.

Turning back from the Chapel Yard, it is best to walk on the west side of Academy Street, so as to look up at the fine mosaics on the gables of what was the Rose Street Foundry. Here were made all the welding machines for Operation PLUTO (Pipe Line Under The Ocean) in which 70 miles of 3-inch diameter pipe were welded together, wound round a 40 foot diameter drum and floated across the English Channel, with one end on the Isle of Wight and the other at Cherbourg, at the time of the invasion of Europe in 1944. It was also the only place 'in the world to weld air-screws from pressings . . . 40 sq. ins of weld taking the 4000 Brake Horse Power developed by the Spitfire, Mosquito or relevant aircraft'.

B

By looking down Margaret Street the fine classical facade of the Public Library is seen. This was originally built as Bell's Institution in 1841. The architect of this 'excellent Greek Revival architecture with a wide central pedimented portico and Doric columns in Moray sandstone' was William Robertson. The school ceased in 1937 and, having been the burgh courthouse, it became the library in 1980. There is a fine Raeburn of Charles Grant in the library, and a good local collection in the Reference Room with plenty of aids to genealogical researchers in the microfilms and microfiches which belong to the Highland Family History Society but may be used by non-members.

On the next corner, that of Strothers Lane, opposite the Cinema is the building that was once the Royal Academy. It has now become shops. Next comes the Station Square, with the memorial to the Queen's Own Cameron Highlanders. It was originally to have been a memorial to mark the centenary of the founding of the regiment in 1793, but was changed to commemorate the Egyptian Campaign of 1882-7.

The garrison of the castle, whether Brude's, Macbeth's or Wade's men, as well as the townsfolk, needed supplies and from the earliest times to today the town provided them, one way or another. Today most of the small family firms of only a few years ago have vanished under the combined assaults of rising rates and big multiples from outside. The Eastgate Shopping Centre is an example of a modern shopping precinct, but the older Markets, opening on to Union Street, Church Street, Queensgate and Academy Street (this has a fine entrance opposite the Railway Station showing carved heads, though the dark glass doors which keep it reasonably warm can discourage visitors from venturing inside) gave a good covered shopping centre, full of every kind of shop, a century ago, and still do, with small, friendly and excellent shops for the discerning buyer.

For a long time the town was largely self-supportive, though it relied on the country round about for many of its industries, such as tanning, or on imports such as hemp from the Baltic for rigging for the ships built on the river and for re-export as ropes. There have been cattle sales in the town for centuries, and these continue at Hamilton's and at Macdonald's marts

Thomas Telford, the great Scottish civil engineer (1757-1834), left his mark on the face of the United Kingdom. In Inverness-shire he built the Caledonian Canal from 1803-23, as well as churches, manses, harbours and miles of roads. 'A man more heartily to be liked, more worthy to be esteemed and admired, I have never fallen in with,' wrote Robert Southey after a lengthy tour with Telford. The first President of the Institute of Civil Engineers, he is buried in Westminster Abbey. His portrait is in the Town House, Inverness.

along the Millburn Road, convenient to the railway. The outward-looking inhabitants were not limited by the burgh boundaries when modern ideas were needed.

These far-seeing men benefited from the good schooling that was available. The landowners sent their sons to the Academy in Inverness, and then they widened their education by travel and by attending universities in Europe. In the seventeenth century, and perhaps before then, boys rode or

walked from Lochaber to go to the schools; in the nineteenth
century some came from London for a better education, or so
their parents thought, than could be had there. The younger
sons were put into business and commerce, into medicine and
the church, and the result of all this was a lively, bustling town.

To get to the High Street by car now involves a circuit round
the Eastgate Centre, but walking is shorter through a
pedestrian precinct which used to be Inglis Street, named after
Provost Inglis. Across the road from the traffic lights, the
Market Brae, or Post Office Steps, lead up to the top of the
escarpment and Ardconnel Street. On either side of the High
Street, if you look up you will see that a variety of styles of
building have survived, though many have been much altered,
up to the corner of Castle Street, which has just been rebuilt
from the ground up; though it is an acceptable building, the
long glass windows are not very attractive. Nos. 21-23, once
The Royal Tartan Warehouse, which had a great influence on
the wearing of good tweeds and tartans in the last century,
have a very good example of the Royal Arms on a central
gable.

The Napoleonic Wars of the early nineteenth century
brought Thomas Telford, the great Dumfriesshire civil
engineer, to Inverness to build the Caledonian Canal, ably
helped by Joseph Mitchell, whose *Reminiscences* give such a
lively, even controversial, view of life in the Highlands in that
century that his second volume was not published for many
years. Not only did they build the Canal, but the road south
was much improved in 1810, and in the 1820s they were busy
building the churches and manses that were put up by order of
an Act of Parliament, though only three manses survive on the
mainland of Inverness-shire. These are often known as Telford
Churches, but are more properly Parliamentary Churches. In
1826 Inverness was one of the first towns in Scotland to light
its streets by gas.

In 1840 there had been talk of a rail link from Inverness to
the south, but nothing came of it. The railways reached
Aberdeen by 1844, and a line went on to Huntly, but then the
traveller had to change to a stage coach for the last part of the
journey. Joseph Mitchell planned a line to run south from
Nairn via Glenferness, a 1320-foot pass, and then over

Air Mail. It was from Inverness that the first regular air mail in Britain ran, from 29 May, 1934, when Captain E. Fresson carried the mail to Orkney. By that time, air ambulances were bringing patients from the Outer Isles to the hospitals in Inverness.

Drumochter itself, 1506 feet, a route that would not have touched many communities to bring business to the trains. But by 1854 a double line was built from Inverness to Nairn and was opened on 5 November, 1855, rapidly extending eastwards. By 1855 there were engine works at Loch Gorm, and in 1869 engines were being designed and built there. The line south from Forres and over Drumochter to Perth was opened on 9 September, 1863 and the Highland Railway made its headquarters in Inverness two years later.

Alarmed by the line to be built from Glasgow to Fort William, the Highland Railway looked south again and fought Parliamentary battles against its rivals; by November 1898 the line through Aviemore, designed by Murdoch Paterson, engineer to the Highland Railway, with its viaducts at Slochd and Tomatin and the magnificent viaduct over the river Nairn at Culloden, was complete. From Inverness the Highland lines went on to Dingwall in 1862 and from there north to Caithness and west to Kyle of Lochalsh. From Fort William the

West Highland line reached Mallaig and ran south to Glasgow. These lines exist today, but a number of branch lines such as that from Fort William to Fort Augustus have disappeared from the map and others, such as a link between Inverness and Fort William, never got beyond the planning stage.

The generations after the pioneer railwaymen were checked by the fearful slaughter of the 1914-18 War, but the survivors of that and the Depression had picked themselves up to such an extent that by April, 1933, Captain E.E. Fresson had raised £2,675 and registered Highland Airways Limited. On 29 May, 1934, Fresson took off from the airport on the Longman in a de Havilland Dragon Moth carrying 2000 letters to Kirkwall, the first regular British internal air mail. In the same year, patients were being flown to hospital in Inverness from the Outer Isles. With few suitable maps, it is said that the pilots often had to fly low enough to read the names on the signposts to know where they were. Some of the black hangars are still to be seen on the Longman, but the airport has moved east to Dalcross.

This has been the briefest view of the Royal Burgh of Inverness, but those more interested should buy the small guidebooks by Edward Meldrum listed among the books to be read.

CHAPTER 2

Ardersier and Fort George

The A96, the Aberdeen road, leaves Inverness to the east by way of the Millburn Road and passes under the A9.

At Allanfearn (716475), a minor road to the north crosses the railway and runs out to Alturlie Point, where there is a row of fishermen's restored cottages. Behind these (715495) is the site of a chapel dedicated to St Columba, and the ridge behind is Cnoc an t-Sagairt (The Priest's Hill). Looking west from here, there are very fine views up the Inverness and Beauly Firths. There was once a family farming here who went regularly to the Tuesday Market in town. At the end of the day, they were usually so drunk that their friends would harness the pony, pile the Macleans into the cart, and the pony would go home. It had to stop at the railway gates, because it could not use the key, but after that everything was easy and it would stop in the yard of the farm. The unusual part of this story is that, while the farmers might be blind drunk, their pony was blind.

Returning to the A96, just beyond this turning are the remains of a cairn and further on still, at Newton of Petty farm, there are a few standing stones of what must once have been a big site, which was largely destroyed when the railway was built in 1854-5.

Leave the main road at 743488, a well-marked turning to the left/north, on to the B9039 towards Dalcross Airport, Ardersier and Fort George. Less than a mile on, Castle Stuart (742497) (not open) can be seen. It is a fine example of a very Scottish building, a tower house. This one was built about 1624 to an E-plan, by James Stuart, 3rd Earl of Moray, son of 'The Bonnie Earl' of the song. It is the third castle to be built at Petty; its predecessor is all but invisible at 754503, on a by-road that goes off opposite the farm. But beyond the Castle a narrow road leads round to Petty Church, now ruinous, but once the burial place of the Mackintosh chiefs. Just east of the church is all that remains of the first castle, a motte hill, the home in the twelfth century of Freskyn of Moray, and in the thirteenth century of Andrew of Moray, the leader of the

31

Northern Scots. With William Wallace, he defeated the English at Stirling Bridge in 1296. In the adjoining bay, in the eighteenth century, the people built a set of turbines, to use the tides to drive their mill. There were native Gaelic speakers in Petty into this century.

Returning from the church to the B9039, there are views across the Inverness Firth to the Black Isle in Ross-shire. There are turnings to the sea that lead down to the little groups of what used to be fishermen's homes. Dalcross Airport lies to the south of the road. In the winter, along this shore, flocks of dunlin may be seen, and black and red throated divers fly in from the sea. Seals are also seen.

To the south of the road, Connage (777533) was the home of the Mackintosh chiefs from 1163 to 1502. In the early 1520s, Lachlan Mackintosh gave Connage to his brother's bastard son, John, so that John might marry Effie, widow of Andrew Munro of Milton, but told him that if he did not mend his ways, he would not keep the farm. John, 'being a man much given to acts of robbery and oppression', murdered Lachlan 'without delay, when he was at his hunting seat' on 25 March, 1524. Caught by Lachlan's nephew, Donald Glas Mackintosh, John was 'beheaded and dismembered on the south side of the Loch of Rothiemurchus' (see p.75).

Beyond the Connage Tollhouse is Ardersier, once two villages Stuarton, built by the Stuart Earls of Moray, and Campbeltown, built by the Campbells of Cawdor. Some of the oldest houses facing the sea used to be thatched with bent grass from the sand-dunes over the hill at Whiteness. Heather thatch was also used, but here the bent grass was more convenient. An awkward turn in the village joins this road to the military road, B9006, built by Major William Caulfeild, whose network of military roads is all too often listed as 'Wade's Road', though Caulfeild long outlived Field Marshal George Wade. At this point it is part of a far older route, the *Via Regis* , the King's Road, from Aberdeen, which divided south of here, to go to Inverness or to cross from the point where Fort George stands today to Chanonry Point in Ross-shire. It was defended by the fort at Cromal Mount (783554), a large motte hill fort, which commanded the surrounding country, including the crossing.

Beyond, the road ends at Fort George. This is considered to

Fort George. This is said to be the finest eighteenth-century fort in Europe. It was built to ensure that no further Rising should take place in the north, but it has never known hostilities. The picture shows the south sally port through the curtain wall. The pepperpot turret (two more can be seen in the distance) would shelter a sentinel who could observe from it the face of the curtain wall and the next bastion.

be the finest eighteenth century fortress in Europe. It has recently had £18 million spent on it, as an Ancient Monument, and this work was awarded a special prize by the Association for the Protection of Rural Scotland in 1987. Although occupied by the Army, it is open to visitors. There is a good guidebook on sale inside, and three of the rooms have been restored to show how soldiers lived at different periods. The Regimental Museum of the Queen's Own Highlanders (Seaforth and Camerons) is in the rooms where the Lieutenant Governor once lived. It covers all the records and uniforms of the two regiments from 1793 to 1961, and of the present regiment since the amalgamation. The walk of a little over a mile round the ramparts is well worth the effort. Fort George is something that should not be missed.

After leaving the Fort, a fork to the left off the B9006 leads to the old walled burying ground of Kirkton. The old parish church has gone, but there are graves of soldiers from the Fort as well as local people, and a Watch House, dating from the time when grave-robbers were active. From here an oil-rig under construction can sometimes be seen to the east (not open). Whiteness Head, the long spit beyond, despite earlier fears, has not been spoiled by the construction yard, for, being now out of bounds to visitors, it has become a bird sanctuary, and presumably the rare Oyster Plant (Mertensia maritima) continues to flourish there.

Continuing along this minor road to its junction with the B9092, turn left and then take the next turning left to see the Kebbuck Stone (826556), a Class 2 Symbol Stone, which is a large conglomerate mass, carved with a worn Pictish-style cross. The Kebbuck Stone is just over the boundary in Nairnshire. From here the B9092 runs on to Nairn, a couple of miles away, but any turning to the right will join the A96, where a right turn goes directly to Inverness, some twelve miles to the west. This is a straight road that makes other drivers take risks, and a low setting sun can be dazzling.

Shortly before reaching the original turning at 743488, on the south side of the road is a prosperous farm, now called Morayston. In 1609, when its name was Termit, it was the scene of the signing of the Clan Chattan Bond, by which the Mackintoshes, Macphersons, Macqueens, Macphails, Macleans of Dochgarroch, Macbains, Macgillivrays and Shaws of Tordarroch (Clan Ay) swore their 'friendship and union' for the future under Mackintosh as their Captain. This 'friendship and union' may still be seen at Moy (see p.00) when Mackintosh holds a Clan Gathering.

CHAPTER 3

Culloden and Clava

The B9006 is the Culloden Road. To follow this road to Culloden, the simplest way is to take the Aberdeen Road along the Millburn Road as far as the Millburn Roundabout, which is large, with flowers on it, and then turn right up the Old Perth Road. On the right are the Cameron Barracks, built in 1884 in the Scottish Baronial style and for many years the depot of the Queen's Own Cameron Highlanders.

At the top of the hill, just by a small roundabout, on the left/ east of the road behind the safety fence is 'Duncan's Well' and diagonally opposite is a stone marked 'King Duncan's Grave'. Shakespeare's influence can be felt here, for King Duncan was killed in battle near Elgin in 1040 and buried at Iona: neither event took place in Inverness. Possibly the names came from the Robertsons of Inshes, who are part of Clan Donnachaidh or Duncan. This family was one of credit and renown in Inverness and the country around from the early fifteenth century, although they were not so flourishing by the beginning of the nineteenth century, and the last laird, Arthur John Robertson, died 17 November, 1881. Inshes had been sold by then. Keeping to the left, the road has Raigmore Hospital to the east and the headquarters of the Northern Constabulary to the west.

The road crosses over the A9, and the first turn to the left/ east wanders along to Cradlehall Farm, on the left, an old farm house, once the home of Major, or Governor, William Caulfeild, the great eighteenth century military builder of 700 miles of road. The story goes that he was very hospitable and gave many parties at his house. As the guests, overcome by the pleasures of the evening, slipped from their chairs and slid under the table, the servants would come in and scoop them up into a 'cradle' and carry them away to sleep off their potations, and so the farm acquired its name. There is a plaque on the western gable end of the house, commemorating William Caulfeild, put up by the Inverness Field Club. His name was given to a nearby road in a housing estate where it is spelled wrong, Caulfield Road. But even if he is scarcely remembered today, his jingle on the state of the roads before he and his first commanding officer came along is still recalled:

> If you'd seen these roads before they were made
> You'd lift up your hands and bless General Wade.

Just beyond Cradlehall turn right up Caulfield Road North to Caulfield Road, turn right and follow that road to rejoin the B9006, turning left at the junction.

If this detour is not taken, the B9006 climbs the hill, passing on the left Castlehill (697442). The name may refer to an early castle of Inshes on this site. The family of Cuthbert of Castlehill was respected in the district over the centuries. Just beyond, on the right, is a fine Gothick gateway which once led to Inshes House, but the drive was cut through when the new A9 was built and the gateway now leads nowhere. Follow any of the blue National Trust for Scotland (N.T.S.) signs for the battlefield, but the ordinary road sign saying Culloden goes north-east down the hill to the new estates and, by following the signs to it, to Culloden House (721465), now a hotel. It was in the house that then stood on this site, the property of Lord President Duncan Forbes of Culloden, that Prince Charles Edward spent the night of 15/16 April, before the battle on the moor above. The present mansion is a handsome classical house, built between 1772 and 1783, probably by John Adam. Again, the N.T.S. signs will bring visitors from Culloden House through Balloch up the hill to the Visitor's Centre at Culloden.

But, for those who are still on the B9006, Raigmore Tower is on the north side of the road, and about half a mile further on, there is a magnificent view to the north at the entry to Blackpark Farm. Walk down past the farm and into the Forestry Commission woods beyond to a very ancient site, marked on the map as Well (723453). This is the Culloden Clootie Well (now called St Mary's Well, Tobar Mhairi). The well is surrounded by a circular wall and the water is often a bright orange colour. The trees all round are festooned with rags (clooties) placed there by people making a wish. No one removes them, for fear that an event wished against will fall on the remover. It was at the beginning of May, the Beltane of the

Leanach Cottage, Culloden, probably looks much as it did from the outside on 16 April, 1746, though it has been altered inside. The low stone walls and heather-thatched roof and the L-shaped design made it as comfortable a cottage as possible. The door faces south and the angle was a cosy spot to sit to spin or gossip, being sheltered from the north and west winds.

Celtic people, that people came regularly to the Well, and in May 1940, when the Highland Division was at bay in France, the crowds were great. Another way of reaching the Well is by walking up the Forest trail that starts in Smithton, where information about the trees and the Forbes Mausoleum can be obtained.

Soon after the Blackpark turning, the road reaches the land owned by the National Trust for Scotland, which starts at the King's Stables, a thatched cottage to the north of the road. Thanks to the N.T.S. the line of the road has now been altered so that it no longer passes right through the burial ground. The forests that had been planted all round have been felled and the site is in much the state that it was on that unforgotten day, 16 April, 1746. There is a good car park betwen the road and the Visitor's Centre. This now includes an audio-visual show, which answers many of the questions that need to be asked, and a display area, which explains why the battle was

37

fought, and the results. There is an excellent bookshop, where guidebooks to the site may be bought, and a coffee shop.

Outside, there are flags to show how far apart the lines were at the beginning of the battle, and markers to identify the regiments involved on both sides. Imagine having to charge in the snow of that day across such rough ground towards the scarlet line of the Government troops. They had to wait and hold their fire until their enemies were less than forty yards away and the whites of their eyes could be seen. After the muskets had been fired, no one could see anything for the pall of smoke from the black powder used then.

The Brahan Seer, who foresaw many events, said in the previous century, 'Oh, Drumossie, thy black moor shall ere many generations have passed away be stained with the best blood of the Highlands. Glad am I that I shall not see that day, for it will be a fearful period; heads will be lopped off by the score and no mercy shall be shown or quarter given'.

Clan Chattan, in the centre, charged first against the cannon fire, just ahead of the Frasers, the Appin Stewarts and the Camerons. The last two penetrated as far as the second line before they were driven back with heavy casualties.

Colonel John Roy Stewart, from Kincardine (see p.84), who fought at Culloden, was a noted Gaelic poet and also wrote in English

> Redoubled are shed my tears for the dead
> As I think of Clan Chattan, the foremost in fight.
> O woe for the time that has shrivelled their prime
> And woe that the left had not stood at the right.

This is a reference to the Macdonald belief that their position should always be on the right of the line; but on this day they were placed on the left wing. Some say that it was customary to move the various regiments so that each in turn had the position on the right and that on this day it was not the turn of the Macdonalds. On the left wing the Macdonalds hoped that by standing still they might induce the Government troops by advance against them. The Clanranald Macdonalds were led by Ranald, younger of Clanranald, and the Glengarry Macdonalds by Donald of Lochgarry; in each case their chief was too old to fight:

Beware of Macdonald! Beware of his wrath!
In friendship or foray, oh, cross not his path!
He knoweth no bounds to his foe or his hate
And the wind of his claymore is blasting as fate.
Like the hill cat who springs from his lair in the rock
He leaps on the foe – there is death in the shock
And the birds of the air shall be gorged with their prey
When the Chief of Glengarry comes down to the fray.

But this day they stood in their place while the battle raged to their right. At last Alasdair of Keppoch advanced alone, saying, 'Mo Dhia, an do threig clann mo chinnidh mi?' (My God, have the children of my clan forsaken me?). He was shot at once, and again, mortally, but his lone attack brought the rest of the Macdonalds into the fight, only to be slaughtered in their turn, on and off the field.

The cairn was erected in 1881 by Duncan Forbes of Culloden 'from a shapeless heap of stones gathered for that purpose half a century earlier, with the view of erecting a monument to the followers of Prince Charles who fell on this fatal field on the 16th April, 1746. The money originally collected for this purpose has been shamefully squandered, but the genial owner . . . has also placed head stones at the end of the long graves or pits – the Mackintosh trench being 54 feet in length – . . . As recent as 1846 the graves are described as 'large green grassy mounds', but for many years past they have, by the complete decay of the bodies which they contained, become green grassy hollows'. So wrote Alexander Mackenzie in 1891, yet the pits are mounds today, and one that was discovered about 1970, when some whins were cleared, was a mound. Mr Mackenzie expected everyone to walk out from town and back, and although they could get a train to Culloden Station, only two miles from the cairn, he suggested that such idle people should complete their excursion by walking on to Fort George and then back to Inverness. Old Leanach Cottage, close to the Centre, survived the day and perhaps looks as it did then, from the outside.

Leaving the car park and continuing along the B9006, we reach a cross road (749453).

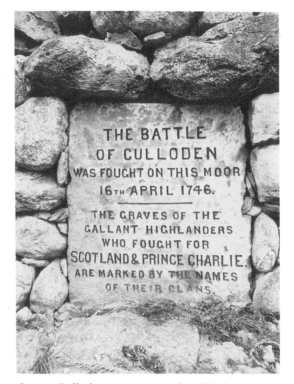

THE BATTLE
OF CULLODEN
WAS FOUGHT ON THIS MOOR
16TH APRIL 1746.

THE GRAVES OF THE
GALLANT HIGHLANDERS
WHO FOUGHT FOR
SCOTLAND & PRINCE CHARLIE,
ARE MARKED BY THE NAMES
OF THEIR CLANS.

The Cairn Stone, Culloden, was put up in 1881 by Duncan Forbes of Culloden, a namesake of Lord President Duncan Forbes, who did so much to mitigate the reprisals after the Battle of Culloden. On the Saturday nearest to 16 April each year a ceremony takes place at the cairn, a sermon is preached, often in Gaelic, and wreaths are laid in memory of the fallen.

For the moment, go forward over the railway. On the south side of the road are acres of soft fruit, which flourish on the south-facing slopes of fertile Strath Nairn and, in the right season, fruit can be bought here.

At a turning to the north (784474), about three miles from the car-park, a minor road leads to Dalcross Castle (779483) (not open) behind its arched gateway. This L-plan towerhouse, originally built in 1621 by Simon Fraser, 8th Lord Lovat, had a wing added in 1703 by the Mackintoshes, who lived here in the winter months, and was well restored in 1898. At Little

Dalcross are the remains of the early mediaeval parish church of Dalcross (field of the Cross), but for many years the parish has been part of Croy. At 779484, north-east of the Castle, is a Clava-type ring-cairn, excavated in 1952.

At the junction, turn right/east to return to the B9006 and then left for Croy, which has an attractive church and burial ground. It is right on the county boundary and, a little to the north, Loch Flemington (810520) recalls the name of Freskyn the Fleming, Lord of Moray, in the twelfth century, who had a castle here, perhaps before he was at Petty (see p.31). In the loch there is Castle Island which has a causeway, not always above the water, joining it to the shore, and it may be an artificial site. Turning left/north at the loch on to the military road, in a short distance the road reaches the A96 at a dangerous cross-road. Turn left/west here for Inverness.

Returning to the Culloden cross-road (7494353), there is a large conglomerate boulder just to the east of the crossing. It is called Cumberland's Stone, but if, as the story goes, he watched the battle from here, he would not see much of it, beyond the clouds of smoke from the muskets.

At this cross-road, take the road to the south, crossing over a minor road with great care, and so down the hill to the River Nairn which is crossed here, not only by the road bridge, but also by Murdoch Paterson's railway viaduct. Seven hundred yards long, it has twenty-nine arches and was built from the local Leanach sandstone in 1897 to allow the Highland Railway to reach Inverness from Aviemore. It is not noticed by travellers by rail, but to see, from the ground, a train crossing it gives an immediate impression of its great size.

After we cross the river, a sign to the right/west shows the way to a car park a little further along between the road and the river. This part of the Strath of the Nairn has been inhabited for thousands of years. A quick look at the Ordnance Survey map will show a large number of standing stones and cairns from the high (947 feet) Dun Davie (718393) almost to Nairn itself. They are thickest on the ground here at Clava (7458444).

Although the trees are not ancient – only a hundred years or thereby – they shelter the three great Clava Cairns, and there is a quite extraordinary sense of peace. There are the remains of five other cairns within a mile of here and they have given their name, as Clava Cairns, to nearly thirty other similar cairns along the banks of the Beauly, Enrick, Ness, Nairn and Spey.

At Clava there are three large cairns and a small stone circle. They take their local name of Balnuaran from the adjacent farm. Balnuaran North East is the nearest cairn to the car park and is a 'passage-grave'. Outside, under the grass, a cobbled pavement surrounds it and this is itself surrounded by a ring of standing stones, about 110 feet in diameter. The entrance to the grave is, as usual, on the south-west point, a narrow passage which would have been covered in, as would the circular burial chamber, by careful corbelling of the walls; this corbelling or gentle shaping in, can be seen inside. At the top there would have been a cap stone. There are four cup-marks on the innermost stone of the passage, but outside, on the north side of the cairn, among the kerbstones that hold the mass of the cairn together, is one that is pitted with them and also has a cup and ring and sundry grooves. No one now knows what these marked stones meant. Their exact meaning must have been lost before they were built into the kerb of this cairn some 4000 years ago, but some memory of their power probably remained. Just inside the gate to the farm house is another heavily indented stone, and others can be seen on other stones within the trees.

The south-west cairn is very similar to the north-east cairn, but between them lies the Ring-Cairn. This has no entrance to the central area, which is about fifty-five feet across. The inside of the four-foot walls are flat slabs of stone. Outside there is the ring of standing stones, but three of these are joined to the ring by strips of stone paving, a unique and incomprehensible feature. It has been conjectured that the bodies may have been exposed inside the ring until only the bones remained and that these were either buried from there or cremated first.

From Clava there is a choice of roads back to Inverness. Turn right/west from the car park and follow the road up some steep slopes and along the ridge. After we cross over the railway, the farm of Castletown recalls the mediaeval Castle Mattoch (749427), the remains of which can be seen by walking under the railway. Crossing the Craggie Burn (732393), there are cairns hidden on either side of the road which shortly joins (729391) the old A9, now the B9154. Turn right/west here to join the new double-tracked A9 at 730384, when another right/ north goes to Inverness.

Alternatively, return across the Nairn and go up the hill to take the left/west turn at the small cross-roads (751451) on to the B851. Within two miles are the gates of Nairnside House (not open). This was once called Culclachy and was the home of an Angus Mackintosh in the early eighteenth century. Angus had two daughters who married twin Mackintosh brothers from Lynwilg in Strathspey. The brothers had set up as ironmongers in Inverness. Their fortunes were made when a barrel of nails that they had ordered was found to be full of gold when they opened it. They did *not* return it to the sender. About a mile further on, in a field east of the road is Daviot Cairn (727412), a Clava-type cairn of which only two monoliths and the kerbstones remain. The next entry is that of Daviot House (not open) built c.1825 on the site of Daviot Castle (729406). The castle was built about 1380 by David, earl of Crawford, and destroyed in 1534 by Hector Mackintosh of Mackintosh. Only a small circular tower remains. At the junction with the A9 turn right/north for Inverness.

CHAPTER 4

Inverness to Drumochter Pass

The A9 is the road south. To reach it, follow the signs for Perth and Aberdeen to the underpass beneath the A9 (685456). The road to Perth is clearly marked and leads up, having passed under the main road, to the southbound carriageway.

The first turning to the left, signposted to N.T.S. Culloden, less than a mile on, goes to the B9006 just beyond where that road crosses the A9 (see p.35). On the west side of the road is Inshes House (695437), formerly the home of the Robertsons of Inshes (see p.35), a family of repute over the years. There was a mediaeval castle, possibly on the site of Castlehill (see p.36). The present house (not open) was built in 1767 and has recently had later accretions demolished. Just south of it, in the garden, is all that remains of another castle, a late sixteenth-century barmkin tower, complete with musket and pistol holes and finished with crow-steps on the gable ends. It is hard to see this when driving south, but easy when coming back north. At 710414, on the northbound carriageway, is Daviot Wood Information Centre, open from May to September, with a picnic area. At 723404 is the junction with the B851 (see p.43), and on the west side of the road is Daviot Church (724394). The building, with its elegant tower, dates from 1826 and stands close to the site of the mediaeval church.

By taking the narrow road that leaves the A9 at 724397 just before the church, it is possible to climb to the ancient stone fort on Dun Davie, 947 feet, but it is not an easy climb and it needs care – not to be undertaken with children, because of the quarry-workings. The road continues in a south-westerly direction. At 708384 it is crossed by General Wade's Military Road, now only a track which can sometimes be walked from here up the hill and through the plantations – depending on the state that the foresters have left the surface in – to Inverness, where it becomes the Old Edinburgh Road. On the way, behind the farm of Druidtemple, is a passage-grave cairn

Daviot Church. There was a mediaeval church here, but this one dates from 1826, with later additions. The unusual tower is particularly attractive. The church stands on a commanding site close to the A9.

at 685420, commanding a good view of the Ness valley. The house now called Castle Heather is by the mound of Castle Leather (Caisteal Leothair, Castle on the Slope) (678426). These last two sites are more easily reached by following the Old Edinburgh Road from Inverness.

Walk down the hill on the old road to Faillie Bridge, an attractive bridge crossing the river Nairn where the soldiers marched dry-footed over the single arch. This minor road crosses the B861 at Balnafoich (686354) and goes on below the Settlement and Field System up on the hill to the west at 674343.

At 686336 a narrow road crosses the Nairn below Tordarroch House (677335) (not open), the home of the Shaws of Tordarroch since the fifteenth century. In 1770 they were visited here by Bishop Robert Forbes, who from 1746 collected the Jacobite reminiscences which were later published as *The Lyon in Mourning*.

In the early sixteenth century the Earl of Moray summoned his Mackintosh vassals to meet him here, where he inquired as

to the whereabouts of Hector Mackintosh, the acting chief, who
had led a raid to Dyke and Darnaway Castle, the property of
Moray. He learned nothing, so he hanged eighteen
Mackintoshes 'over the balks of the house where the court was
held'. From this day came the saying, 'Chan ann a h-uile latha
'bhitheas mòd aig Mac an Toisich' (It is not every day that
Mackintosh has a gathering). The late Lachlan Mackintosh,
who farmed Tordarroch, said that he once found a boot with a
foot in it. Just beyond Tordarroch is Croft Croy cairn
(683332), an unusual Clava-type cairn, having a long narrow
chamber instead of the usual circle.

Returning over the hump-backed bridge to the road, a mile
along is Dunlichity Church. Standing among the carved stones
on the graves of members of Clan Chattan, the little church,
successor to an early building dedicated to St Finnan (whose
statue was taken to Inverness and burned in the market-place
there in 1643), was rebuilt in 1758, but parts of the 1569 church
still survive. In what may be the original chancel lie the Shaws
of Tordarroch, with some fine modern stones. A survivor from
earlier times is the Watch House, where men spent days and
nights after a funeral to foil the grave-robbers who, when they
could, sold 'resurrected' bodies for medical research.

The road opposite the church leads across past Brin House
to the B851 at 669295. For those who like a scramble and a
view, stop and climb to the unmarked fort at Creag Bhuidhe
(665314).

Past Dunlichity Church, Loch a'Chlachain is to the south of
the road. Next comes Loch Duntelchaig, part of the water
supply for Inverness. Leaving the car at 646320, near the
locked gate, which must be surmounted, there is a pleasant
walk along the east side of the water. The road goes on past the
north side of the loch, across a plain where there are many
cairns and signs of our predecessors, for it is part of the drove
road from the Aird that crossed the Ness at Bona (see p.103)
and went south by Farr and Glen Kyllachy to the Findhorn and
the southern trysts. It is possible that the large circle of stones
to the south that can be seen from the road was used, whatever
may have been its original use, as a fank to fold the beasts or,
more likely, the sheep when they had fed enough.

Loch Ashie lies to the north of the road. At 621343, just

inside the plantation fence on the north of the road, is a stone with a hole in it. This is the Clach na Brataich (the Banner Stone). Some think it is linked with the 'Phantom Battle' which is occasionally seen across the loch. There is no history or legend about this battle. One account tells of an American family on a fishing holiday. The landlord of their hotel sent them out one Sunday, when fishing was forbidden, with a picnic lunch and directions for a pleasant drive. They returned with graphic descriptions of the 'pageant' that they had seen here.

Beyond Loch Ashie there is a cross-road, 621345, where General Wade's military road of 1729 crosses the old drove road, and here a choice must be made. To the left/south the road will meet the B682, and a right turn there goes back to Inverness via Dores (see p.94).

To the right/north at the cross-roads, the road, on which a phantom car has been seen, goes straight back to Inverness, passing Essich (647396). The house barely survives, but up a narrow turning to the right/east just before it, 648394, are, first, the foundations of the village of Essich, which flourished from the middle ages to the nineteenth century, and then, at the 600-foot level, to the west of the road, Carn Glas (Grey Cairn) (649381), the largest burial mound in the North of Scotland. This is not a Clava-type cairn, but is three Orkney/Cromarty-type cairns joined together to form a single unit about 978 feet by 57 feet. Even further up this road is a Bronze Age, c.1700 B.C., cemetery (635378), and also hut circles and clearance cairns, which is the name given to heaps of stones gathered from the fields before they are cultivated.

Back at Essich, the next thing of interest is seen just after crossing the burn at 635378, in a field at the right/east of the road. Protected to such a degree that the carving is almost invisible is the Knocknagael Boar Stone, an Ancient Monument. This is a Pictish Class I Symbol Stone, carved with a Boar (now the symbol of the Inverness Field Club) below the 'mirror-case' symbol. It dates from the late sixth century and, for whatever reason, the lines of the carving are fading fast. This road runs into Inverness along Stratherrick Road.

But straight over the crossing, the old road runs down some steep turns, with wonderful views of Loch Ness, over to

Urquhart Bay on the other side (see p.112). At 614358, pull in
to the side of the road to visit the MacBain Memorial Garden.
This is a heather garden with paths leading up to a seat at the
top, sheltered by a curving wall and guarded by two bronze
wild cats, the emblem of Clan Chattan (the Children of the
Cats) of which the MacBains form a part. The cats are the work
of the late Pilkington Jackson, who also designed and made the
great statue of King Robert the Bruce at Bannockburn. There
is a tablet listing the descent of the Macbain chiefs, and it is a
very good place for a picnic. In the season, these slopes are
covered with blaeberries and also fungi, but it is necessary to
know about fungi before venturing to eat the latter. The road
continues down the hill and then rises to join the B852 at
608368. The curiously named Antfield marks the place where
there was once a religious centre, Annat. Turn right/north at
the junction, and the road goes to Inverness.

At the bottom of the hill, a sharp turn left/east, which was
once the A9, is now the B9154, the road south to Edinburgh,
and the advised tourist route as being more interesting than
the main road, even if not so speedy. On either side of the road
as it climbs the hill are cairns, and to the south (730382) there
are hut circles and field systems. At 748379 is Meallmore,
which was built as a shooting lodge by the Mackintoshes in the
last century. King Edward VII was among the guests who
stayed there. At the top of the hill, on the north side of the
road, is a marker stone commemorating the improvement of
this road in 1925. It reads, *Reconstruction of the Inverness to Perth
road. The first turf was cut by Mrs Mackintosh of Mackintosh, wife of
Colonel Mackintosh of Mackintosh, C.B.E., Lord Lieutenant and
Convener of the county of Inverness, on 5 May 1925 and this stone
was erected to mark the occasion. The road was originally constructed
by General Wade who began the work in 1728.* After passing under
the railway, a glance to the right will show one of the few
remaining wooden railway bridges at 760349.

Moy (Magh, a plain) has been a home of the Mackintosh
chiefs since the fourteenth century, and their principal place of
residence since the early eighteenth century. It lies to the east
of the road at the north end of Loch Moy. The present Moy
Hall (768351) (not open) dates from 1957 and is the latest of

their houses in the area. There are two islands in the loch; one has an obelisk to Sir Aeneas Mackintosh, d.1820, and the smaller has the remains of a house about 58 feet by 21 feet, built by Lachlan Mackintosh in 1665. One of the islands was the summer home of the Bishops of Moray until 1336, when the then Bishop granted the Barony of Moy to William Mackintosh. Since the Reformation it has been held from the Crown.

When Lachlan Mackintosh died in his new house in 1731, Moy was considered to be 'inconveniently remote', so his body was carried to Dalcross (see p.40) where it lay in state for two months until his successor arrived and it could be buried.

Malcolm Mackintosh, who fought at Harlaw in 1411, was the Chief when the Comyns hanged some of his men in 1424, so he led a reprisal raid to Nairn and killed all the Comyns in the Castle there.

Following this the Comyns returned to Badenoch and drove the Mackintoshes on to the island in Loch Moy and, to complete their destruction, they dammed the loch to raise the level of the water. One of the Mackintoshes swam to the dam at night and bored holes in the planks which formed it, which he then plugged. By a skilful use of ropes, he pulled out all the plugs at once and the rush of water demolished the supporting turf banks. The Comyns were encamped below the dam and were overwhelmed.

It is at Moy that the Highland Field Sports Fair is held on the first Friday and Saturday in August. This is not a Highland Games, but includes Fishing, Shooting, Terrier Racing, Falconry, Shetland Pony racing (to those who know the work of Norman Thelwall, this alone is worth the entrance fee!) and so on. The Clan Chattan always has a tent not far from the house, where members of the Clan are made welcome. The A.G.M. of the Clan is on the Thursday evening, and from time to time a full Clan Gathering is held on the Saturday, with a march past of all the Clans in the Confederation, the Mackintoshes, Macphersons, Shaws, Macbeans, Farquharsons, Davidsons, Macgillivrays, Macphails, Macqueens, and Macleans of Dochgarroch.

Moy Church (772342) is a plain building, dating from 1765, on an ancient site. There is an early nineteenth-century watch house in the burying ground. The grave of Donald Fraser, the

Smith of Moy (see p.52), is said to be marked by a marble
stone which was sent from Rome by some Jacobite admirers.
To find this stone, go in by the first gate, and in a couple of
rows to the right is a tall polished red granite pillar, crowned
with an urn, which was put up in 1903 in memory of Donald
Fraser, the Smith of Moy, who died at Corriebrough in June,
1804. To the east of this, at the foot of the grave, is a carved
grey stone, with a cherub's head in the top. It is covered with
lichen, but the words *In Memory of Donald Fraser* can just be
made out. This is the stone that is said to have been sent from
Rome, by Jacobites living there.

This detour rejoins the A9 just north of Dalmagarry
(788323), now a farm, but originally a King's House. These
were built along the military roads as rest houses where
refreshments could be had and a change of horses provided
evey ten miles or so. Once one of these has been identified, it is
not too difficult to find others at about that distance from each
other, though some of the intervening ones may have gone.

On the right/west, as the road climbs beyond the turning to
Moy, is the B851, a road to Fort Augustus at the head of Loch
Ness.

This road, the B851, leads to Fort Augustus from the
turning at 718377 as the A9 rises after crossing the Nairn.

A few hundred yards from the turning, an unmarked road
to the right/north, once part of the military road, runs down to
Faillie Bridge, a well-preserved single-arched bridge. The
military road crossed the B851, but this part has now been
overlaid by the access to a large gravel-pit.

About 3½ miles from the A9 the B861 joins from Inverness.
Turn right/north and in about a mile the great Gask Cairn is
on the right of the road. Look for a tall stone at 679358. To
reach the cairn, the largest of all the Clava-type cairns, drive
past it and walk through a gate and back along the fence. The
outer ring is 126 feet in diameter and the tall monolith is 11
feet high above the ground, but it is only 9 inches thick.

Returning to the B851, the road runs along the south side of
Strath Nairn. Beyond Farr, at 678316, a narrow road leads
over the hills to Strath Dearn (see below). It is an old drove
road, but it can be driven over, opening and shutting the gates

as they are reached, although the finest views are seen when driving towards Farr from Strath Dearn.

At East Croachy (651277) another, less exciting, road turns right/north-west to wander through the hills past Dalcrombie, the home of John MacGillivray, one of the early partners of the North West Company of Canada, to the south end of Loch Duntelchaig and on to join the B862 at 599300. To the south of this road, and easily seen from Dalcrombie, Loch Ruthven has a crannog (an artificial island) in its south-west corner, and there may well be more than this one. Crannogs, lake or bog dwellings, often fortified, were occupied from ancient times up to the late Middle Ages.

At East Croachy is an Episcopal church. This was an Episcopalian area, the congregation often having to worship quietly in different houses until the first church was built in 1817. This was burned in 1859, but rebuilt by Duncan Mackenzie (Parson Duncan), and the congregation has continued until today.

Just off the road is Dunmaglass Mains (611238) which is almost on the site of the home of the Chiefs of the Macgillivrays, part of Clan Chattan since the fourteenth century. In 1745 Mackintosh was a serving officer in the 42nd, Royal Highland Regiment, the Black Watch, so Clan Chattan was raised for the Prince by his 20-year-old wife, 'Colonel Anne', and commanded by Alasdair Macgillivray of Dunmaglass who fell at Culloden. There is a well-known picture of him by Logan in *The Costumes of the Clans*, 1826. An Episcopalian family, they gave much help to Bishop Robert Forbes in compiling *The Lyon in Mourning*.

Just beyond the entry to Dunmaglass, a narrow road leads to Abersky and Ruthven (602269). North of Ruthven, on the edge of Loch Ruthven is Tom Buidhe (604274), a fort overlooking the crannog in the loch. This road joins the B862 at 585267.

Continuing south, just off the A9, near the line of the old military road, now in the forest, near the place where the dual carriageway ends on the way south, is the site of the Rout of Moy (745346). On Sunday, 16 February, 1746, with an escort of Camerons, Prince Charles had arrived at Moy to pass the night there. His hostess was Lady Mackintosh, a passionate

Jacobite, the 'Colonel Anne' whom we have already met. The news of the Prince's arrival reached Lord Loudon at Inverness and he sent 1500 men to take him. It is likely that the boy who brought to Moy the news of the advancing troops was sent by Mackintosh, who was with Loudon.

'Colonel Anne' had already posted Donald Fraser, the Smith of Moy, with four other men, on the Inverness side of the Camerons, who were guarding the house. The weather was appalling and the five men sheltered by some peat-stacks until they saw against the skyline the advancing Government troops. From their different positions they fired their muskets and shouted as if each block of peat were a body of Jacobites. 'Upon this the blacksmith huzzaed and cried aloud, "Advance, Advance, my lads. Advance (naming some particular regiments). I think we have the dogs now!"' By the flashes of lightning the peat-stacks seemed to Loudon's men actually to be firing at them and they fled back to Inverness, about ten miles. Only one man is known to have been killed, Macleod's piper, who was with his master among the Government troops. He was the famous Duncan Ban MacCrimmon, who had already been taken prisoner by the Jacobites. His captors returned him to Macleod, for pipers were precious men, and Duncan Ban was one of the most famous. It is said that before he left Skye he composed his great *Cumha Mhic-criomain, MacCrimmon's Lament,* as a result of a premonition of his death. The Prince was saved and the Jacobites entered an undefended Inverness the next day.

In 1763 'Colonel Anne' was elected 'Burgess, Freewoman and Guild sister of the Burgh of Inverness'. She died in 1784 and is buried in Leith with her family.

At 785324 the B9154, formerly the A9, which has passed through Moy on its way south, rejoins the present A9. At 790321 a minor road leads east by the Funtack Burn and past Ruthven, but beyond that it is best to walk.

At 794303 a turning to the right/west, once the A9, goes into Tomatin. The Freeburn Inn is the successor to and on the site of a long line of inns and change houses on this main road. Here is the largest distillery and bonded warehouse in Scotland, but at present it is not producing to its full capacity.

Fishing on the upper reaches of the River Findhorn. Salmon fishing is a popular pursuit and many Highland rivers carry these fish. Today there are fish-farms around the coasts and in some of the lochs, but fish from them do not bring the excitement of a successful day on the river or loch.

There is the inn, and little more.

Immediately before crossing the Findhorn Bridge (804277), a road turns abruptly off the old main road to run the length of Strathdearn for miles along the valley of the river Findhorn. At 766243 is the ancient church of Dalarossie. It stands on a peninsula sticking out into the river, on the other bank of which there is a cairn. It is necessary to walk across a field to reach the church, but it is worth the visit. There is a key at the Keeper's house at Dalmigavie Lodge, further up the Strath.

A short distance beyond the church, a turning to the right/ north leads up Glen Kyllachy and on through the hills to reach the B851 at 6793318 at Farr (see p.51). This road, which reaches a height of 1518 feet, has very good views to the western hills, but it is a gated road, and those that have to be opened, also have to be closed.

The valley road does not have a surface for much further,

but cars can be taken on, if permission is obtained first at Coigs Cottage.

The old A9 crosses the concrete Findhorn Bridge and climbs the hill, finally crossing the railway by a right-angled bridge and joining the new A9 at 826264, just before the Slochd summit.

Where the present A9 crosses the Findhorn at 808290, it is worth stopping in the lay-by just north of the bridge, to look over the parapet at the river below. When the water is not too high, the old ford can be seen and some of the supports of a much earlier bridge.

As the road rises to the Slochd (pit), the old Military road can be seen on the hill to the left/north, since all the roads, and the railway, too, must pass by this narrow gap in the hills. Sometimes groups of Wild Goat *(Capra hircus)* may be seen on these hills. When beginning the descent from the top, 1333 feet, of the pass, The German's Head can be seen. It is a curious formation of stones almost hanging from the hill on the north side, that resembles a man in a German helmet which is not so obvious on the way north. The road then crosses the Black Mount, a dreary place in the winter, on its way south.

Badenoch (the drowned place) was a large district, reaching from Slochd (840252) to the county boundary at Drumochter (631760). It is bounded on the east by the central Grampians, one of the largest single areas of high ground in Britain, 300 square miles, of which 200 square miles are over 2000 feet high. They include Ben Macdhui (4300 ft.), Cairn Toul (4241), Braeriach (4284) (Braigh Riabhach, speckled slope) (954999) and Cairngorm (4084) (Blue heap) (005041) – an enormous lump of granite. The first two peaks are in Aberdeenshire, the last two in Inverness-shire. To the west Badenoch is bordered by the summits of the Mondahliath (stony moor) hills, the highest of which is Cairn Mairg, (deplorable heap), 3093 feet (636025).

The Lordship once belonged to the Comyns, who picked the wrong side when they opposed King Robert I. In 1371 it belonged to a younger son of King Robert II, Alexander Stewart, better known as *The Wolf of Badenoch*. He passed Badenoch to the Earl of Mar (see p.16), his son by Mariota, who was not his wife but was the mother of his children. Later King James II gave Badenoch to the first Earl of Huntly.

Badenoch is watered by the Spey which, because the fall is small, floods frequently. The river is usually about 10-20 yards wide, but it can widen to more than half a mile, 880 yards, so Badenoch is a good name for the district, of which the other name is Strathspey (the wide valley of the Spey). The Spey is always 'she' and was inhabited by a White Horse which walked beside weary travellers, inviting them to ride it. If the invitation were accepted, the White Horse would gallop off into the river and the rider would not be seen again. 'Who is so foolish as to talk now of the White Horse of Spey?' said an old lady in the 1920s, 'Dear me! That's old talk, – but all the same, she's a bad, bad river.' She is said to take at least one life each year.

The whole area was once well endowed with naturally growing woods as opposed to the present-day commercial and tax-assisted forests, and a tale tells of a projected attack on these woods and forests. The King of Lochlann was jealous of the Scottish forests and sent a witch to destroy them by fire. She started with the Sutherland forests, but remained in the clouds so that no one could see her. As she advanced on Badenoch, a wise man had an idea to make her show herself. He gathered large numbers of sheep, cattle and horses, then separated the ewes from their lambs, the cows from their calves and the mares from their foals. The cries of the separated young for their mothers were so loud that the witch stuck her head through the clouds to see what was causing the noise. The wise man had loaded his gun with a silver coin – he shot her and saved the Badenoch trees.

At 876241 a well advertised road leads to the left/north to Carrbridge. Take this, another part of the old A9, for a more interesting road, with less traffic (see p.61).

At 822047, to the right/west of the road, is Dunachton Lodge (not open). It is on the site of a castle that was built by William Mackintosh when he married the heiress about 1500. In 1689, as the latest move in a long quarrel between the Mackintoshes and the Macdonalds of Keppoch, Coll of Keppoch, whose house had been captured by the Mackintoshes before the battle of Mulroy in 1688 (see p.203), burned Dunachton as part of his harrying of the Clan Chattan lands.

Shearing or Clipping. This shepherd is using the old-fashioned shears, which can leave the sheep as smooth as velvet. They are not as fast as the electric clippers, but they can be used where power is not available. Shearers from Australia and New Zealand can often be found at the clippings in Scotland.

Only the back wing survived to shelter the family. Edward Mackintosh (see p.90) lived here at one time. The chapel in the hollow between the two roads is dedicated to St Drostan.

Nechtan, one of the Pictish kings, who reigned from c.706 to 732, is said to have fought a 'King Harald' near here. Harald is said to have sat on An Suidhe (the Seat) (813072) to watch the fight. He was, of course, defeated, and was buried on Creag Righ Tharailt (crag of King Harald) (792053). Dalnavert (dail na bheart, place of graves) (857064) is said to be where the rest of the slain were buried.

According to the Account Book of William Mackintosh of Balnespick (816301), which runs from 1769 to 1780 while he lived at Dunachton, there were then on this estate, 1 Tailor, 3

Millers, 5 Weavers, 1 Carpenter, 3 Fox Killers, 4 Wrights, 2 Shoemakers, 1 Mason, 2 Smiths and 2 Fiddlers. Sir Aeneas Mackintosh, at the same period, said that 'on a farm rented from me by McIntosh of Balnespick for £84.13.4 sterling, 240 people are supported, of which 60 are able to bear arms'.

At 792026, to the right/north of the road, is Balavil (not open), sometimes written Belleville. This was the home of James 'Ossian' Macpherson (1736-96), who was born at Ruthven (see p.79) and became a schoolmaster at Kingussie (see p.71). He published some fragments of Gaelic verse with translations in 1760 and the Faculty of Advocates sent him round the Highlands to collect some more. As a result, he published in 1762 *Fingal, an Epic Poem in Six Books* and in 1763 *Temora, an Epic Poem in Eight Books.* A great argument followed, and still rages, as to whether he was a fraud or not, but Napoleon carried his works with him on all his campaigns. He became Surveyor General of the Floridas in 1764 and in 1779 agent to the Nabob of Arcot and M.P. for Camelford from 1780. He built Balavil – his architect is said to have been Robert Adam – on the site of Raitts Castle (see p.90) where a Regularity Court was held on 13 October, 1380 by Alexander Stewart. This house was burned out in 1903, but rebuilt in 1904-5. When Macpherson died there, on 17 February, 1796, his body was, by his wish, enclosed in three coffins, the first being of Glen Feshie pine, the second of lead and the third of mahogany, before he was carried to Westminster Abbey for burial.

In the 1829 floods, which started on the Spey where the Calder joins it at 706978, south of Newtonmore, 'about Belleville and on the Invereshie estate, *the meadows were covered to the extent of 5 miles long by 1 mile broad'.* At Invereshie the bridge, normally 22 feet above the water, had flood water 3 feet above the keystone of the arch, 25 feet above its normal level.

The A9 sweeps south of Kingussie, giving a good view of the ruins of Ruthven Barracks (see p.80), which are often floodlit. At Raliabeag (704970), just south of the junction of B9150 from Newtonmore with the A9, is a pleasant picnic place, easy to get at from the north and the south.

At 693952 a turning to the right/west crosses the railway and

C

Ruthven Castle, Badenoch. The ruins of the eighteenth-century barracks stand on the site of the castle once inhabited by the Wolf of Badenoch. Today cattle graze in the foreground, but this part was by no means always a peaceful place, standing, as it does, where the passes through the hills join.

the river Truim and runs above the right bank of the Spey to join the A889 at Catlodge, just beyond Breacachy (Breac-achadh, speckled field) (638928) (not open). A Mary Macpherson of Breacachy was very beautiful and she loved Macpherson of Uvie (675957). Her family disapproved, but the two continued to meet in the woods until one day Mary's brothers caught Uvie, bound him hand and foot and laid him on an anthill. Mary fled across the Spey to Uvie to tell the people what had happened, but no one thought that the young man was in any danger, so there was no rush to rescue him. When they did find him, he was dead. Mary went mad and thereafter lived in the woods where she had once been happy.

Macpherson of Breachacy led the mutiny in the 42nd (Royal Highland) Regiment, the Black Watch, in 1743 and, with a neighbour, Malcolm Macpherson, from Druimard Farm, Laggan, was executed in the Tower of London. A few years later, Donald Macpherson of Breachacy was the go-between and messenger when Prince Charles Edward was hiding in Cluny's Cage (see p.210).

Further down the A9 the old road leaves the main road to run along the west bank of the Truim to Dalwhinnie.

At 683922 the old A9 leads off to the right/west to Dalwhinnie (636848). The old Crubenmore Bridge (677914) is worth a look, but the new road, lying further up the hill, blocks the view of the Crubenmore Falls (677911) from this road. At 639858 the military road to Fort William, the A889, leaves the old A9 by the railway bridge and climbs into the hills (see p.210).

Dalwhinnie, at 1188 feet the highest village in the Highlands, has a station, hotels, a school and a distillery, which is open to the public. The village having been by-passed, it comes into its own when the snow gates at 639819 are closed. The inn, now the Loch Ericht Hotel, had links with General Johnnie Cope, and perhaps Prince Charles wrote his letter to Glenlyon from here. His army, having crossed the Corrieyairick from the Great Glen, with Cope retreating in front of it, camped here. The letter was photographed about a century ago. The photograph survives, but the whereabouts of the original, then or now, are unknown today.

Dalwhinny Camp
Agst. ye 29, 1745.

You must have heard before this time of my arrival in Scotland with a firm resolution never to abandon the Island. Therefore lay my account that you will with all expedition possible raise what men you can and join the Royal Standard. You may give credit to the bearer and after concerting matters with him let me hear from you. The more dispatch you make will be the more useful and when I see you, you may depend upon all due marks of my favour.

Charles P.R.

For
The Laird of Glenlyon.

Just by the snow gates the roads rejoin, near one of General Wade's most attractive bridges. Running south-west from Dalwhinnie is Loch Ericht, a gash in the hills nearly fifteen miles long by three-quarters of a mile wide at 1153 feet. It is almost invisible from the old road, just a glimpse through the railway arch, but rather more is seen from the new road. Its water is used to power hydro-electric turbines.

The main road runs on to the south, reaching the county boundary at the Pass of Drumochter (Druim uachdair – ridge of the top) where the road summit is 1504 feet and the railway reaches 1484 feet. The hill to the right/west of the road at the summit is An Torc (the Boar, generally called the Boar of Badenoch). To the south, in Perthshire is The Sow of Atholl.

CHAPTER 5

The Old A9 to the South

This chapter covers most of the line taken by the old A9, which changes its number as it goes south. The road past Moy is included in the A9, the road from Inverness to Perth and Edinburgh (see p.48).

The A938, which was once the A9, leaves the main road at a well-marked turning to Carrbridge at 875241. It passes under the railway and in a couple of miles reaches Carrbridge, where it keeps left at the fork in the road by the hotel, where the B9153, demoted from its former A9 status, keeps to the right (see p.63). The A938 runs generally eastward, with a double turning off at 928245, where the B9007 runs north to leave the county at Beum a' Claidheimh (slash of the swords), a pass that carries it first into Moray and then into Nairnshire on its way to Forres and Nairn on the Moray Firth.

At Duthil (935243), two miles from Carrbridge, on the right/south of the road, is the abandoned church of St Peter, dating from the early fifteenth century. Matilda, or Bigla, daughter of Cummin Gibbon Mor of Kinveachy, Glencairnie and Pitlac, is credited with founding this church. Her second son was Patrick MacIain Roy, ancestor of the Clan Phadruig Grant of Tullochgorm. It replaced an older church on another site, possibly at Baile an t-Seapail (Chapelton) (918191) or at Deishar (deisear, having a southerly exposure) (928196), where there is a burying ground.

The Chiefs of Grant, whose home was in Moray at Castle Grant (formerly called Freuchie) (042303), were buried at Duthil from 1585 until 1913, when 'in terms of the Testamentary writings of Caroline Stewart, Countess Dowager of Seafield, this mausoleum has been closed and is not to be used for further interments'. Because of family quarrels there are two mausoleums at Duthil. One was built in 1837 and has the arms on it. It is this one that was closed in 1913. The other is just outside the consecrated burial ground and was built in 1884. The whole complex has recently been bought by a Clan Association and will, it is said, be turned into a Visitors' Centre

Carr Bridge. This attractive little bridge has given its name to the village. It once had parapets, but these were washed away in the great flood of 1829 and were never replaced. The modern bridge gives photographers a good opportunity to capture the beauty of the curve of its predecessor, which cost £100 in 1717.

of particular interest to Grants. Services are now held in the former United Free Church in Carrbridge, built in 1909, and the monuments from inside Duthill Church have been moved here.

On the left/north of the road at 9986251 is the recently restored Muckrach Castle (not open). Built by Patrick Grant, the second son of John Grant of Freuchie, in 1598, it was the earliest possession of the Rothiemurchus family. It stands in a much stronger position than appears from the road. The hotel, a little further on, is acclaimed at present for the excellence of its sandwich lunches. Just beyond the hotel, where the burn from above it reaches the river Dulnain, is the county boundary, but carry on the short distance to Dulnain Bridge and there join the A95 from Grantown-on-Spey, cross the bridge and return to Inverness-shire.

Just across the bridge, a turning to the right/west runs

through the oddly named Skye of Curr, where there is a Show Garden of two hundred varieties of heather. This road joins the A95 at 977226. At 994225 a turning to the left/east crosses the abandoned railway just south of Broomhill station and crosses the Spey on its way to Nethy Bridge (see p.86).

Between the road and the river at 969214 is Tullochgorm (not open). Isobel, the laird's daughter, was courted by a Macpherson and several Robertsons. A Robertson decided to get rid of Macpherson, but the victim escaped and went to a barn where he struck down his attackers with his sword and a musket that Isobel loaded for him. Her brother was among those killed. In celebration, Macpherson composed and danced the Reel of Tullochgorm, but their joy was short-lived. Isobel was imprisoned for her part in the fight. Macpherson was soon shot; his head was presented to Isobel and she died not long after.

The A95 runs through pleasant farming land, with turnings at 944199 and 924192 to Boat of Garten. This name 'Boat' can be seen along many rivers, reminders of the time when a boat was necessary to cross the water. The bridge at Boat of Garten was built in 1898. The golf course here has been called 'a miniature Gleneagles'. The road is joined at 913188 by the B9153 and carries on along the old A9 to 902152, where it turns sharply to the right/west to join the A9.

Returning to Carrbridge, the old main road, now the B9153, leaves the A938 and enters the main part of this holiday resort. Here, where Stone Age implements were found about a century ago, was the first all-winter ski-resort in Scotland. The first ski-school was opened about 1958, using the Austrian method of teaching.

A few yards down the slope is a turning just below the famous Bridge, which was built in 1717 for the easier access of funeral parties. The mason, John Nicolson from Pluscarden, was to build it for 'ane reasonable Breadth and Height as will receive the Water when in the greatest speat', which he did for £100. It had parapets until the great flood of 1829. This turning passes under the A9. At 878216 a track to the right (leave the car here) leads up to the Sluggan Bridge (869220) which, although a ruin today, carried General Wade's Military

Landmark, Carrbridge. Seated in a Spey coracle outside the Landmark Visitors' Centre is David Hayes, who felt that there was a need for something more than the rather dull collections which were all that existed in the 1950s to show the history of the Highlands. He filled the gap with his Centre, where an audio-visual presentation of history can be followed from comfortable seats, trails at ground level and at tree-top height give views, food can be had and souvenirs bought. The museums have been much improved, perhaps as a result of his work.

Road from Inverness to Stirling over the river Dulnain. Upstream of Sluggan Bridge is another which leads across the river to Inverlaidnan (862214). The ruin to the north of the farm is where Prince Charles Edward spent the night of 15/16 February before going to Moy (see p.51).

The road goes on to Dalnahaitnach (not open) (853199). Here lived Iain Beg (small Ian), a famous archer. One day eight men came looking for him when he was in the house. His wife, pretending that he was out, said that she would send the herd for him and sent Iain Beg off with a blow to his head. When the men, who were not after him for his good, came out of the house, Iain Beg picked them off, one by one, and buried their bodies down by the river. Across the river and easily reached by crossing the Inverlaidnan bridge and walking upstream is a monument to Iain Beg.

The turning from the main road a few yards beyond the Bridge, on the left/east, runs through gentle country to near Dulnain Bridge and so on to Grantown-on-Spey. Taking the turning there marked for lorries just before the town, this road joins the A95 for the A939 (see p.86).

Passing through Carrbridge, the Visitors' Centre of Landmark is found on the right/west of the road. There is a good car park and picnic site and the whole family is catered for. Not only is there a Nature Trail, but also a Tree Top Trail, a Multi-vision show, a good shop and restaurant and a Sculpture Park.

Keeping to the old A9, now the B9152, and continuing south along it, ignoring the turning where the A95 turns off to the A9, the old road carries on to Aviemore (Agaidh Mor, big gap). This is now a premier holiday resort, where Father Christmas appears all the year round! Here are hotels and chalets, an ice rink and a solarium, a cinema, restaurants, dances and discos — everything that is needed for some sorts of holidays or conferences. It is also a good centre for exploring the country round.

It was not always so. Although there is a ring cairn (sign-posted) to the left/east of the road, Aviemore is really a railway village on a main road. In 1768 John Grant, a vintner, lived here, but in 1786 a traveller wrote, 'It hurts me to say I found the Inn I now put up at differing from those I passed, it being but very indifferently kept; the rooms very dirty; whereas when I was here before no Inn could be in better order'. In 1839 Lord Cockburn wrote, 'There are only two things wanted to make Aviemore one of the grandest places in Scotland. They are wood and a house'.

Not until the railway was opened on 9 September, 1863, on the line between Perth and Forres, and 1884, when the plans were passed for the direct line to Inverness by Carrbridge, did Aviemore grow towards its present eminence. The Highland Railway from Aviemore reached Carrbridge in July, 1892, and in November, 1898, it arrived at Inverness. Aviemore was then a junction and a place of importance for travellers. The line from Aviemore to Forres via Grantown was closed in 1965, but the Strathspey Railway enthusiasts have taken over the rails as far as Boat of Garten. They run steam trains between the two stations in the summer and work hard to restore their collection of ancient engines to their former glory. Their base is well marked.

To the west of the A9 there is Craigellachie National Nature Reserve (885125), with a Nature Trail. Sir Thomas Dick Lauder, writing of the great flood of 1829, said, 'Nothing could equal the sublimity of the scene on Tuesday morning. An entire river poured itself over the rugged brow of the hill of Upper Craigellachie, converting its furrowed front into one vast and diversified waterfall'.

The B9152 runs on south from Aviemore, passing the Lynwilg Hotel, once a Stage House, at 874095. The Inverness to Perth coach started in 1814, and in 1831 no fewer than seven coaches passed daily to and from Inverness. By 1835 they ran three times a week each way for nine months of the year and twice a week for the remaining three months.

After Aviemore, the ninety-foot pillar erected on the top of Tor Alvie (885089) to the 5th and last Duke of Gordon, who died in 1836, catches the eye. It was completed 'in a year, to the joy of the Building Committee', in 1840. Not so visible is the cairn raised by the Marquis of Huntly in August, 1815, to the memory of two Highland colonels, John Cameron of Fassfern, of the 92nd Regiment, the Gordon Highlanders (see p.215), who was killed at Quatre Bras on 16 June, 1815, and Sir Robert Macara, of the 42nd, Royal Highland Regiment, the Black Watch, who fell at Waterloo on 18 June, 'pierced through the chin until the point of the lance reached the brain', when attacking French lancers were thought, until almost the last moment, to be friendly Brunswickers. The Waterloo Cairn belongs to the Gordon Highlanders and there is a public right of way to it, which is reached by turning in to the left/east through a gateway marked for Kinrara a few yards beyond the Lynwilg Hotel and following the drive round the hill to the first house on the right. Leave the car here and follow the path to the south of the garden up the hill to the cairn.

Tor Alvie is on the Kinrara estate (not open) which was once

Highland Wild Life. Mr Eddie Orbell, the Managing Director of the Highland Wild Life Park near Kincraig is seen with four bear cubs which were born in the Park. Many other animals which used to roam these hills can be seen here, but modern dogs must be left outside. The Park is an out-station of the Edinburgh Zoological Gardens.

the home of the beautiful and famous Jane Maxwell, Duchess of Gordon, who is said to have helped her son, the Marquis of Huntly, to raise the 92nd regiment by asking recruits to take their enrolment guinea from between her lips. She is buried at St Eatha's (or Bride's) chapel (868077). Her funeral cortège from London, the hearse drawn all the way by six black Belgian horses, was long remembered.

At 864094, on a headland above Loch Alvie, is the attractive parish church. Here the Reverend William Gordon was minister to the age of 101, and was preaching to within six

months of his death. He gave help to the fugitives from
Culloden and was duly arrested and taken to the Duke of
Cumberland. He is said to have been 'a small portly man' who
'addressed the Royal Duke with great calmness. "May it please
your Royal Highness, I am exceedingly straitened between two
contrary commands, both coming from high authority. My
Heavenly King's Son commands me to feed the hungry, to
clothe the naked, to give meat and drink to my very enemies
and to relieve to my utmost power all objects in distress,
indiscriminately, that come my way. My earthly king's son
commands me to drive the homeless wanderer from my door,
to shut my bowels of compassion against the needy and to
withhold from my fellow mortals in distress the relief which it
is in my power to afford. Pray, which of these commands am I
to obey?" Surprisingly, Cumberland answered that he should
obey those of his Heavenly King, and Mr William Gordon
returned safely to Alvie'. This story was told to Dr I.F. Grant
(1887-1983) by her nurse, though by the 1920s it was largely
forgotten.

St Ailbhe (pronounced Alvie) was an Irish missionary, a
bastard son of Olchu. His mother fled before his birth, but was
found by Cronan, Olchu's master, who ordered her to put the
baby on the hill. She put him by a sheltering rock (all, rock)
and he was suckled by wolves and fostered by one Lochlan,
who gave him to some passing Britons. They baptised him and
took him to Britain. He later went to Rome and, on his way
back to Ireland, he founded an unidentified monastery, which
he left to the care of the MacCillie (sons of the sacred cell). It is
possible, with the matching names, that the monastery was
here. The church is mentioned in the Bishop of Moray's
records in 1107. Other religious sites in the district were: two
dedicated to St Eatha or Bride, one at Kinrara and one at
Banchor (see p.73), two to St Moluag, at Balavil and Chapelton
(see p.61), and one to St Drostan at Dunachton (see p.56).

The present Alvie church dates from 1768. It was repaired
in 1833 and later, by Sir Basil Spence, in 1952. During the re-
flooring in 1880, the skeletons of 150 soldiers were found
buried under the cobble stones. There is no history or legend
to account for them and, unfortunately, no one thought to take
any notice of what remained of their clothes and weapons. The

bones were removed to the graveyard, where a stone was put up:

Buried here are Remains of 150 human bodies
Found October 1880
Beneath the floor of this church.
Who they were, when they lived, how they died
Tradition notes not.
Their bones are dust, their good swords rust,
Their souls are with the saints, we trust.

There is a tradition that Nighean Bhan (the fair washer) was seen on the shores of Loch Alvie washing many bloody shirts, which she laid to dry around the loch, complaining loudly at the size of her task, so there may have been a battle, long since forgotten, in the neighbourhood, or the shirts may have belonged to the dead of the battle a bit further south (see p.130). The white waterlilies on Loch Alvie, *Nymphea Alba*, are a rare flower: perhaps they represent those shirts.

The 1829 flood took place when it was a Sacrament Sunday at Alvie and a number of ministers had come to assist. They were all marooned in the church until the following Wednesday.

In 1901, Sir George Henschel, the famous musician, built his house at Alltnacriche (873110). He and his family spent their summers there and Sir George would row across the loch to play the organ for the service at Alvie church. His daughter now lives at Ballintean (845018) with her ponies, which people come from far to ride.

When the railway was built, a skeleton was found with a pair of very large hart's horns laid across it, and, on the Moor of Alvie, Roman urns are said to have been found, placed under small arches of half-burned bricks.

Alvie House (not open) (842075) was built by Sir James Ramsden from Huddersfield in Yorkshire in the early nineteenth century, after he had moved all the cottages that were on the site down to Spey Bank (845067). Although Alvie is on the fringes of the old Caledonian Forest, Sir James planted a further 2000 acres of woods, but eventually sold Alvie and moved to Ardverikie (see p.207), on the south side of Loch Laggan.

At 830056 the turning to the left/south-east leads to Kincraig and on to Insh church (835054) overlooking Loch Insh, now a bird sanctuary. Kincraig is a railway village. The line came in 1863 and the station was called Boat of Insh; it was closed in 1965. When the river is low at the north end of Loch Insh, the stone with the ring set in it for the ferry boat can be seen. This is all that is left of the Boat of Insh, which ended in 1880, when the bridge was built. Prince Charles Edward is said to have stayed at the Boat Inn. This has now gone, though its roses remain, which Queen Victoria found interesting when she came here.

Mrs Grant of Laggan wrote that in the eighteenth century in Badenoch 'in every cottage there is a musician and in every hamlet a poet'. At the same time Miss Grant of Rothiemurchus said that every tenth Highlander could play some instrument tolerably well. This disproves the general supposition that the Calvinistic ideas of the Church of Scotland destroyed all the artistic side of Scottish life. William Wordsworth, the composer (d.1988) lived in Kincraig. He named some of the tunes that he wrote for the *Cambridge Hymnal* from this district *Speyside*, *Glenfeshie*, *Gynack* and *Morlich*. He also wrote a *Highland Overture* and *Variations on a Scottish Theme*.

Insh church claims to be one of the few places in Scotland where worship has continued since the days of St Columba. The present building was repaired in 1830 when a Parliamentary manse was built, now called Insh House. But its origins probably go back to a pre-historic religious site, for it is said to be one of the places visited by the Swan Children of Llyr, and it has the by-name of The Swan Chapel.

Llyr was the son of Manannan, the sea god, who is often 'christened' as St Michael. Llyr had four children by his first wife, three sons and a daughter. They were hated by their stepmother, who turned them into swans for 900 years. Through all these centuries they flew, and swam, singing, until they were found on a small island in Ireland by a Christian priest. Day by day they came to his bell and, linked by a silver chain, they worshipped in his chapel. At last they were taken to meet Deoch, the wife of the king of Connacht, and there in the court they regained their human form – but they were 900 years old. The priest baptised them before they died.

To this day, two types of swan, Bewicks and Whoopers, visit Loch Insh. One tenth of the British wintering population of Whoopers spend the winters here before flying to Iceland to breed. The Royal Society for the Protection of Birds has set up hides on the south side of the marsh for the benefit of bird-watchers. Although there is a centre for Water Sports on Loch Insh, the loch is said to be the home of giant eels, which is why bodies are rarely recovered from its waters.

In the early years of this century the fittings of Insh church were renewed, and again in 1964, when clear glass, inscribed with an Iona Cross by Helen Munro, of Edinburgh, was fitted. The parish minister, the Reverend A. Hutchinson, took the service, the Reverend George Macleod, now the Very Reverend Lord Macleod of Fuinary, re-dedicated the church and the Right Reverend Kenneth Carey, Bishop of Edinburgh in the Scottish Episcopal Church, preached the sermon. No doubt the collection was taken in the long-handled wooden ladles.

The church is dedicated to St Eonan, or Adamnan, who lived c.690 and was the biographer of St Columba. His bell is still in the church. If it is removed, it cries 'Tom Eonan' (Eonan's hill, one name for this site, but it can also mean the hill of birds) until it is safely home again. Each clang brings a year of bad luck to whoever took it. Taken to an exhibition in Edinburgh or Glasgow, it flew back, but hit a stone in Drumochter, which accounts for its broken edge.

Continuing along the main road, a turning to the right/north at 810036 passes under the A9 to the Highland Wild Life Park, an outstation of the Edinburgh Zoological Gardens. Here visitors drive through birchwood and grassland where they can see examples of once-native animals, such as wild horses and European bison, living freely. There are enclosures for smaller mammals and birds and a Centre shows the changing story of Highland wild life. No pets are allowed in, but free kennels are provided.

As the road nears Kingussie (pr. Kin-you-sie), it passes under the A9, changing its number yet again, becoming the A86, and runs into Kingussie (Cinn a' Ghuithsaich, head of the pine wood).

The village, though founded as such by the 4th Duke of

Gordon, who was trying, vainly here, to encourage the manufacture of linen, is an old place, for there was a priory here, dedicated to St Columba, which was endowed by the Earl of Huntly in 1490, and in the churchyard there is a stone commemorating the saint and 'according to tradition, planted by himself'. The former parish church was built on this site, and was rebuilt in 1624. It can be reached by walkers turning off the High Street more or less opposite the Royal Hotel. In 1792, when the new church was built on Tom a' Mhoid (hill of the court), it was said that there was no village in the parish. This church was replaced in 1824.

A signposted turning to the left/south leads to the Highland Folk Museum. There is a large car park adjacent to the house. This Museum started as a collection made by the late Dr I.F. Grant in the 1920s and '30s, and in 1935 she kept it on Iona. Later, as she acquired more examples of the everyday things of our predecessors, she moved her collection to Laggan, and then to Am Fasgadh (the shelter) here in Kingussie. In 1954 she handed it over to the four Scottish Universities but under their control things did not go well. It is now run by the Highland Regional Council, and Miss Grant was happy to come and see it in their good hands before she died in 1983.

Not only is the house, itself a Listed Building, full of things to see, but in the grounds are reconstructions of early dwellings and a Farming Museum. The whole includes transport, dairy, cultivation, costume, furniture and other displays. It was the first Folk Museum in Britain and one of the very first in Europe. It is a fine monument to one determined woman, who also wrote books for sixty years, many of which are still in print.

Kingussie has most kinds of shops catering for local people and visitors. It was here in 1952 that Ewen Ormiston started pony-trekking, now enjoyed all over the country. Yet it was a Kingussie man who said, 'Kingussie was forgotten when Sodom and Gomorrah were destroyed – and the people who were too bad to live in Kingussie are in Newtonmore!' The two villages are great rivals when the shinty season comes around.

Only 2½ miles south of Kingussie on the A86 is Newtonmore. This village, with its useful shops, was essentially the work of James Macpherson, the son of 'Ossian' Macpherson

Going for a Drive. Only a few years ago, this was the main means of transport, and elegantly dressed ladies would trot round the roads to visit their friends. This exhibit is in the Highland Folk Museum at Kingussie, together with many other treasures gathered originally by Dr I.F. Grant to form the first Folk Museum in Britain.

of Balavil. As with other places, the district has an unrecorded history that goes further back, for there is an ancient chapel of St Bride with a burial ground at Banchor (710987) approached by a road which it took an Act of Parliament to keep open, as the notice board shows, and another at Nuide (731986).

At the west end of the village, where the roads divide, the A86 to the west (see p.211) and the B9150 (once the A9) to the south, is the Clan Macpherson Museum. This contains a number of treasures of that clan, including the Black Chanter and the silver centrepiece showing Cluny holding the Officer's horse at Dalchully (see p.212). Taking the B9150, just beyond the village on the right/west is The Eilean, the home of the famous Newtonmore shinty team, the rivals of the Kingussie men and many others in the north. The road crosses the Spey just below its confluence with the Calder, then, after an awkward railway bridge, it joins the A9 by the picnic site at Raliabeg (704970).

There is at present a well-advanced plan between Ross Noble, the Curator of the Highland Folk Museum, and the Highland Regional Council for the creation of a Highland Folk Park at Newtonmore. It will cover some ninety acres and give a vision of how things were, good and bad, no doubt, in 'the good-old days', when life was hard and uncomfortable for most people.

Returning to Aviemore, at 893116 the road to the mountains and chairlift turns left/east and over the railway and the Spey to join the B970 at Inverdruie. Here there is a fish farm, where trout are reared in ponds and visitors may catch their own fish, if they so desire. Shortly after the fish farm, on the left of the road at 901112, is the small Episcopal church of St John. It was dedicated in 1930 and consecrated, being free of debt, in 1931. It is the work of Sir Ninian Comper, the architect, who was often a guest of the Grants of Rothiemurchus and found that it was a long way to the nearest Episcopal church. The silk on the baldachino came from China.

Just beyond the church is the turning to the Dell (not open) which was the house that Patrick Grant of Muckrach built and lived in while he was building the Doune (see p.75).

Taking the right/south fork by the green, the B970 runs south along the right bank of the Spey and the western side of the once vast Rothiemurchus Forest, formerly twenty miles long by about seven miles wide. This forest, although quite a lot now remains (see p.80), is 'the last sad remnant of the Caledonian Forest which stretched from Glen Lyon over the Moor of Rannoch to Strathspey and from Glencoe to the Braes of Mar'. It is now part of the Nature Reserve and is not always open in the stalking season. From 1764 the London water supply was carried in pipes made from the long straight trunks of the Rothiemurchus pines. Some, marked P.G. (Patrick Grant), were replaced within the memory of people alive in the 1960s.

At 891097 there is a turning to the left/east to Loch an Eilean (of the island). A handsome carved stone pillar stands in the turning, a memorial to Dr James Martineau, brother of Harriet Martineau, the novelist. He was a leader of the Unitarian movement and lived in Rothiemurchus for many years, where he set up a school of drawing and carving. His pupils made the monument in 1900. The Old Manse, which lies at 894096, off this road to the left, is an unspoiled example of a Parlimentary Manse of the single-storeyed design. It was built without a new church being built alongside. There is a parking place at the north end of the loch and an Information Centre. There is a very pleasant Nature Trail all round Loch an Eilean, good for dogs, and the more energetic may extend it to Loch Gamha (of the stirks) (893097) where a bronze cauldron, dating from the Bronze or Early Iron Age, was found in 1964.

The castle on the island was once occupied by the Comyns, but its best-known inhabitant was Alexander Stewart, son of Robert II, better known as *The Wolf of Badenoch*. He ruled this part of Scotland with an iron hand and was an energetic castle-builder, for he either strengthened or rebuilt this castle, Ruthven (see p.80), and Lochindorb (975364). On 25 March, 1524, Lachlan Beg Mackintosh, the Chief, was murdered by his foster-brother and his nephew while he was hunting at Ravoch (Raigmore) near Tomatin (see p.32). The murderers were later caught and, after eight years' imprisonment in Loch an Eilean, they were tried, found guilty, and tortured; then one was beheaded and the other hanged. In very hard winters the loch freezes over and the castle can be reached on foot.

At 889095 the drive down to the Doune (not open) (886097) leaves the B970. The old dun (fort) is a boat-shaped mound by the Spey. Here the Shaws had their fort, which they lost to the Comyns, but they regained it for a short time before the Crown acquired it. Whether it was destroyed by the Comyns or by Patrick Grant when he acquired the lands of Rothiemurchus in the late sixteenth century is not known, but a curse was laid on the next builder to use the site. Perhaps for this reason, the present house is at the foot of the mound. The Doune has been in the hands of the restorers since 1979, and will be for some time yet.

It was at the Doune that Elizabeth Grant of Rothiemurchus wrote her *Memoirs of a Highland Lady*, which gives a lively description of life there nearly two hundred years ago. She mentions Black Sandy Grant, who was forced to flee after cutting off a girl's ear. His son, Ulysses Grant, commanded the Union forces in the American Civil War and was elected President in 1868.

The ancient church of Rothiemurchus (886093), which fell into disuse in 1929, is marked on the map as a ruin. It can be reached by a white gate on the right/west of the road, next to a lodge (886089), and a path down through the woods. Here, on a flat gravestone, are five loose stones. The headstone is modern and says,

THE GRAVE OF
SEATH MOR
SCORFHIACLACH
VICTOR IN THE
COMBAT AT PERTH
1336.

This is the grave of Farquhar Shaw, who 'led and was one of the 30 of this Clan who defeated the 30 Davidsons of Invernahavon on the North Inch of Perth, 1396. He died 1405'. The stones, which are said to resemble cheeses, are older than 1405 and probably came from the old dun, complete with magical powers, for they are dangerous things to move. Once a footman of the Duke of Bedford took a stone and threw it into the river. He was made to replace it almost at once, but was drowned in the Spey within a week. Two men, more recently, moved the stones and both died within the year.

Further down the B970, on the right/west of the road is Inshriach House (873073). It was built by Adam Black, the publisher, for his son, who was killed in the First World War. In 1938 Jack Drake started his Alpine Gardens here. There was a gap between 1939 and 1945, but since then the name has been established and the plants are now exported to many countries. The gardens are open.

Off the road, at 857065, is Dalnavert, once the home of Helen Shaw, whose son was Sir John Alexander Macdonald (1815-91), the first Prime Minister of Canada, who was mainly instrumental in the creation of the Dominion of Canada and,

Tossing the caber, Newtonmore Highland Games. This heavy caber (stick) is thrown in such a way that it lands on the end that is at the top in the picture and then turns over to lie at '12 o'clock', i.e. straight ahead, from the thrower. It is not an easy thing to do and some contestants cannot toss it at all.

with Donald Smith (see p.147), in the construction of the Canadian Pacific Railway.

Near Dalnavert lived Duncan Mackintosh, the most handsome man in the district. His wife Betsy and seven daughters were very ugly, though they were splendid workers, so that the farm was the richest for miles around. Despite this, Duncan felt that he was being pitied by the local women for having such an ugly family. Betsy suspected that he was not faithful to her when he took to going out every evening. She followed him and found him with a very beautiful woman dressed in green. Betsy fell on her. She only got the green dress, but at once she became beautiful. A strip of the dress was

torn off by a nail on the house door and the daughter who
picked it up immediately became beautiful and so did the
others when given a piece of it. Very soon they were all
married to the most eligible men in the district. But (there is
always a 'but') the beautiful Betsy became useless on the farm,
which soon went to pieces, leaving Duncan longing for the days
of his plain but useful Betsy. It does not appear that Duncan
ever worked at all.

Beyond the Dalnavert turning there is another to the right/
west through the woods to a Heather Farm, with thousands of
tiny sprigs growing into strong plants. Just to the south is Loch
Geal (white) (0854058) which is said to contain 'hairy trout'.
One account says that they had 'very thick scales, from each of
which a fine hair, light in colour and about half an inch in
length, protruded, giving the creature a most unnatural and
revolting appearance'. It is possible that this loch is connected
underground with the Feshie or the Spey.

At 853044 a sharp turning to the left/east through the woods
goes to Glen Feshie Gliding Club, which has a landing strip
here. Visitors are very welcome. In the woods behind the
landing strip there is another Nature Trail.

The road crosses the gorge of the Feshie at Feshie Bridge
(852044), which survived the 1829 flood. General Wade
planned to build a road through Glen Feshie to link Strathspey
with Deeside, and the idea is revived from time to time, but so
far it has not been built. The present road up the glen is part
of a Nature Trail and can be driven over to the old house at
Achlean (853975) before walking on.

Well up the track, at 846927, a little further up than Glen
Feshie Lodge, and on the right bank of the river, is Ruigh-
aitchean (cultivated field). There used to be several buildings
here, called *The Huts*. Sir Edwin Landseer (the painter of *The
Monarch of the Glen)* painted the inside wall of one of the huts.
Nothing now remains. Queen Victoria, riding through from
Balmoral on 4 September, 1860, wrote in her diary, 'then we
came upon a most lovely spot – the scene of all Landseer's
glory – and where there is a little encampment of wood and
turf huts, built by the late Duchess of Bedford: now no longer
belonging to the family and alas! all falling into decay'. In 1861,

she wrote, 'We got off and went to look at a fresco of stags of Landseer's, over the chimney piece'. This time she was riding from Balmoral by Glen Feshie to stay with the Duke of Atholl at Blair Atholl.

At 839044 a turning to the right/north to Kingcraig passes Insch church (see p.70). Continuing south, the B970 runs along the south side of the Bird Sanctuary and reaches Tromie Bridge.

It was up Glen Tromie that Captain Macpherson of Ballachroan (733003), the Black Officer, set off in December, 1800, to go hunting in Gaick Forest. The party passed the night in a bothy, 'the only human habitation for many miles, at the head of Loch an t-Seillich (of the willows)'. Late in the night they were woken by the sound of someone or something scrambling about on the roof. There were loud bangs and a 'swishing sound such as a fishing rod would make if used as a whip'. The men and their dogs were silenced by terror. After a time Captain Macpherson went out and the others could hear him talking and being reproved in 'goat-like tones' for not bringing enough men. He came back and later in the day they all went home.

On 31 December the Captain set forth again, but only one of his previous companions, a Macfarlane noted for his piety, would go with him. It happened that the Captain had left his watch and keys at home and so a party of men went out on New Year's Day to find him, knowing that the two men would be staying in the bothy, which appeared to have been demolished as by an avalanche. They found Macfarlane's body some way from it. Captain Macpherson was not seen again.

At 764997, on the right/west of the road, is Ruthven Castle. Although it is clearly a very ancient site, surprisingly little written evidence is easily found. It would seem to be a natural mound in the swamps of the Spey which has been improved over the centuries so that it is now a very strong site. At one time the Comyns had a castle here, but when they had fallen from power it came to the Crown. The end of the Comyns is said to have come when 'the wicked Lord Walter' was torn to pieces by eagles in Gaick at Leum na Feinne (leap of the Feinne). He was said to have been on his way to force the

Ruthven women to work 'unclothed and naked' in his harvest fields, so he deserved what he got:

> While in the wood there is a tree
> A Cumming will deceitful be.

Two of the better-known occupiers of Ruthven were Alexander Stewart, *The Wolf of Badenoch,* and his son, Alexander, the Earl of Mar, who became Justiciar of the North (see p.16). It passed to the Earl of Huntly in 1451, and in 1646 Huntly imprisoned Lochiel and Keppoch here before executing them at Elgin. Dundee's men, under Coll Macdonald of Keppoch, burned the castle in 1689 and the Crown bought the ruin in 1715, building the barracks on the mound in 1719. They were so strong that in 1745 they were held by a sergeant and ten men against two hundred Jacobites, who could not break into the solid walls. In 1746 it fell and the Jacobites burned everything in it that could be burned. After Culloden quite a number of them rallied here, some say 8,000 men, only to get the message that each should look out for himself. The ruins are worth scrambling up to see and they are dramatically floodlit in the evening.

From here the B970 turns right/north and goes to Kingussie, the old road having been destroyed by the new A9.

Returning to the green at Inverdruie (902109), the old school on the northward B970 is now a Visitor's Centre. Here is the place to find out all about the Rothiemurchus estate, some of which is explained by entertaining drawings in one of the rooms. The estate entered into an agreement with the Nature Conservancy Council in 1954 in order to conserve the forest, which contains, among other things, naturally regenerating pine forest, in which no exotic species may be planted, and, on the high tops of the Grampians, an Arctic tundra wilderness. Eighty-five per cent of the estate is now protected as a site of Special Scientific Interest (SSSI). As a result, the characteristic fauna and flora of all the differing types of land have survived. Free information leaflets are available, showing many of the walks that can be taken, and there is a Ranger Service to advise and guide. For the less

Winter in the Cairngorms. These slopes have become a favourite resort for skiers, and the ski-lift takes them almost to the top of Cairngorm itself. In the summer it provides an easy way to the top for the spectacular views that can be had from there.

energetic, there are Estate Tours by tractor and trailer.

At 903107 a side road goes right/south to Upper Tullochgrue, and from there it is not far to walk to the old field settlements at 915086. But from a short distance further along the B970 the tracks go to Loch Einich (915990) in the Cairngorm National Nature Reserve. This was set up in 1954, nearly sixty-four square miles, much of it a sub-arctic plateau, where introduced reindeer may be met. Loch Einich is cradled in the crags of Sgoran Dubh Mor and Beag (big and little precipitous dark heights), and Sgor Gaoith (of the wind) and Einich Cairn (937993).

Soon after the start of this track, the old drove road bears away to the left on its way to the better-known Lairig Ghru. It is popular with long-distance walkers, the distance from Aviemore to Braemar being about twenty-eight miles, climbing

81

to 2,733 feet on the county boundary at 974014. The meaning of Lairig Ghru is doubtful. Some say that it should be Lairig Cruaidh (hard pass), or Ruaidh (red) or Dhru (of the oak) or Gruamach (gloomy). The map-makers preferred the last and, apparently without any authority, shortened it to Ghru, which means nothing at all. This ancient road was widened in 1842 to allow the large herds to continue to use it until late in the nineteenth century.

The B970 leaves Inverdruie, passing the big hotel, for Coylum Bridge (cruing leum, narrow leap) and turning north (see below).

The road up to the ski-lift runs straight on through the forest. Between the road and the river are several Picnic Places, from which there are paths through the heather, just some of the signposted foot paths in the Rothiemurchus forest.

At 954100 the road enters the Glenmore Forest, nearly twenty square miles of which have belonged to the Forestry Commission since 1948. Soon it reaches Loch Morlich: 'Glen More, entered by a narrow mountain pass, opens into this scene of gloomy grandeur having in its bosom Loch Morlich, a lake nearly circular of 2 miles diameter'. It is not so gloomy now, but is a favourite place for swimming and sailing. Just beyond the loch is a group of buildings on the left of the road, and here, at 976097, between the car park and the chapel, is the monument to the Free Norwegians who trained here from 1940 to 1945 and introduced ski-ing to Scotland. Beyond is the National Outdoor Training Centre at Glenmore Lodge. Further on still is a large car park at the bottom of the ski-lift which reaches the Ptarmigan Restaurant (004048). From here it is an easy walk up to the summit of Cairngorm, 4084 feet. On a good day the view from the summit is spectacular.

From the turn north on the B970 at Coylum Bridge, Loch Pityoulish is soon reached, reputedly the home of a White Kelpie. It appears on moonlight nights to carry off its prey. Between the road and the east end of the loch is a hollow where nothing will grow but blaeberries. It was here that the Shaws annihilated a party of Comyns. The blaeberry is the badge of the Comyns.

Summer in the Cairngorms. Loch Morlich, cradled in the hills, has a splendid sandy shore and is a popular place for picnics. The Loch Morlich Water Sports Centre provides training for those who wish to learn how to be safe on water, and to enjoy themselves at the same time. The way up to the high hills can be seen in the background.

At 943163 a narrow road to the right/east runs up into Abernethy Forest and circles Tore Hill (989172). The turning at 983176 goes to Loch Garten (see p.86).

In 1728 Sir James Grant allowed the York Building Company to take 60,000 trees over fifty years from the Abernethy Forest. The smelters at Balnagown were fed by this timber and with ore from the Lecht, but they went out of business in 1737. During the French wars the Royal Navy needed a great deal of timber to keep its 'wooden walls' afloat. Aaron Hill designed the first rafts used to move quantities of trees down the Spey to the coast. They were manned by local men called Floaters. One of the *Dog Heads* used in this work is in the Kingussie Folk Museum. So fast ran the river that Floaters leaving early in the morning were said to have walked

83

home from Garmouth, some thirty miles, at the end of the day.

The Royal Society for the Protection of Birds bought the Abernethy Forest in February, 1988. The thirty square miles of the new Nature Reserve include 4,000 acres of the ancient Caledonian Forest, the largest surviving fragment and the richest in wildlife, with golden eagles, peregrine falcons, and the Scottish crossbill, as well as ptarmigan and snow bunting. It is the largest land purchase in Europe made by a voluntary conservation organisation.

Aaron Hill lived at Coulnakyle (997216) and used to head his letters home 'From the Golden Groves of Abernethy'. During the first Jacobite Rising, in 1689, General Hugh Mackay had his Headquarters at the same house. Aaron Hill was the author of

> Gently stroke a stinging nettle
> It will sting you for your pains.
> Grasp it like a man of mettle
> And it soft as silk remains.

Not everyone thought that felling was a good thing, and one man, known as Peter Porter, because his trade had been, and his family's before him, to carry goods across the river, decided to buy a tree to save it. He was successful, for the Canadian loggers in the Second World War did not touch his tree. It still stands, though rather battered by the weather without the protection of its former neighbours.

Kincardine church (938155) is off the road on a mound, with a well, now filled in, called the Well of Tomhaldidh (Tom a'h-allaidh, mound of the wolf) and a dew cup which is never known to be dry. In the churchyard is a stone to Sir Walter Stewart, grandson of Robert II. He was the third son of the Wolf of Badenoch and was knighted after good work at the Battle of Harlaw in Aberdeenshire, a major but indecisive battle in 1411 between the Crown and the Lord of the Isles. 'Macdonald had the victory, but the goverment the printer'.

Colonel John Roy Stewart was a native of Kincardine and a Jacobite who fought at Culloden (see p.38). Although he had to hide after Culloden, he emerged to dance at a wedding at Balnagown, and eventually went to Cluny's Cage (see p.210),

A Solitary Skier. From this spot, high on Cairngorm, there is a fine view to the west, covering Strath Spey with the Monadhliath hills beyond. Aviemore is in the middle distance, and below the white curve of snow the car park and ski-lifts can be seen.

and on to France, where he died soon after. He was a well-known poet and amused himself when skulking near his home after Culloden by composing in English variations on the metrical psalter:

> The Lord's my targe, I will be stout
> With Dirk and trusty blade,
> Though Campbells come in swarms about
> I will not be afraid.
>
> The Lord's the same as heretofore,
> He's always good to me;
> Though redcoats come a thousand more
> Afraid I will not be.

At 961196 there is a turning from the B970 to the right/ south of Loch Garten in the Abernethy Forest. At the right time of year, the early summer, there are AA signs *To the Ospreys*. At 977184, by Loch Garten, is a Nature Reserve, principally for the protection of the first Ospreys that returned to Scotland to nest in 1954. For fifty years there had been no Ospreys (Fish Eagles) nesting in Scotland and this nest, despite being watched at night and day by the R.S.P.B., has been robbed several times. In the spring of 1987 there were fifty-one nests in Scotland, though their locations, except for this one and those at the Loch of the Lowes in Perthshire, are not made known to the public.

There are now two good car parks, one by the loch, and one between the B970 and the loch. Leave the car (and the dog) in one of them and walk along the marked track to the Observation Point, where large binoculars focused on the nest allows people to have a close-up view of the Osprey family at home, and sometimes to see one of the parents flying in with a fish in its claws to feed the young ones.

Nethy Bridge is a small village, convenient for both summer and winter holidays. In 1730 the York Building Company had a smelter here, but the exact site was lost until the great flood of 1829 uncovered it. At 002206 the Bridge crosses the Nethy, which runs from high in the Braes of Abernethy to the Spey. Just north of the bridge a turning to the right/east (part of the crossroads of which the left/west road goes past Counakyle to Broomhill (see p.63)) runs up into the hills and eventually joins the A939 at 067215. South of Nethy Bridge there are many walks through the Abernethy Forest, the longest of which leads past the Boiling Well at Rynettin (010150), where a well of white sand contains a tiny geyser which rises some inches above the level of the water, though it is very cold, and on by the Ryvoan bothy and An Lochan Uaine (the little green loch) (002105) to Glenmore Lodge.

The B970 goes north and on the left/west is Abernethy church and then, next door, the ruins of Castle Roy (006218). In 1203 the parish of Abernethy went east to Tomintoul in Banffshire (167190), north to Cromdale (076285) and south to Rothiemurchus (886094). In the churchyard is another dew cup which does not dry out. Castle Roy (ruadh, red) dates from the thirteenth century and was probably built by the Comyns.

At 036263 the B970 bears left, turning itself into the A95

An Osprey's Nest, Loch Garten. The picture shows one of the parent birds approaching the nest, which is wedged in the top of a dead pine tree. The Royal Society for the Protection of Birds has been guarding this tree since the first pair came in 1954, fifty years after the last pair had been known to nest in Scotland. In 1987 the R.S.P.B. knew of 51 nests.

and, crossing the Spey by the modern bridge, runs out of Inverness-shire into Grantown-on-Spey in Moray. But, keeping to the right, after a short distance the old Bridge of Spey, dating from 1754, can be walked over. The scramble down the bank to river level on the north side is worth the effort. The A95, on its way to Keith, leaves Inverness-shire at 064169.

Soon after the old Bridge, the A939 leaves the A95 and climbs the shoulders of the hills, following for much of the way an old military road. This is a beautiful road, with little traffic.

There is a View Point at 104202 and then the road runs
steeply down to Bridge of Brown (124204) where it leaves
Inverness-shire for Banffshire.

CHAPTER 6

The East Side of Loch Ness to Fort Augustus

The B862, leads out of Inverness along the east side of the river, between the water and the Castle, starting at the Ness Bridge. Go to the bridge and turn left/south at the east end of it and follow the river bank, with views of the Cathedral, the Eden Court Theatre and the Royal Northern Infirmary, to a T-junction. Turn right/south, just by a small garden, the Cavell Garden, where the Town's War Memorial stands. This road is liable to be choked, but not impassably so, by parked cars, so another road bears up the hill to the left under the Castle Wall, a few yards from the Bridge. Take this and keep right at the top to join the riverside road near the War Memorial. Alternatively, go up Castle Street on the east side of the Castle and keep right at the fork just south of the Castle. This road leads down to the Haugh, and is joined by the two roads previously described.

In the river, and approachable on foot from either bank, are the Ness Islands, a pleasant place to walk in and formerly a favourite resort of the Magistrates. Beyond the Islands, at 654437, is the turning to the right/west to the Holm Mills. These have been here since 1771 and it is possible to see them at work and to buy some of their products. It is from here that the material came to hold the banks of the Canal (see p.102).

At 651423 a turning to the left/east will lead round to Holm Motte (653421). It is on the right of the road, a little way up the slope, and has some fine Scots Pines on it. It is an Ancient Monument and is all that remains of a castle that controlled the ford, so the river has probably changed its course a little. It is in a defensible place, with the burn close by and deep ditches on the south and east. The motte is sixteen feet high and forty-five feet across inside its six-foot ramparts. The later Holm House (652421) (not open) was the home of the Mackintoshes of Holm. It dates from the sixteenth century and has crow-stepped gables. At present a new road is being built within feet of this turning, so it may be altered in the future.

At 642409 a turning to the left/east of Torbreck makes it

possible to walk across to the Stone Circle (645404), the only free-standing stone circle in the county. It is only seventeen feet across, but has nine tall stones, one of which is seven feet above the ground. It may be a later development of the Clava cairns.

Just beyond Scaniport, to the north-west of the road at 623400, is Borlum (not open). This is a name frequently found in the Highlands. In origin it is Bordland, the land that kept the table (board) of a local castle well filled. In this case the castle could have been Inverness, Holm or Aldourie. It is now a pleasant eighteenth/nineteenth century laird's house of a fairly ordinary design, but it stands on the site of the homes of the Mackintoshes of Borlum, who, with one exception, seem to have been a particularly quarrelsome lot; the worst 'who surpassed them all for fiendish ferocity', being the Mackintosh who married Bessy Innes. She was known as 'The Witch of Borlum', but probably not to her face, for in 1618 she organised the murder of Provost Junor by her two sons because he had remonstrated with her in Inverness. Although the Town Council knew full well who had murdered their Provost, they could not bring them to justice, since Borlum himself was on the Council and was under the protection of the Earl of Huntly.

But, from that day the star of the family Borlum waned until at last they had to leave their old home and Edward, the last laird, moved in the middle of the eighteenth century to Raitts, now called Belleville (see p.57), in Badenoch. Here he continued his wicked ways, more or less as a highwayman, finally fleeing to France before the Revolution of 1789, but leaving his illegitimate brother Alastair to face the wrath of the people for crimes that were certainly Edward's. Alastair was hanged at Muirfield, still protesting his innocence, which was believed by many people, but not by the judge.

Set against his forebears, Brigadier General William Mackintosh, 'Old Borlum' (1662-1743), shines like a star. 'His indomitable courage, enterprising character and unshaken constancy was conspicuously displayed in his daring expedition across the Forth – his skilful and masterly retreat to Kelso – his bravery at Preston – his escape from Newgate, and subsequent flight to France have left for him a proud name in the annals

Eden Court Theatre, Inverness. This fine modern building is as interesting inside as outside. The original Eden Court, now part of the theatre complex, can be seen on the right of the picture. It was the home of Bishop Robert Eden, who was Bishop when the adjoining St Andrew's Episcopal Cathedral was built in the 1860s.

of his country'. He was a staunch Jacobite in both the '15 and '19 Risings and died after a long captivity in Edinburgh Castle, during which time he wrote an early and valuable book on arboriculture.

A little further on, on the left/east of the road at 621389, is Kinchyle Cairn, a Clava-type cairn which was visited by James Boswell on his journey with Dr Samuel Johnson in 1773. On a narrow parallel road is Kinchyle (not open), formerly the home of the Chiefs of Macbain (see p.48).

Before reaching Dores a road to the right/west at 608370 leads down to the east end of Bona Ferry. This was a major crossing of the Ness, where it leaves the loch at 604375, until the building of the Caledonian Canal raised the water level and the ford could no longer be used. The ferry itself is now only a name. On the south side of this by-road are the gates to Aldourie Castle (601372) (not open). This is a fine Victorian castle which incorporates an earlier tower of the sixteenth or seventeenth century.

Nearly opposite this turning is one that leads past Darris (an old spelling for Dores), once another Mackintosh house, and up the hill to the Macbain Memorial Garden (see p.48).

The road divides at Dores (600350). The Dores Inn was once a King's House on the Military Road. It is the lower road, the B852, that is the Military Road, built by Wade in 1732. The view across the loch is dominated by the round head of Meallfourvonie (see p.116).

Starting from Dores, the B852, the Foyers road, runs through the woods along the east side of Loch Ness. There are at present five Picnic Sites set out at intervals along the road from which it might be possible to see Nessie. The fifth site has a View Point. A quarter of a mile past this site, on the side of the road between the road and the loch is a small inscribed stone, with a rather faded notice board behind it which was put up by the Inverness Field Club. This is An Ire Mhor (548278), where once stood a cottage which was visited by Boswell and Johnson in 1773. 'It was a wretched little hovel of earth only, I think, and for a window had only a small hole, which was stopped with a piece of turf, that was taken out occasionally to let in light . . . Our hostess asked us to sit down and take a dram. I saw one chair. She said she was as happy as any woman in Scotland. She could hardly speak any English except a few detached words'. At Rudha Ruadh (Red Point) (541271) are the remains of a Ferry House, from which a boat used to cross to Castle Urquhart on the other side of the loch, and, not so long ago, took the children from this side of the loch to the Secondary School at Drumnadrochit (see p.113).

At Inverfarigaig, take the turn to the left for the Forestry Commission's Farigaig Forest Exhibition Centre (see p.96).

Further south, Boleskine House (509222) (not open), on the left/east of the road and above it, was the home, early in the twentieth century, of Aleister Crowley (1875-1947), the self-designated 'wickedest man alive'. He was fascinated by the occult from his youth and quite appalling rumours followed him, but how 'wicked' he really was is unknown. It is said that his mistress lived on the other side of the loch at Grotaig (see p.116). Below the House and the water, at 507224, is Boleskine

Peat Cutting. Peat is still cut by hand in many places to provide fuel for the winter months. The curiously shaped spade is designed to cut and lift the slices of peat. The peats are then carefully arranged so that the prevailing wind will dry them before they are carried down to the house where they will be burned. In some parts the cutting is done on a commercial scale, with large machinery to slice away the peat. The whisky distilleries use a large amount of peat.

Burying Ground, with the remains of the ancient parish church. It is reputed to be a haunt of witches. The curious-looking yew trees at the northern end were defended by the people against the would-be destroyers, workmen from the District Council, in 1986. Parts of the trees had been cut and the new growth is now noticeable round the older centres.

At Foyers in 1896 William Murray Morrison of the British Aluminium Company (later Sir William) took the advice of Lord Kelvin and built the first electric reduction plant powered by hydro-electricity to produce aluminium. In spite of having a bomb dropped on it during the Second World War, its original turbine and water wheel continued to work until 1970, by which time it was considered to be too small to be practical. The machinery was not destroyed, but was carried up the Canal and shipped to Norway. The famous Falls of Foyers are

93

not quite as fine as they were since they have been harnessed, but are worth a visit.

British Aluminium has now gone, but the North of Scotland Hydro-Electric Board has built in its place a giant pumped-storage hydro-electric power-station down by the loch. From the west side of the loch it looks like an enormous barn. By day the turbines are fed by the water falling from Loch Mhor (see p.97). At night, when the demand is low, the power is used to pump water from Loch Ness 200 feet back up the hill to Loch Mhor so that no drought can affect the water supply. This power house produces 300,000 kw of generating capacity.

The B852 winds up the hill from Foyers and runs along the river Foyers to join the B862 at 496173 and that road goes on to Fort Augustus (see p.125).

The B862 climbs steadily from Dores, giving views across Loch Ness. At 595324 a narrow road to the right/south-west leads to Drummond and Erchite. Drummond was the home of Angus Mackintosh, the younger of the twins who found the barrel of gold (see p.43). He bought land which was then on the edge of Inverness, which he called Drummond, after his country home. His son, Phineas Mackintosh, 'a very wicked man', according to the late Captain William Mackay, was Provost of Inverness four times. He married Barbara Hossack in 1748, the daughter of Provost Hossack, who was kicked down the steps of the Town House by Cumberland (see p.20). His portrait hangs in the Council Chamber in the Town House. At Erchite are the scanty ruins of Erchite Castle, a Fraser stronghold, destroyed by Government troops after Culloden.

At 597315 the earlier Military Road from Inverness via Essich (see p.47) joins the B862. North-east of the junction across a field is Dun Riabhachaidh (601316). It is a large stone hill fort, oval in plan with two ruined stone walls. On the west side there is also a ditch and an outer turf rampart; on the east the rock face is a sufficient defence. It is not a difficult climb. Between the fort and Loch Duntelchaig are the remains of huts and field systems.

The road runs along the north side of Loch Ceo-glas, and across the water can be seen the rocky peak of Tom na Croich (Gallows Hill) where the Frasers of Lovat made an end of

'Milking time in the Highlands'. This painting, by Thomas Woodward, of a house at Garthbeg by Loch Killin, was exhibited in the Royal Academy in 1847 and is shown here through the kindness of C.W. Graham-Stewart. It would have been painted when it was still the custom to take the cattle, sheep and goats into the hills for the summer. The wife is milking the goat in the old-fashioned way, from behind. The family would have been very snug in their little stone house with its turf-thatched roof.

offenders among their Stratherrick tenants. At 577279 the roads divide.

The minor road runs straight on, a single-tracked affair with passing places to allow for overtaking or meeting other traffic. This is marked on some maps as a Military Road which, as a forestry track, leaves the road to the left at 547255 and goes down through the plantations to cross the River Farigaig by a modern wooden bridge. It goes a little further, but soon comes to an end.

At Balchuirn (542254), on the right/west of the road, is a cleared village and beyond it, at 538251, is Kilmoluag (St

Moluag a sixth-century contemporary of St Columba), an ancient abandoned burying ground, where some stones can still be seen within the stone wall.

The road goes down to Loch Ness by a series of extremely steep bends, to be taken in very low gear. 'This last route is well worthy of the tourist's notice, were it only for the sake of the splendid burst of Loch Ness from the plateau above these traverses.' The river Farigaig runs to the east of the road, down in a cleft which divides it from Dun Garbh and the great hill fort of Dun Dearduil. This narrow road meets the B852 at Inverfarigaig. Turn left/south, cross the river and turn left again for the Forestry Centre, or carry straight on along the B852 for Fort Augustus.

The B862 turns abruptly to the left/south-east at 577292 and across open moors with hut settlements on either side. Part of the Military Road runs past abandoned houses a short distance to the west to join the newer road before arriving at Errogie at the north end of Loch Mhor.

At Errogie (556225) a turning to the right/west from the B851 runs west through the plantations and down to the B852 at Inverfarigaig. 'This ravine is called the pass of Inverfarickaig, than which there is none more picturesquely beautiful and wild, or even stupendous, in the Highlands.' Almost at the foot of the Pass is the car park of the Forestry Commission's Faragaig Forest Exhibition Centre. From here there is a Forest Walk up the braes south of the Allt Mor. Almost opposite, at Fasnagruig (524236), a path, not used much and so a bit overgrown, leads, not easily, to Dun Dearduil (527238), the summit being 925 feet. Legend, and perhaps its name, link this great fortress with the story of Deirdre and the Sons of Uisneach, as one of the homes that they shared in Scotland. If they did, they chose one of the most spectacular sites possible. The stonework, once laced with timber, is vitrified in part. This is a sign of destruction, probably accidental here, when the interior timbers have caught fire. There would have been wooden buildings inside the walls, using the walls as a support. Had one of these gone on fire, the flames would have spread to the timbers inside the outer walls. Experiments have shown that the heat generated

Fort Augustus. This rather naive oil painting by an unknown artist shows the second fort at Fort Augustus and is shown here by kind permission of Mrs Robertson. Behind the Fort, Loch Ness stretches into the distance and the old military road from Inverness comes down the hill on the right to cross the river by Caulfield's bridge on its way to the west coast at Glenelg.

by such a fire would have been enough to melt many of the stones comprising the wall, to such an extent that they have melted into a glassy mass.

Returning back up the pass for a short way, there is a turning to the right/south which goes through Glen Liath, passing, on the left, the memorial to the famous geologist, Dr James Bryce, who fell to his death in this glen in 1877. This road joins the B852 above Foyers at 502198.

Loch Mhor, to the east of the B862 at Errogie, is the result of joining Loch Farraline and Loch Garth and is part of the North of Scotland Hydro-Electric Board's work at Foyers (see p.93). Often it is said that the shortest river name in Scotland is the Ae in Galloway, but the river that flows into the south end of Loch Mhor is the River E.

Past Errogie on the right/west side of the road is Old Gorthleck House (544210) (not open). It is an eighteenth-century two-storey, harled laird's house, nothing out of the ordinary, but it was here that Prince Charles, having fled from Culloden on 16 April, 1746, met Simon Fraser, Lord Lovat, who would lose his head on Tower Hill in London. Though the Prince had been welcome here on his previous visit, the news of the battle had gone before him and he was not encouraged to stay. Tom-a-mhoid (the Meeting Hill) (531205) was the site of the court of justice for Lovat's Stratherrick lands in the Middle Ages.

The next turning to the right/north leads to Boleskine Church (508183), dating from 1777. Before the junction with B852 is a low 'Resting Cairn' used by funeral parties where the bearers would change over on their way from the house to the burying ground. This one is known as Carn Bhean Ardachy (the Cairn of Ardachy's wife). One Ardachy (379075), still in the parish of Abertarff and Boleskine, lies south of Fort Augustus. There is an Ardochy at 477123, but this seems a bit close to have given its name to the cairn. Ard-achaidh means High-field. At 495171 is a Roman Catholic church, dating from 1859.

The foundations to be seen at 493171, on the east bank of the Fechlin, are those of the camp of Wade's men while they were working on the road. This road crossed the Fechlin by the White Bridge, an elegant structure dated 1732. The present road uses a modern bridge, just downstream, but it is worth a stop to walk over the high single arch of the old bridge and have a look up the river. The White Bridge Hotel, further up the hill, is said to have been originally a King's House. Knockie Lodge, dating from the eighteenth century, was the home of the Frasers and then Grants and is now a hotel.

At 485148 is a well-marked turning to Loch Killin, which lies in a deep cleft in the hills about four miles from the turning. 'The bottom of the glen, except that part of it covered by the lake, is a perfectly level tract of land, upwards of two miles in length, covered with the richest pasture and traversed by a small winding stream which flows into the lake. This extensive 'shealing' is frequented for the summer-grazing of the cattle and its surface is dotted in many places with little huts – the temporary residences of those in charge of them. Several hundreds of cattle are kept here from the beginning of June till the middle or end of August.' So wrote an anonymous author in 1847, but today the custom of 'shealing' or 'shieling' the cattle has died out. They were taken from the land round the houses to the higher grazing grounds for the summer, until the harvest was gathered, when they, with the younger people who had spent the summer with them, returned laden with the butter and cream for the winter.

The same writer says firmly that the eight miles on to Fort Augustus are 'along a hilly and tiresome road, and through a country by no means interesting', but it must be remembered that steep slopes, either up or down hill, meant that the traveller had to get out and walk, so probably when he reached the top of the pass (448104) at 1275 feet it was a day without views. Today, if the weather is clear, stop the car here, get out and look north. The road goes on down past Loch Tarff, where the wooded islets shows what the country would look like without either sheep or rabbits. The road crosses Allt Doe just above one of Wade's bridges, and runs across the south end of Loch Ness, with another Borlum (384082) to the south of the road. On the right/north of the road as it joins the A82 in Fort Augustus is Fort Augustus Abbey and School (open but ask at the Tourist Office, p.125), built on the site of the later Fort.

CHAPTER 7

Inverness to Glencoe, by Drumnadrochit and Fort William

The A82, the Fort William to Glasgow road, is reached by crossing the Ness Bridge or the new Friar's Bridge and taking the road to the west. It leaves the town when it crosses the Caledonian Canal at the Tomnahurich Swing Bridge.

On either side of the road is the eighteen-hole Torvean Golf Course. On the right/west along the side of the hill are two hospitals, Craig Dunain, built in 1864, and Craig Phadrig, finished in 1969. On the left/east is the Torvean quarry at the southern end of which, high in tangled brushwood and trees, are the scanty remains of Torvean Motte Hill. In its day it commanded the western end of the ford across the Ness, of which Holm Motte (see p.89) held the eastern end.

Close by was Kilvean (St Bean's church) where Gruoch, the wife of Macbeth, is said to be buried. She is still sleepless and her ghost is seen from time to time washing its hands in the river. In 1952 she was seen by some visitors, who thought she was acting in some film or other. She is known to be interested in the Royal family, and this was the day before Princess Elizabeth and the Duke of Edinburgh were flying out to Africa, so some anxiety was felt for their safety. In fact, it was the King who died.

On the right/west of the road at 627424 is Dunain House, now part of Craig Dunain Hospital, but from 1452 the home of the senior line of the Baillie family.

At 624416 a road, signposted for Blackfold and Abriachan, bears away to the right and into the hills as part of the old road south (see p.107). It was not until 1798 that the road along the west side of the loch reached Drumnadrochit. The military road built by General Wade ran along the east side of the loch (see p.92).

Keeping right up the road to Blackfold and Abriachan, the entrance on the left/south is that to Dochgarroch (not open)

Rescuing a Wellington Bomber. The aircraft was on a training trip during the Second World War when its engines failed and it dropped neatly into Loch Ness. One of the crew was killed, but the rest survived. It was lifted from the water in 1985 and moved by road to Weybridge, in Surrey, to be restored.

along the line of a railway that never was. The road, which is part of the old high road from Inverness, climbs steeply, with glimpses of Loch Ness and the other side of the loch through the trees. The plain white house on the far side is Borlum (see p.90).

At Blackfold (591407) a track comes in from the right/north which was once the high road from Inverness via the Leachkin. At 569399 the road zig-zags over a burn. Just before this, in the field on the right/west, is An Fuaran Dearg (the Red Spring). In fact, there are several springs and the water from them is a bright orange colour, as if from iron oxide, and it will keep its colour for a year, if sealed up in a bottle.

All the way along this road there are views into the western hills with distant peaks appearing one after another. This is true whether travelling north or south.

Passing through the plantations, there is an entry to Woodend on the right/west, and further along this entry, at 545365, can be seen the little farm that was the centre of Katharine Stewart's *A Croft in the Hills,* an account of what it was like, not so long ago, to work and live in this high (875 feet) valley. A little further along the road on the left/east, at 548361, is what seems at first glance to be a rough heather-covered slope. It is the site of a Bronze/Iron Age village which was not planted over by the Forestry Commission when its existence was pointed out to them. There is an information board at the fence and, from a few minutes' study, it is not difficult to pick out the curved turf walls of the huts and the lynchets (field strips) as well as the clearance cairns. There is access to the 'village' by the stile near the board.

A little further on, beyond the white house that is Druim, which was built by the grandfather of Eona Macnicol, who wrote *The Jail Dancing,* and other books, this road joins the Abriachan road (see p.106) at 556355.

On the west of the A82 at 617408 is Dochgarroch (not open), a pleasant nineteenth-century house built by the Baillies when they had bought that estate from the Macleans of Dochgarroch, who had owned it from about 1550. Their old home was demolished. On the hill behind, at 608405, a site marked on the map as Battlefield is a reminder of the successful attack on the English Sir William Fitzwarine, then Constable of Urquhart Castle for Edward I of England, by Sir Andrew of Moray and Alexander Pilches, burgess of Inverness. It took place on the Sunday before Ascension Day, 1297, and Fitzwarine was lucky to get back to Urquhart.

The entry on the right is to Dochfour House (604392) (not open), the home of the junior line of the Baillies, which inherited the whole estate when the senior line died out. On the left, the Canal runs by the road, separated from the river by a solid bank covered with whins. When this embankment, which runs for several miles from Inverness, was built, it leaked until Thomas Telford had the idea of wrapping it with woollen lengths specially woven at Holm Mills on the other side of the river (see p.89) and then planting it with the whins. This unlikely combination has held the water in the Canal for nearly

Hunting Nessie. In 1987 a flotilla of small ships was formed up in line across Loch Ness to see what could be found by using all the latest technology available. Although the Loch Ness Monster did not surface for the photographers, some curious blips appeared on the screens which were not there on a second pass over the same place. So the elusive Monster had hidden once again.

two hundred years. At the south end of the bank, a weir divides the Ness from the Canal. The road here runs on an embankment which divides Loch Dochfour into two parts. The closed church of Bona, on the left/east, was dedicated to St Curitan.

At the sign for Lochend, turn down to the left/east on to a narrow road that leads to Bona Ferry (Ban Ath, the White Ford) where the river leaves Loch Ness. This was a major crossing place, not only for droves of cattle but also for people, until the Canal was built, 1803-22, raising the level of the water by six feet, so that a ferry was needed, but this has also gone and it is a long way round to the other side. At Bona is the Light House which shows the way by day and night to the traffic on the Canal.

Post Office, Drumnadrochit.

Drumnadrochit Post Office about the turn of the century. Third from the left is a telegraph boy, with a badge on his arm and a pouch on his belt. Note the long black over-sleeves which protected the white blouse. This building is now part of a shop east of the bridge and the present Post Office overlooks the green. Fashions may have changed, but the service there is still good and personal, with a welcome for all who come in.

Just north of the crossing, at the end of the field at 603380, are the tree-grown foundations of Bona Castle, which commanded the ford. It is also called Caisteal Spioradan from an event which took place there about 1450 when the Macleans, later of Dochgarroch, held the Castle. The details vary, depending on which clan history is read. The opponents were Hector Maclean and the Cameron chief (they were not 'of Lochiel' for another hundred years). The Camerons refer to Hector as a 'robber baron from the north' who had tried to take over Lochaber. The Macleans and other northern accounts say that they had been down south to avenge Cameron atrocities in Glen Urquhart. The Macleans had got home with some prisoners, including Cameron of Glen Nevis. The stories vary as to the order of events, but at the end there were dead Camerons hanging round the battlements and Cameron had killed two of Maclean's sons in their father's

Throwing the Hammer. One of the 'heavy' competitions to be seen at Highland Games. This splendid photograph has caught the moment when the thrower has just released the hammer, which weighs 16 lbs.

sight. From that day Bona Castle was Caisteal Spioradan, the Castle of the Ghosts, because of its haunting by the dead men. It was demolished by Telford's men, in case it might have got in the way of the Canal, but no doubt the stones were useful.

From the safety rails just south of Lochend there is a view of Aldourie Castle across the loch (see p.91), and it was in the water just off the first big lay-by that a Wellington bomber lay for over forty years until it was raised, almost complete, in 1985. When a battery was connected to the electrical system as the aircraft hung dripping from a giant crane, the lights came on. It has been moved to Weybridge, in Surrey, for restoration and safe-keeping.

At 574349 a narrow road leaves the A82 to climb very steeply from the loch to Abriachan. This is a scattering of houses in a fertile high valley, some 750 feet above sea (and loch) level. If the car is left at the roadside at 564348, where there is a turning to the left/south, there is a very pleasant walk of about 1½ miles to Corriefoyness (Corrie bho an eas, corrie below the waterfall), with views across the loch. A little further along the road, there is a bridge, with wooden rails on either side, and if the car is taken off the road and left here, there is another walk with good views by Balmore to Achculin, where there are the remains of a group of eighteenth-century houses in a very sheltered nook in the hills. This is a short half-mile.

The next building on the right/north of the road is the former Abriachan School, which now has the Post Office and the County Library in the front porch. Leave the car in the yard just before the school and call in to collect the keys for the small Croft Museum. This is a few yards further along the road, in what was once the Village Hall. Here there is a collection of bygones, relics of the crofting life of this part of the world, largely collected by Katharine Stewart, the author of *A Croft in the Hills*. There is something here for all ages, a wildlife section, and a small but good geological collection, as well as a tiny schoolroom, with pictures of the pupils who worked in the school, bringing with them a peat for the schoolroom fire and a bannock for dinner. There are craftsmen's tools of the many trades that were once common in the district – blacksmiths', masons', foresters', shoemakers' – as well as a good collection of domestic gadgets that may seem primitive now, but which were hailed as 'the latest thing' when new. This is one of the two collections in Inverness-shire made by women who treasured the everyday implements and pictures and so preserved them (see p.72).

The first schoolhouse was just beyond the Museum, on the other side of the road, at Leault. Sometimes there were a hundred pupils on the register, sometimes only a dozen. The school was finally closed in 1958, but, at the time of writing, it is necessary to send a mini-bus to collect the children and take them to the school at Dochgarroch. Driving past the school, take the left fork, about a quarter of a mile further on to Loch Laide. The right fork goes back to Inverness by the old main

Urquhart Castle. The ruins of the keep still dominate the site of Urquhart Castle on Strone Point on the west side of Loch Ness. There has been a fortified place here from the Bronze Age. Sometimes it was held for the Crown, sometimes for the Lords of the Isles, and on occasions the invading English held it for short periods.

road over the hills by the Caiplich and Blackfold (see p.100).

This part of the world was renowned for its illicit whisky stills. 'The strong pot ale that overtopped the rich gilt flaggons that lined the board, was home-brewed; the genuine mountain dew that filled the capacious vessel that occupied the centre of the table, was distilled in Abriachan's most secret shade.' Holinshed, writing in 1597, said of whisky, 'Being moderatlie taken, it sloweth age, it strengtheneth youth, it helpeth digestion, it cutteth flume, it abandoneth melancholie, it relisheth the harte, it lighteneth the mynde, it quickeneth the spirite, it cureth the hydropsie, it healeth the stranguary, it pounceth the stone, it repelleth gravel, it puffeth away ventosotie, it kepyth and preserveth the head from whirling – the eyes from dezelyng – the tongue from lyspyng – the mouth from snafflyng – the teeth from chatteryng – the throte from rattlyng, the weasand from stieflyng – the stomach from wambling, the harte from

107

swellyng – the bellie from wirtchyng – the guts from rumblyng, the hands from shiveryng – the sinowes from shrinkyng – the veynes from crumplyng – the bones from soaking . . . trulie it is a soveraigne liquor'.

In January 1873 the *Nairnshire Telegraph* recorded, under the heading Seizure of Illicit Still: 'It appears that smuggling still goes on in certain districts of the Highlands. Early on Saturday morning, acting on information, Messrs Fraser and McLeod, preventive officers, Nairn, proceeded to a remote part of the country, at the head of Loch Ness, and discovered in the woods of Abriachan an illicit still and still head in perfect working order. The still was an uncommon one, being what is known as a double-horned still, having two worms, and capable of containing 40 gallons. The still was brought to the seizure store, Inverness.'

Some of these stills were set up against the slopes of the hills south of Loch Laide, where the thin wisp of smoke would be hard to see against the trees. At 545348 are the foundations of the small bothy which belonged to Donald Fraser, *The King of the Smugglers*. It is said of him that he once disguised his father as a corpse, covered him with a sheet and put the telltale cask of whisky by the side of the 'corpse'. Abriachan was not the only haunt of distillers, for, in 1823, 400 people in the district, including the Aird to the north, Strathglass to the west and Glen Urquhart to the south, were fined 20 shillings each for illicit distilling and another 4 guineas for selling whisky without a licence.

One of the islands in Loch Laide is said to be a crannog, or artificial island. Black-headed Gulls nest on it, and from time to time Slavonian Grebe are seen, and even nesting here, as well as the more ordinary Mallard and Tufted Duck. It seems peaceful, but people would not pass the loch at night. Did a kelpie once lure someone to a watery grave? History does not say.

The next narrow turning to the left/south looks like a forestry road, but it is the continuation of the old high road from Inverness (see p.100) which goes on through Achpopuli. There used to be a fair here, where the people from Glen Urquhart would come up to sell to the Abriachan folk. From there the road ran on to Drumbuie in the Glen and to the A82

Fort Augustus Locks on the Caledonian Canal. A fishing boat is making its way through the canal to Loch Ness from the west coast. When it needs to pass the road bridge, which is seen in the background, the road will be closed to traffic. The towers of Fort Augustus Abbey rise from the trees a little further off. The Abbey stands on the site of Fort Augustus, illustrated on page 97.

there (see p.112). It forked on its way over the hills and one branch came down behind the Drumnadrochit Hotel and carried on up Glen Urquhart on its way to the west coast. At 529378 a sharp turn to the right/east runs north along the west side of the Caiplich from the old road to South Clune and Moniack.

At an irregular cross-road at 523387, the left/south road leads to the A833 at Convinth (see p.155), and the road straight on does the same at 516505. The road to the right/north-east runs to Moniack, joining the road through South Clunes at 555424. Before this, at 541420, to the north of the road, is Castle Spynie (not be be confused with the Castle Spynie near Elgin, where the Bishops of Moray used to live). This one is a circular stone dun on top of a rock with great views to the north. It is reached by a walk along the road, and a scramble.

At the T-junction is Moniack Castle (552436). The original castle is an L-plan tower-house, dating from the sixteenth or seventeenth century. It has been altered a good deal, the latest additions dating from 1830. A Fraser house to this day, it is now a Winery.

Turning right at Moniack, and right again in a few yards at the next T-junction, about half a mile south is the car park and picnic place of the Forestry Commission's Reelig Glen Forest Park. Reelig has been the home of the Frasers of Reelig for more than 500 years. Reelig Glen, with its interesting trees, was given to the Forestry Commission in 1949 by Major Charles Ian Fraser of Reelig, the noted historian and herald. Most of the older trees were planted by his predecessors, particularly by James Bailie Fraser (1783-1856). There are two well-marked walks. The Low Glen walk is easy enough for wheelchairs to go along it for part of the way. Leaving the carpark, drive straight on north and either take the first turning to the right and cross the bridge to join the A862, turning right/east to go back to Inverness, or else go straight on to join the A862 at 549446, with care, and on to Beauly (see p.00).

On the A82, just beyond the Abriachan turn and marked by two large cypresses, is Killianan churchyard. It is best to drive past it and to leave the car in the parking place beyond the bridge and walk back. There was an early church here, dedicated to St Adomnan or Eonan, the biographer of St Columba and Abbot of Iona c.679, or, as some say, to Fianan, a monk who lived at about the same time. There is a very interesting flat gravestone, possibly dating from the fourteenth century, with an ornate cross on steps with *fleurs de lys* ornamentation. About a hundred yards into the woods is St Columba's Font, a stone with a hollow in it, which is said never to be dry.

Eona Macnicol, the writer of *The Halloween Hero,* says, 'Above the graveyard is a beautiful old stone. Large and flat and almost heart-shaped, it has in it a round man-made hole. This has been thought to be the foundation stone of Fianan's house-cell, the hole supporting the central wooden pole for the roof. The sanctity of the worship cell has, I believe, become

The Well of the Heads, Loch Oich. This monument was put up by Alasdair Macdonald of Glengarry in 1815 to commemorate the Keppoch Murders, which took place in 1663, though his forebear did not do much to help Iain Lom Macdonald when he cried to him to avenge his kinsmen. It was to Glengarry that the heads of the seven men were shown when Iain Lom was on his way to Sleat to prove that justice had been done. The heads were washed in the spring that lies below the monument.

transferred to the house-cell. And this stone is called a Font Stone. It is even called by a name greater than Fianan's – St Columba's ... The power attributed to the stone agrees with what is known of St Columba, a special interest in women in childbirth. It was believed up to a generation ago that the water held in the round hole was of benefit to women in childbirth. My parents remembered also that infants had a few drops of the water put into their baptismal bowl. There is mystery about the water. It is present even in dry weather and if the hole is emptied it fills quickly, though there would seem to be no inlet to allow the entry of spring water'.

The road now approaches Urquhart Bay, with views of the Castle on Strone Point (sron, a nose) at the south side of the bay. At 529300 there is a parking place above Temple Pier, one of the few surviving piers on Loch Ness, once the landing place for the steamers bringing coal, goods and passengers. Temple (Teampull, a church) is the site of St Ninian's missionary centre. Now all that is left is the well on the north side of the road, which was a *clootie well* (see p.36) until the road works in the 1880s; the stone set up to mark the site; the name of the farm above it, St Ninian's; and the name of the hill, Creag Nay on the map, but formerly Craig Neamh, the hill of heaven. Until the road was improved in the 1930s, there was a fine ash tree by its side, said to have been planted by St Ninian, although it must have regenerated many times since he was here in the fourth century. When the road builders wanted it out of the way, no-one would lay an axe to it until 'foreigners', who had no idea of the sanctity of the tree, were engaged to fell it. The white house just above the road, dating from 1851, was once an inn, convenient for those waiting for the boats. The steep road up the hill by Drumbuie is the old high road from Inverness, but there is no way through now for other than walkers at some points.

Urquhart Bay is one of the places that have produced sightings of the Monster, and at Drumnadrochit there is the Official Loch Ness Centre, where visitors may study the matter and make up their own minds about it. For the botanically learned, the vegetation running inland from the bay to the bridge is a *hydrosere,* that is, some of the trees like having their feet in water, but those further inland like it less.

At 508303 the A831 forks right for Cannich (see p.00), but the main road keeps left over the bridge across the Enrick. Drumnadrochit (Druim na dhrochaidh, the ridge of the bridge) is one of the few Highland villages with a green in the middle of it, and this one is triangular. The Grants, who owned Glen Urquhart for 400 years, allowed this to be a market stance and a place where the droves of cattle might spend a night on their way to the markets in the south. After the Seafield Estates were sold the green was acquired by the Glen Urquhart Association, and the Christmas Tree is put up here.

From the car park, just beyond the green, where there is a direction board, a well-marked route leads along the Pitkerrald road, and through the woods to the very top of Craig Monie, 450 feet, where there are the remains of a hill fort. The path is in good order by the kindness of the Forestry Commission and the Woodland Trust. This hill is named after a 'Viking Prince' who was defeated in a battle here, and fled up the glen to Corriemonie (see p.160). There is a splendid view, and below in the flat field are some stones that are said to be where St. Drostan lived. The hill is also sometimes called Queen Mary's Hill, but the name has nothing to do with Mary, Queen of Scots. Drostan used to climb to the top to meditate and he commended the Glen to the care of St Mary, Queen of Heaven, hence the name.

The walk from the car park goes past the attractive group of council houses to the Pitkerrald turning and joins the woodland track after a short walk along that road, which eventually reaches a farm called Pitkerrald, named after St Coirell (see p.204), and a place where courts were held. Just to the north of the hill is the site of the battle which Monie lost and from which he fled to Corriemonie (see p.160). The old names of this area perpetuate the memory of the battle: Blair na Geilt (the field of terror), Poll a'Ghaorr (the pool of gore) and Lag na Cuispairean (hollow of the archers).

The turning to the left/east at the cross-roads leads down past the Secondary School. Just before the school a turning to the right goes back to the A82, passing the Parish Church of Kilmore, built 1836, the British Legion's club house and Blairbeg Hall, the Public Hall, on the corner of the main road. Past the school, the hotel on the left was once the manse. The road reaches the ancient church yard of Kilmore (515295) where the early church once stood. The ruins of the church built in 1630 are among the graves, and beyond is the gravestone of Corporal Roderick Macgregor, V.C., 2nd Battalion, the Rifle Brigade, one of the recipients of the Victoria Cross from Queen Victoria at the first presentation in 1857. It is a reddish stone, with the V.C. carved on it, and often there is a wreath of poppies there. Although the church is known as *Old Kilmore* (the Great Church, or possibly St Mary's Church), it seems likely that the original dedication was to St

Drostan, a Pict still remembered as a local saint. Indeed, Glen Urquhart used to be called Urchadainn mo Dhrostan (St Drostan's Urquhart) and his relics were preserved at Temple until the Reformation. The road goes on through East Lewiston, part of a planned village, with some unplanned modern houses, and joins the A82 at Borlum Bridge.

But, continuing along the main road, in a few yards the Bowling Green and Playing Field are on the right. On the last Saturday in August the Glen Urquhart Games take place on the Playing Field, one of the amateur games, held more for the Glen people than for tourists, though visitors are made very welcome. On the other side of the field on a low mound is the burying place of the Grants who once owned the Glen. *The Inverness Courier* of 25 April, 1825 reported: 'The obsequies of the late Colonel Grant of Moy which were recently celebrated in Glen Urquhart, may be noticed as another lingering instance of a genuine Highland funeral. Beside the gentlemen who attended from all parts of the country, it is calculated that about 4000 Highlanders were assembled, chiefly from Kintail, Strathglass, Glen Moriston and Glen Urquhart. The quantity of whisky expended on this occasion is variously estimated'. Some of those men must have walked a hundred miles to attend the funeral and to get home again.

The road past Kilmore Parish Church comes in on the left, making a cross-road with Balmacaan Road, named after a house now demolished.

Take this turning to the right/south-west and drive straight on, crossing the river Coiltie by a right-angled bridge and up the hill, taking the right fork for Diveach (pronounced Jee-vach) and on to the Forestry car park. From here a walk through the woods (splendid for dogs) goes to a view of the Falls of Diveach. Further along the road, Diveach House (not open), a confusion of buildings, mostly dating from 1864, but possibly incorporating earlier buildings, was the holiday home of a number of interesting people, including John Philip the artist, Anthony Trollope, who wrote *Ayala's Angel* while staying here, Kate Terry (when Mrs Arthur Lewis) and her grandson, Sir John Gielgud, Edward VII and – was it Lily Langtry? The house can be seen, teetering on the brink of the abyss, from the viewpoint below the Falls (495274). On the way

The Commando Memorial, near Spean Bridge, Lochaber. This fine bronze group of three soldiers was made by Scott Sutherland and was unveiled in September, 1952 by the Queen Mother. The Commandos trained in these hills and the giant soldiers stand out against the background from whichever angle they are approached. The peak to the left of the group is Ben Nevis, at 4406 feet the highest mountain in the United Kingdom.

back, take the right turn at 503285 and then left to Lewiston.

Sir James Grant of Grant had a plan made for this village as early as 1767, but it was stolen from his carriage in Inverness in 1769. By 1789 a row of houses had been built along what is now Balmacaan Road, west of the Food Market. They were 'temporary-type thatched dwellings' and Lady Grant thought that they were too close to Balmacaan. So the village was, slowly, moved to its present site along the banks of the Coiltie as a planned village designed by George Brown, one of Telford's surveyors, in 1808 for Sir James Grant as part of his hopes of keeping his people from emigrating. The Good Sir James died in 1811 and the village was still being actively worked on in the 1820s. It is now a Conservation area, despite which some houses have recently been built in the gardens between the road and the Coiltie. This road, too, reaches the A82 at Borlum Bridge.

The A82 runs straight from Drumnadrochit to Borlum Bridge. The green slopes on the hillsides to the right/south of the road show the terraces that were left by the glaciers that once stretched up into Glen Urquhart and can be matched with those on the other side of the Bay.

Immediately over Borlum Bridge a narrow road to the right/ west can be taken, which leads up by sharp bends and along the ridge to Grotaig (491236). This is the continuation of the old road (see p.112) which came down to the present A82 at 517302 and crossed the Enrick by a ford. It is possible to walk down to the A82 through the Forestry Commission woods to Ruiskich (479217). But it is easier to walk from Grotaig to Dun Scriben (491235), with views across Loch Ness to Dun Dearduil (see p.96).

The dominant hill to the south is Mealfourvonie (Meall fuar mhonie, the round cold moor), and between there and Grotaig is Lon na Fola (Bloody Meadow) (472219), the scene of a clan fight in 1603 between the Macdonalds and the Mackenzies. The Macdonalds, enraged by the capture of Strome Castle in Wester Ross (864354) by the Mackenzies, were on their way home, driving seventy head of cattle and nine horses which they had taken in a raid on the Mackenzies of Kilchrist in the Black Isle. Their leader, Allan Dubh (Black Allan), the young heir of Ranald Macdonald of Lundie in Glengarry, had spent some time in the guise of a pedlar exploring the Black Isle before the raid. He, alone of the Macdonalds, survived that day. One story goes: 'There was never one left alive of them but Allan himself, who escaped naked, without cloathes or arms by a leap that he gave desperately over a most ill-favoured lynn [pool] which he nor any other man did never before nor afterwards. Allan, being asked thereafter how he got such a leap done, answered that providence had brought him through and he would choose rather to die than try it again, though he were put to such a necessity'. He is said to have fled down the hill and into Loch Ness, where he was rescued by Hugh Fraser of Foyers. He is also said to have lived for some time on an island in Loch Lundie (295035). The place (472213) where

Allan made his leap is known by the Glen Urquhart people as Leum a' Cheannaiche (the Merchant's Leap), linking it with his disguise when reconnoitring the raid. The Glenmoriston people call it Leum Ailean Mhic Raonuil (Allan MacRanald's Leap).

The Reverend John Mackenzie, whose lands had been destroyed and five of his men killed in the raid, sued Allan Macdonald in 1622, but got no satisfaction. During one of the court cases against Glengarry, following the Raid, Mackenzie of Kintail proved that Glengarry was a 'worshipper of the Coan', 'which image was afterwards brought to Edinburgh and burned at the cross'. St Coan was a Prince of the House of Leinster, and also patron of Knoydart. The story that the Macdonalds had burned the congregation of Kilchrist inside the church while their piper marched round the outside, playing loudly to drown the sound of the screams, seems to have no foundation in fact, the church being a ruin long before 1603.

The large building at Borlum Farm (517291), across the field by the A82, is the Riding School of the Highland Group of the Riding for the Disabled Association, where disabled riders and drivers are made very welcome, and so are the able-bodied. As a result, pony carts are seen round some of the roads. Please given them plenty of room and do not come charging past them with a happy blast of the horn. The ponies are safe, but the drivers, being handicapped in one way or another, may not be very experienced or very strong.

Borlum (Bord land, table land) was the farm that supplied the garrison at Urquhart Castle on Strone Point, a mile along the road. There is a good car park above the Castle, and from there the path is steep but easy and a guidebook can be bought at the kiosk. Looking north across the bay, a house high on the opposite side can be seen, Tychat (tigh chait, house of the cat) (533303), basking in the sun. It has been suggested that Emchattus, the Pict who was baptised by St Columba, may have been the Governor of the fort at Strone, and have lived at Tychat, in a house on that site. At one time it was known as St Adamnan's Croft.

When the invading king, Edward I of England, heard of the affair at Battlefield in 1297 (see p.102), he ordered reinforcements to Urquhart Castle, saying, 'We learn that certain malefactors and disturbers of the peace, roaming about, have killed some of our servants and imprisoned others . . . and are maliciously laying ambushes for our beloved and faithful William Fitzwarine'. Despite the reinforcements, Urquhart fell to the Scots, who put in a garrison of their own. When the invasion was renewed in 1303, the invaders decided that they would starve Urquhart into submission, Inverness having opened its gates to the English. During the winter the stores in the castle were very low and it was clear that something had to be done. The drawbridge was lowered and an expectant mother came across it. She explained that she had been caught inside the castle when the siege began and was now wanting to have her baby in more comfortable quarters. The besiegers agreed to let her pass and, while they were discussing the matter, the garrison rushed across the drawbridge, but in the ensuing fight they were all killed, including Sir Alexander Forbes, Governor of the Castle. Only the woman, who was Lady Forbes, got away.

Between the road and the water at 517268 is the cairn erected to the memory of John Cobb, the famous racing driver, who was killed on Loch Ness when trying to break the world water speed record. He was much loved by the people of the Glen and they built the cairn themselves, setting into it a fine bronze plaque made by George Bain, the Celtic Art expert, who also taught art. It reads: *On the waters of Loch Ness John Cobb, having travelled at 206 m.p.h. in an attempt to gain the world's water speed record, lost his life in this bay, Sept. 29th, 1952. This memorial is erected as a tribute to the memory of a gallant gentleman by the people of Glen Urquhart. Urram do'n treun Agus do'n iriosal.* (Honour to the valiant And to the humble).

At Alltsigh (456193) is a Youth Hostel. It may have been the site of a Change House, but the present building dates from the 1930s, when it was a tearoom.

At Invermoriston is the home of the Grants of Glenmoriston since the fifteenth century, when John Grant, *The Bard*, was put in by the Crown to pacify the district after the collapse of the Lordship of the Isles. His natural son Iain Mor (d.1548) was the first Grant of Glenmoriston. Near the house (428114) (not open) is a building which in the eighteenth century was a linen-weaving centre; now it is holiday flats.

The Ben Nevis Race. Although they are not yet at the summit, these men are beginning to feel the strain of the race, which takes place every year. In the background are the British Alcan works, fed by the water pouring through the pipes on the right of the picture, which have passed for fifteen miles through the mass of Ben Nevis. Inverlochy Castle is hidden in the trees in front of the railway bridge across the Rover Lochy.

The Forestry Commission plantation above the house is called on the map Creag nan Eun (Rock of the Birds) (438175), but it used to be Creag Iain (John's Rock). In the late seventeenth and early eighteenth centuries John Grant of Glenmoriston (1657-1736) was a staunch Jacobite and from time to time it was expedient for him to take to the hills, for instance, after Killiecrankie, 27 July, 1689, when Invermoriston House was burned to the ground, which happened again after Sheriffmuir, 1716. He thus acquired the by-name of Iain a' creagain (John of the rocks). No doubt this convenient 1355-foot hill was one of his refuges, Craig an Daraich (Oak Rock) above Blairie being another. John knew his grandson, later Colonel Hugh Grant of Moy, a son of Grant of Shewglie, who was born in 1733 and who died in 1825 (see p.114).

In the burying ground at Invermoriston (422167), which shows by its circular shape that it dates from the Celtic Church, there is a stone to Iain a'Creagain. Another grave in this old burying ground is that of the poet Alexander MacIain Ban. He was a soldier for many years and was on his way home when he collapsed and died. Some say that he died at Drumnadrochit, others that he reached his father's house at Achnaconeran (416180) and died there. The day after the funeral his sweetheart visited the grave and heard groans from under the ground. She rushed for help and the grave was speedily opened. Alasdair was found to be dead, but face down in his coffin. He was straightened and the earth was replaced over him.

Here the A887 leaves Invermoriston at 4321168 for Kyle of Lochalsh, fifty-six miles to the west.

In 1746 Ewen Macdonald left his home at Livishie (403177) with other Glenmoriston men in answer to Ludovick Grant of Grant's disgraceful plan to hand them over to the Duke of Cumberland. His wife implored him not to go, but he took no notice until he was beyond Achnaconeran (416180) on the old road. There she threw their child into the heather, and told her husband that he could either pick it up or let it lie there and die. Ewen had no real choice: he took his child home and stayed there in safety.

Blairie (381166) was the home in the mid-eighteenth century of Paul Chisholm, whose sons, Alexander, Donald and Hugh, were three of the Seven Men of Glenmoriston, who protected Prince Charles after Culloden. Alexander was dead by 1751, and his grandson William emigrated to Glenmore, Glengarry, in Canada. Donald stayed on at Blairie until 1769 and then he emigrated to Glengarry. Hugh went to Edinburgh, where he knew Sir Walter Scott, who helped him with money when he fell on hard times. He returned to Glenmoriston, but later moved to Balnabruaich in Strathglass, where he died. The others were Alexander Macdonald, who was also dead by 1751, Gregor MacGregor, who was still alive in 1751, Patrick Grant, from Craskie (255123), and John Macdonald, whose real name was Campbell, also from Craskie, who emigrated in 1775, aged about 75. Patrick Grant was pressed into the British Army in 1753 and served in North America. He retired in 1763 and returned home, as an Out-Pensioner of Chelsea

Hospital. He gave a good deal of information to Bishop Robert Forbes when the Bishop of Ross was collecting memories for his book, *The Lyon in Mourning*.

These seven men, as result of the devastation of Glenmoriston, swore an oath never to surrender themselves or their arms to the Government, and lived at Uamh Ruaraidh na Seilg (cave of Roderick the Hunter) in Corrie Sgreumh (1614). It was here that Prince Charles came on 29 July, 1746. On 2 August they moved to another cave at 138155, where they remained for some days. Eventually the Seven Men delivered the Prince and his companions, via a cave in Glen Cannich and Fasnakyle (see p.165), to the care of the Camerons at Achnasaul (153894) (see p.190).

At 357158 the river is dammed just west of the Glenmoriston Power Station. At Dundreggan (315140) the track from Tomich meets the road (see p.164). In 1746 Major Lockhart, who had been a prisoner of the Jacobites and had bribed a guard to release him, was busy with some Government troops in Glenmoriston. He saw three men at work in a field and shot them without warning. Then he ordered Grant of Dundreggan to collect his cattle. To fill in the time while this was being done, he stripped Dundreggan and forced him to watch the three dead bodies being hanged at the gallows. Only when Lockhart was persuaded that Grant was far from being a Jacobite, but had, on the contrary, helped the Government troops, was his life saved, but his cattle were taken, his house was burned and his wife's rings were torn from her fingers and her clothes stolen.

In 1827 Finlay Munro was preaching to a group of Glenmoriston people on the hillside at 312138 when some of his audience disagreed with him and heckled him. 'I tell the Truth', said Munro, 'and, to show it, the marks of my feet here on the ground will not disappear.' They are there to this day. To see them, look out for a passing place sign on the right/ north of the road, not far after a new house just west of the spot where the road narrows. There is room to leave the car on both sides of the road. At the passing place sign on the north side of the road there is a small cairn of stones, more noticeable when driving east and a notice saying FOOTPRINTS. Pass through the fence by the wooden gate and follow the track a

E

short distance to the cairn that stands by Finlay Munro's footprints.

Just before Torgyle Bridge (309129) is a turning to Dalcreichart. It is another stretch of the military road to the west, but its interest is also linked with the saints in Strathglass (see p.172). When Erchard, or Merchard (Mo Erchard, my Erchard) set out from Crunaglack in Strathglass, he went south and over the hills to find the place where his bell should ring for the third time. He came to Suidhe Mhercheid (Merchard's Seat, 301179, now An Suidhe), which lies above the track from Tomich to Glenmoriston (see p.164), and here his bell rang for the first time. Down in the glen, at the spring, Fuaran Mhercheid, at Ballintombuie (282130), the bell rang again, and rang for the third time at the place where the burying ground is (276127), and there he set up his church, Clachan Mhercheid. It is fairly easy to find. Past Ballintombuie farm and a new bungalow there is an iron gate on the left, between two high deer fences. Go through the gate and walk on down the clear tracks towards the river to the old site, where there still remains Merchied's Font, which, like the one at Killianan (see p.110), is never without water. Here he lived and taught for a time, but it is said that he later went to Rome, where the Pope consecrated him bishop. Passing through Poitou on his way home, he fell ill. He prayed that he might seem his home again and his prayers were granted. He reached Kincardine O'Neil, met his own kin again and there he died. His body, at his request, was put on a cart drawn by two horses, and where they stopped, there he was buried and the church of Kincardine O'Neil was built over his grave. His bell survived at Dalcreichart, being kept on an old tombstone after the church was moved, until 1873, when someone stole it, a stranger, it was thought, who knew nothing of its healing powers.

At Torgyle Bridge (309129) one branch of the military road from Fort Augustus reaches the river, coming through Wester Inverwick. The other branch (see p.125) joins the present road at Achlain (279124).

Across the bridge at 249116, where there are some sheep fanks today, once stood the inn at Aonach, where Alexander Macdonald, one of the Seven Men, once lived. The Government in 1770 spent £80, and another £60.5.0 the next

A Night Rescue. When there is a major mountaineering disaster, rescue teams will come from all over Scotland. This picture shows the members of the Cairngorm Mountain Rescue Team bringing a casualty down from the hills after a night rescue, which may have kept them out for many hours.

year, on out-houses and a stable. The money probably came from the Forfeited Estates. This was not only an inn, but also the base for the men who were still working on the military road in 1773, and had been since 1750. On 31 August, 1773, when Boswell and Johnson arrived at the inn from Fort Augustus, the innkeeper was 'a M'Queen' who had 'made the whole with his own hands' and whose 'pride seemed to be much piqued that we were surprised at his having books'. The building was of turf and there were three rooms in a line, with a smaller room sticking out to one side. Inside, the rooms were lined with wattles. When Miss M'Queen made them tea and chatted with them, Dr Johnson was so impressed that he gave her a book which he had bought in Inverness, but whether she really enjoyed *Cocker's Arithmetic*, history does not say. The family were intending to emigrate to America the next year, because the rent for their farm had gone up from £5.00 to £20.00 a year, and although they could have managed with a rent of £10.00, the £20.00 was too much and so they were going. 'His wealth consists of one hundred sheep, as many goats, twelve milk cows, and twenty-eight beeves ready for the drover.'

At 238112 on the left/south side of the road there is a cairn with a plaque. This a monument to one of the real heroes of the '45 Rising, Roderick Mackenzie. He was a native of Edinburgh, probably a son of Colin Mackenzie, a Jacobite jeweller. Some say that he became one of the Prince's bodyguard, some that he was an officer. The two are not incompatible. It was acknowledged that there was a remarkable likeness between the two young men. Tradition says that Mackenzie used this likeness on more than once occasion to suggest that the Prince was somewhere other than where he was. But who Mackenzie really was, and even the date of his death, have not been established.

In the summer of 1746 the Highland glens were being ravaged by Government troops, commanded by brutal officers and actively encouraged by William, Duke of Cumberland, who 'marched his Army with safety as far as the Roads could carry him and extinguished the Rebellion with Dignity and Teror unknown before in that part of the Island', as a certain William Taylor recorded twenty-five years later. 'Few districts, if any, in Scotland suffered more cruelly from the atrocities and the rapacities of the English Butcher and his demon gang than Glenmoriston,' wrote another commentator. One of Cumberland's aims was the capture of his cousin Prince Charles.

Roderick Mackenzie was in Glenmoriston in July, 1746 when he was attacked by Government troops who thought that he was the Prince. He made no attempt to undeceive them but refused to be taken alive. As they shot him he exclaimed, 'You have slain your Prince!' The delighted soldiers cut off his head and took it in triumph to Fort Augustus, and Cumberland either took it or sent it to London. The Government soon realised that Prince Charles was alive, but the hunt had been relaxed long enough to ensure his survival.

Mackenzie's body was buried between the road and the river. At the end of the nineteenth century a sword was found nearby; perhaps it was his. In 1973 the Inverness Field Club placed a carved teak cross on the grave, made by one of their members, Dr James Bruce.

At Ceannacroc, on the north side of the road, a large hydro-electric station is buried inside the hill. At 212101 the A87 joins the A887 (see p.181).

The A82 keeps to the left at Invermoriston and it is worth stopping a hundred yards beyond the turn to get out and look upstream and downstream from the old bridge over the Moriston, near the craft shops. On the south of the river is Dalcataig, once the home of Ewen Macdonald, whose poem on Coire Iaraidh is said to have been the model for Duncan Ban Macintyre's *Coire-Cheataich.*

Just beyond the Inchnacardoch Hotel the main road takes a left turn but a road marked Jenkin's Park goes straight on and leads, by turning right at the first opportunity, to the end of the road at some Forestry Commission gates near a group of Forestry houses (371095). From here the old military road to the west climbs the hill in a series of hairpin bends, but so well were they graded by Major Caulfeild's men (see p.35) that it is no great effort, and enjoyable for dogs, to climb 500 feet to the edge of the forest for magnificent views up and down the Great Glen and across to Glen Tarff and the military road over the Corrieyarick Pass, which can be walked from Ardachy (379075) to Garva Bridge (522947) in Strathspey (see p.212). The walk through to Achlain (280124) on the A887, which was the road used by Boswell and Johnson in 1773, was re-opened in November, 1986, after the Forestry Commission had repaired about nine miles of it.

The main road runs on into Fort Augustus, formerly Kilchuimen (St Cumein's church). There is a good car park on the right/west of the road and a Tourist Information Office. Just south of the Canal bridge, which opens for boats making the passage through the six locks, is a small free museum with some interesting exhibits. The walls of the first fort lie in the gardens of the Lovat Arms Hotel further up the hill. The later fort is now almost completely lost under the buildings of the nineteenth-century Benedictine abbey and school. The fine modern chapel is open to visitors, but ask first at the Tourist Office for the times of opening. Several monks from the Abbey have seen the Monster over the years. It is just by the gate to the Abbey that Wade's military road from Inverness joins the A82 (see p.97) to cross the river Oich by the old bridge and join the part that has been described near Jenkin's Park.

The A82 is now on the line of Wade's Great Line of Communication, or military road, to Fort William, and it is just south of Fort Augustus that one of the most amazing winter exploits in military history had its start. On the night of 30/31 January, 1645, the Marquis of Montrose at the head of the King's Army had camped on the flat area by the Straight Mile betwen Kilchumein and Aberchalder. He was on his way north to deal with Lord Seaforth, who was holding Inverness. He was woken by Iain Lom Macdonald (Satirical John) (see p.129) with the news that the Campbells were at Inverlochy (see p.134) and were harrying Lochaber. Alasdair MacColl Ciotach, Montrose's able general, threatened to hang Iain Lom if he were not telling the truth, but as a result of the news the army was roused and moved south, but not by whatever track may have run through Glen More.

Up into the snow-covered hills to the east they went, by Cullachy (376064) and Glen Tarff and south by Glen Turret to Achvady in Glen Roy (296867), where they rested. Although it is sometimes said that they went up the track that can still be walked up the Allt Leachdach to Tom an Eite (238694) and then down by Glen Nevis to avoid being seen by the Campbell sentries, it seems unlikely that they would have added some fifteen miles to their march. By crossing the river at Dalnabea, a ford below Corriechoille, and then moving by Killiechonate, Lianachan and Tomnafet (203781 and now covered by forests), down the river Lundy using the ground as they would have known how to do, and with some care during the short hours of daylight, unless the Campbells had out-pickets, they would not have been seen. A few of them actually were seen, but were not thought to be a danger. On 2 February, St Bride's Day, or Candlemas, Montrose and his men fell on the unsuspecting Campbells and defeated them at Inverlochy. Argyll, the Campbell chief, who was not commanding his forces, remained on his galley at Camus nan gall, and got safely away. Iain Lom refused the offer of a sword from Alasdair, saying, 'If I fall in battle, who will sing your praises?'

Running along the west side of the road is the line of the old railway which once ran to Spean Bridge. It was opened in 1903, but it never paid and was finally closed in 1946. The line ran from Fort Augustus to Aberchalder, then down the east side of Loch Oich, lying here on the track of Wade's road, and it is quite possible to walk along the track from the north end of Loch Oich to the A82, just south of the Swing Bridge at 399983. The railway continued above and to the east of the road on the military road to 229886 and then crossed the A82 at 223865 to run near Loch Lochy and up the east bank of the river Spean (often written Speyn or Spain in old papers, it should be pronounced that way), crossing it at 206814 and joining the Glasgow-Fort William line at 214813.

At Aberchalder (342034) Prince Charles gathered his forces before crossig the Corrieyarick to Edinburgh and England. The A82 crosses the Canal and the river Oich and soon reaches the boundary between the Inverness and Lochaber Districts as it runs along Loch Oich, the highest level of the Canal system. At 314013 is the turning to the left/south to Invergarry Castle Hotel, built between 1866 and 1868 by Edward Ellice as his home, David Bryce being the architect. By driving down almost to the house and turning right in front of it, the tall ruins of Invergarry Castle are soon reached.

The Castle was the home of the Macdonalds of Glengarry, though how early they had a building on this site is not known. Possibly it was built after the loss of Strome Castle in 1603 to the Mackenzies. On 24 April April, 1654, General Monk said that the met 'Col. Morgan's Brigade near Glengarrie's new house, which was burnt the day before, and the remayning structure I ordered to be defaced by the pyoneers'. It must have been repaired fairly soon, for it was used by a garrison of Government soldiers from 1692 to 1715. They did a great deal of damage, which was assessed in 1703 at at least £3,542, but the money was not paid. In 1715 Glengarry recovered the Castle, but next year the Government troops re-took it and it was burned again in August of that year. In the 1720s, when Thomas Rawlinson was manager of the Invergarry Company (see p.176), he spent £100 on making it habitable and lived there until 1731, when Glengarry moved in again and stayed there until the Duke of Cumberland had it destroyed in 1746, after Prince Charles had slept there before and after Culloden. The marks of the various conflagrations can be seen on the walls.

Alasdair Macdonald of Glengarry (1771-1828) was the subject of a magnificent portrait by Raeburn, but he was a bad Chief, and his son Aeneas had to sell all the family lands except the Castle, the Well of the Heads and Kilfinnan (see below).

Alasdair's mother, Marjory, daughter of Sir Ludovick Grant of Dalvey, began the evictions from the Glengarry lands as early as 1772. Later, Alasdair wrote to his agent in Knoydart, 'Enclosed you have a list of small tenants belonging to my Knoydart property. Their leases being expired by Whitsunday first, And having refused to serve me I have fully determined to warn them out and turn them off my property without loss of time'. Mrs Macdonald of Glengarry cleared Knoydart in 1853, telling the people that they were to go to Australia, which pleased them, as a good place to go, if go they must. When it came to the point, they were taken to Nova Scotia instead. In 1746 the population of Glengarry alone was between 5000 and 6000; by 1911 it is doubtful if there were twenty men left there.

Alasdair's brother, Sir James, was the hero of the defence of Hougoumont during the battle of Waterloo, 1815, and later, in 1832, he became Governor of Canada. Many of the Glengarry men had emigrated to Canada, where they founded the Gaelic-speaking settlement on the banks of the St Lawrence which they called Glengarry.

At Invergarry another road, the A87, leads on at 308012 to Skye (see p.176). The A82 crosses the river Garry, and just beyond the little Roman Catholic chapel on the right/west of the road, Invergarry Castle can be seen over the wall of the field and an entry on the left/east leads to it. It is hard to get this view when driving north. At 350992, opposite a shop, between the road and the water is the monument to the Keppoch Murders, set up in 1815 by Alasdair of Glengarry. It has recently been cleaned. Known as Tobar nan Ceann (the Well of the Heads), the heads can be seen carved around the top of the pillar which is surmounted by a hand holding a dagger. The story is told, though not altogether accurately, in Gaelic, French, Latin and English on panels in the base.

Briefly, Donald Glas Macdonald of Keppoch (see p.201), who had fought at Inverlochy with Montrose and died c.1649, left two sons who were later sent to Rome for their education. After their father's death the estates were run by their Tutor, or Guardian, their uncle Alasdair Buidhe. In due course the boys returned and Alasdair of Keppoch, perhaps full of foreign ideas, soon made himself unpopular. One one occasion he attacked the Siol Dughaill, a Macdonald family who had moved into Inverlair (339799) about a hundred years before and had recently taken a lease directly from Huntly, the Superior of the district, to the annoyance of Keppoch. So he attacked Inverlair and drove off his cattle. Inverlair complained to the Privy Council and Keppoch counter-claimed.

Early on 5 September, 1663, Inverlair, his sons and supporters broke into 'the place of Keppoch, armed with swords, dirks, and other weapons' and slaughtered Alasdair Keppoch and his brother Ranald, apparently to no great grief in the district. But when Iain Lom, the Keppoch Bard who had led Montrose to Inverlochy in 1645, heard of the murders, he asked for help from Glengarry to bring the murderers to justice, but in vain. On he went to Skye to ask for help from Sir James Macdonald of Sleat, who had fostered the fatherless boys. Sleat refused at first, but after several visits from Iain Lom he gave way, obtained from the Privy Council a Commission of Fire and Sword and lent the poet fifty men. They arrived at Inverlair to find the house barricaded against them, but the avengers broke down the doors, set the place on fire and, as the defenders staggered out, they killed all seven men, though whether any of the seven were involved in the murders is unknown.

Iain Lom cut off their heads and arranged to have their bodies buried on a mound to the east of the present house. Then he set off north with the heads. At Tobar nan Ceann he stopped to wash them in the trough into which the spring falls. This spring had some link with the Celtic cult of The Head, for he could have washed them much nearer Invergarry before showing Glengarry that he, at least, knew his duty. Iain Lom later either sent or took the heads to Sleat as proof that justice had been done and Sleat sent them on to the Privy Council, who thanked him for 'the good service done to his majesty'. Iain Lom finally wrote *Mort na Ceapaich* (Death of Keppoch) — and seems to have become a bit of a bore about the whole thing.

Access to the trough is by a scramble down to the water-level, taking a torch if possible, and along a vaulted passage. It lies well below the modern road, for the level has been raised over the centuries. There is a picnic site just south of the monument, and on the other side of the loch the highest point is Creagan nan Gobhar (Crag of the Goats), 1624 feet (316985). From the top is about the best view along the whole Canal, for there are no intervening hills and, on a clear day, both the North Sea and the Atlantic can be seen. It was on this summit that the beacon was lit when Glengarry wished to summon his clan.

Just beyond the picnic site a narrow road signposted Kilfinnan leads south behind the cottages. Take this road to a farm just across a modern bridge over a burn. Leave the car off the road here and walk through the farm yard and down to the burying ground and the curious tower-like structure which is all that is left of St Finnan's church (278956). This was the burying place of the Macdonalds of Glengarry and there are three large flat stones inside the 'tower' with inscriptions on them. In 1643 'An Idolatrous Image called St Finan' was burned at Inverness cross, presumably from this church, or from Dunlichity (see p.46). Before the canal was built, the droves of cattle had an easy crossing of the water below the church, because it was dry ground where the loch is now.

Further on, the A82 crosses the Canal and at 294972 there is a Youth Hostel, which stands approximately on the watershed of Scotland. The old name is Laggan Ach an Drom (the field on the ridge) and, being a central place, fairs were held here, deeds were signed, and a gallows meted out justice to wrong-doers.

At 287963 a side road turns off to the right/west to Laggan Locks. There is no further passage for cars, but walkers can cross the water and walk on to Kilfinnan.

At the side of Loch Lochy, in 1544, was fought Blar na Leine (the battle of the shirts) between Frasers and Grants and an allied force of Clanranald Macdonalds, Glengarry Macdonalds and Camerons. As a result of Government policy over several years, the Macdonalds were in a state of ferment, and decided to avenge their wrongs by raiding the estates of their opponents, principally those of the Earl of Huntly and his allies, the Frasers. Accordingly John Macdonald of Clanranald, with Macdonald support, and with more from Cameron of Lochiel and MacIain of Ardnamurchan, made a successful raid into Abertarff and Stratherrick, to the east of Loch Ness, and

High Street, Fort William. This was a collection of wooden houses, which could be easily destroyed by the garrison in the Fort, until the nineteenth century. A busy town at any time, with an excellent Museum, Fort William becomes crowded in the summer, but the ring road that keeps the passing traffic out of the High Street has made life easier for everyone.

came home after harrying Urquhart and Glenmoriston, on the west side of the loch, and even occupying the Castle at Urquhart. Lovat and Grant, whose lands had suffered most, under Huntly's command chased the allies into 'thair awan cuntrye apoun the west seis, quhair Lawland men cuid haif no acces unto thame'. Content with this, Huntly made his way home, probably by Glen Turret, while Lovat and Grant went on north along the Great Glen. The allies soon knew of the division of forces and sped along the western hills to fall on their enemies. At the end of the hot day, in every sense, for both sides threw off their belted plaids and fought in their shirts, of four hundred Frasers and Grants, only four were alive, and of the six hundred allies, only eight survived.

131

At 253913 an old white house right on the edge of the road was built in 1735 to house the officers of the troops building Wade's road. It later became an inn, largely for drovers, and many men, making for home after Culloden, died here. The landlord, careful of his safety, threw the bodies into the loch. Some floated to 'the site of Blar na Leine and were buried there', presumably at Kilfinnan; others came ashore at Clunes Bay (203885) on the north side of the loch.

At 223864 the turning to the left/east is Wade's road, which lies further up the hill than the A82, and crosses the Gloy Burn by the Low Bridge. It is pleasant to walk north along the old road, but the side road forks right and runs on for about six miles into the hills before it comes to an end. It was a useful road for the drovers to get to the Corrieyarick by walking on to the north-east.

The A82 runs along Wade's road as far as Stronaba (207844), where the old road bears away to the south-west, because it had to cross the Spean at the High Bridge (see p.133). In the 1841 Census, James Munro, the official collecting the details, wrote of Stronaba. 'The enumerator for this district writes me as follows: "All the people in Stronaba are in very miserable Circumstances. The proprietor has been warning us off for these 35 years, and causing us to pay a Share of the law expenses incident on the process of removing. He has this year raised an action of Ejection against us, and altho' he has not yet executed it, it hangs over us, and we do not know what to do. We have not yet been allowed to cut our peats, tho' the Season has been so very favourable." I believe there are as poor people in this district as in any in the Highlands'. Ten years later, in the 1851 Census, it is noted that most of the country has been cleared of crofters, but the 'small village of Stronaba still under crofters, But these are presently under Summons of Removal at this term of Whitsunday first, 1851'.

At 207824 is the Commando Monument, a magnificent bronze group of three more-than-life-size soldiers by Scott Sutherland, A.R.S.A., which was cast by H.H. Martyn of Cheltenham, the firm that later cast the statue of King Robert I at Bannockburn. The group was unveiled by Queen Elizabeth the Queen Mother in September, 1952. During the Second World War the Commandos had their headquarters at

Achnacarry (see p.187) and trained in the Lochaber hills and to the west. Immediately below the memorial the B8004 turns to the right/west for Gairlochy (see p.187), but the A82 goes on, passing the parish church of Kilmonivaig on the right/south of the road at 213819. The church dates from 1812, but was altered in 1891 and in 1928. The original church was down by the river Lochy at about 173834 or perhaps at Gairlochy (see p.187). Before crossing the bridge at Spean Bridge, the A86 turns off to the left/east (see p.199) and about a mile further on, at a cross-road (2208813), a narrow road to the right/north is signed to High Bridge, the other side going to Lianachan, once the home Dr Kennedy (see below) and now surrounded by forests.

Taking the turning to High Bridge, built in 1737, the remains of the old bridge can be seen by leaving the car where the road takes a right-angled turn at 199819, just by a newish bungalow, and finding the way down through the birch woods to the river Spean. It is a very steep and slithery route, but even the remaining pieces of the bridge give an idea of how talented were the engineers in the first half of the eighteenth century, for the bridge was high above the water with one arch resting on a boulder in the middle of the river. It was superseded by Telford's bridge at Spean Bridge. Continue along this road, which is a quiet and pleasant drive with views across the river and the canal, until it rejoins the A82 at 144373.

The land to the right/west of the A82 for about six miles was, between 1945 and 1961, owned by Joseph Hobbs, the son of a Hampshire farmer. He went to Canada at the age of nine, was a naval airman in the 1914-18 War, made a fortune in shipping in Canada, but lost over £80,000 in the depression and came to Scotland with £100 to set up another career in whisky. By 1940, he controlled seven distilleries, which he then sold for £38,000, plus an option on the stocks, which was said to be worth £250,000. He made this estate into the Great Glen Cattle Ranch, so improving the land by draining and working the once-barren moors, that the area of arable land, which was some thirty acres in 1945, had by 1961 grown to more than 1200 acres. He is buried at Onich.

Close to Shelter No.2 are three stone cairns, one of which was erected to the memory of Dr William Kennedy of

Lianachan (1810-51) whose coffin rested here when the men from Spean Bridge took over the carrying of it. 1400 men attended him to his burial. The other two cairns were erected later in memory of his brothers.

At 144773 the road that was signposted for High Bridge rejoins the A82. The Inverlochy Castle hotel on the right/west side of the road is mis-named, for this Victorian mansion was formerly and more correctly known as Torlundy. It was built between 1863 and 1891 by the second and third Lords Abinger. There is an underground mausoleum in the grounds where several of the family are buried. In August, 1869, Jefferson Davis, once President of the defeated Confederated States of America, stayed here with the Abingers, and in 1873 they entertained Queen Victoria.

By this time the great mass of Ben Nevis should be visible to the left/east of the road, though often the top is hidden by the clouds which drift in from the west. Further on can be seen two small buildings up on the side of the hill, with pipes running down from them to the British Alcan Works at the foot of the hill. One old lady, seeing these for the first time said, 'I cannot be thinking what the people in those wee houses can be at, that they should need such enormous drains!' In fact, a six-foot man can stand upright inside the 'drains'. They carry the water from Loch Laggan (see p.206) which has passed through a tunnel driven right through the Ben for fifteen miles to power the turbines at the works.

At 125757 the A830 leaves the A82 on its way to Mallaig (see p.213). About half a mile further on there is a turning to the right/west, with a notice saying 'Freight Depot Area Manager'. Take this road which passes a small burial ground, and the first turning, forbidden to coaches, goes to Inverlochy Castle. It is now an Ancient Monument and some work has been done to the ten-foot thick, thirty-foot high walls, which date from the end of the thirteen century. It was built by the Comyns, who were Lords of Badenoch and Lochaber from about 1200 until they picked the losing side and quarrelled with King Robert I. The south-west tower, which is the largest, is known as Comyn's Tower. A good view of it for a camera is seen from the Mallaig road (see p.213).

Just before the road crosses the river Nevis at 113784, a

narrow road turns off to Achintee (125731). After passing through an industrial site, take the first turning to the right. There is a monument with information about the war memorial cairn on top of Ben Nevis just by this turning. The car may be left in the car park just south of the house, before climbing Ben Nevis, the highest mountain in the British Isles at 4406 feet. Although, in one sense, the route to the summmit can be walked, no one should undertake it 'unadvisedly, lightly or wantonly, but reverently, discreetly, advisedly and soberly', for not only is the actual track rough, but the weather can change in a matter of minutes from brilliant sunshine to thick mist and, even in summer, sleet and snow. F.H. Smythe, in *The Spirit of the Hills*, wrote: 'I have crawled on hands and knees over the ice-bound plateau of Ben Nevis in the teeth of a snow-laden hurricane worthy of Everest at its worst'. So, leave a note under the windscreen wiper giving the time of leaving the car, take warm clothes and stout shoes or boots and any advice that is offered. The Ben is worthy of care and respect, and so are all the Highland hills.

To reach the other side of the river Nevis and to drive up the length of the glen, continue along the main road to the small roundabout.

Over the bridge, the left/east turning out of the small roundabout leads up Glen Nevis for about five miles along the west side of the Nevis to Achriabhach (145684) where the road crosses the river, just before a parking place, turns right and in about two miles more reaches a final parking place. On the way up the glen, at 123736, the north end of the West Highland Way reaches the road. From here it is possible to walk south to Balloch at the south end of Loch Lomond – ninety-five miles and some of it rough going.

Glen Nevis is considered to be one of the best examples of a glaciated valley, the ice having left it only 9,000 years ago. It had the same reputation for illicit stills as had Abriachan (see p.107). Beyond the old burying ground of the MacSomhairle Camerons of Glen Nevis, a track climbs the hill and goes on to join the Lundavra road at 097725. It is an easier walk to start from that end and to come down into Glen Nevis, with splendid views. The hill that dominates the view up the glen is the quartz peak of Stob a' Mhaim, 3,601 feet. Glen Nevis

House is where Lochiel had his headquarters during the siege of Fort William in 1746, but the earlier home of the MacSorlies is thought to have been at Dun Dige (Moated Fort) at the Youth Hostel (128717).

To the right/south of the road at 127702 is another Dun Dearduil (see p.96), and more or less opposite, hidden in the trees across the river, is the abandoned burial ground of Achnacon. By going down to the flat picnic field on the left, the ford to the burying ground can be seen. The water from it was considered to be holy, being used by the living and the dead.

Where the road crosses the river by the first car park, a track to the left/west goes to the Pol-dubh (Black Pool) or Lower Falls. But it is a beautiful drive to go for another couple of miles to the last parking place to see Allt Coire Eoghainn (burn of Ewen's Corrie), a 'water-slide' 1,250 feet long as it falls from the hill above. Beautiful it may be, but it is a dangerous place, so take note of the Police Notice at the car park.

It is worth walking on through the gorge to the Upper Falls at 186687. Here An Steall Bhan (the white gusher) leaps from a hanging valley to fall 350 feet. From here the really energetic walker, properly equipped with stout shoes and a map, can go on past Tom an Eite to 264684 and there turn north to reach Glen Spean, or go on across the south end of Loch Treig and then south along the railway line to Corrour Station (356664). The third option is to go south and west nearly ten miles to Kinlochleven. But most people will walk gently back to the car park.

As the A82 goes into Fort William, An Gearasdan (the garrison), it passes the Craigs burying ground on the right/ north of the road. Here the path that leads up to the arch divided the ground, so that the soldiers from the Fort lay to the west, the town's people to the east of it. To the west of the path is an outcrop of rock, and it was from here that the Jacobite guns bombarded the Fort in 1746. The arch that stands there so oddly, astride the old road from the Fort, has an inscription on it: *This arch was erected in 1690 over the main entrance to the Fort and re-erected here in 1896 where Sir Allan Cameron of Erracht in 1793 raised the 79th, or Cameron Highlanders, a regiment which distinguished itself on many a hard-fought field for King and Country.*

At the time of the Disruption, in 1843, the Free Church congregation of Fort William, having no place to build a church, worshipped at the Craigs, among the graves of their forebears. There is a monument to Ewan Maclachlan, the Gaelic scholar and poet, but, although it is known that Donald Macbain, who fought at Mulroy in 1688, is buried here, the site of his grave is now unknown.

The best way to see Fort William is to follow the road round the large roundabout and into the car park near the station and to leave the car there.

Just west of the car park, between it and Lòch Linnhe, is all that remains of the Fort, which once stretched to where the railway station is today, but it is enough to show how it commanded both Loch Linnhe and Loch Eil. The Fort was built in a strong position between the river Nevis and Loch Linnhe by General Monk in 1654 as a small turf and timber affair, to hold about 250 men. In 1690, General Hugh Mackay of Scourie greatly improved it, to the point where part at least was of stone and a thousand troops could be accommodated. It was he who named it Fort William after the then king. From here the troops marched to Glen Coe in February, 1692. General Wade had work done on it in 1725, and in 1787 it was considered to be larger than Fort Augustus. In 1752 James Stewart of the Glen was held here after the murder in Appin of Colin Campbell of Glenure before he was tried in Inveraray and again before his execution at Ballachulish (see p.143). The Fort was garrisoned until 1854, when the Crimean War started, but by this stage the twenty-four men were here mainly to discourage smugglers. In 1864 it was dismantled and the buildings were sold to the husband of Mrs Campbell of Monzie, who was the Superior of the town. He turned part of it into a housing development. In 1889 the West Highland Railway Company bought the site. The block of officers' quarters was occupied by railwaymen until 1935, when it was condemned as unfit for human habitation, but it was not finally demolished until 1948.

After the subway under the dual carriageway, the Parade, an open green space, is seen. The two statues there are to the Donald Cameron of Lochiel who died in 1905 and to the men from the town who fell in the two World Wars, one hundred and twelve between 1914 and 1918, and twenty-four between 1939 and 1945. Perhaps the fact that the Highland Division was taken prisoner at St Valery in 1940 and that there was a pause before it was re-formed to fight in the Western Desert and in Europe had some effect on the casualty lists. To the north of the Parade is Belford Hospital to which so many casualties are brought from the moutains, and beyond it is the Roman Catholic church. On the other side of the Parade is the elegant spire of St Andrew's Episcopal church. Unfortunately a supermarket has been built almost against the church's north end, thus spoiling the view from the Parade. This very handsome church was built in 1880 to replace the old Rosse Chapel which stood on the same site. Lochaber is one of the areas where a considerable proportion of the people continued to be Episcopalians.

About a hundred yards further on is Cameron Square where there is an excellent Tourist Information Office. Here also is the West Highland Museum, which has grown from the original collection made in the early years of this century by Victor Hodgson, of Onich, who founded it in 1922. There is a particularly rich collection of Jacobite relics, and one of the panelled rooms from the old Fort has been rebuilt here. There are also weapons and domestic bye-gones, as well as other interesting objects. Until 1965 there stood in Cameron Square a monument to Dr William Kennedy, a much-loved local physician. He caught typhus while looking after the poverty-stricken family of Macphee the Outlaw, who had lived on an island in Loch Quoich (see p.180). After Macphee was captured and imprisoned, his family moved into Fort William and lived in the poorest part of town. When they became ill, Dr Kennedy nursed them, and is said to have cleaned out their hovel, but he caught typhus from them and died of it in 1851 (see p.133). Macphee died in prison.

Fort William was the first town in Britain to have its streets and houses lit by electricity from its own water power. In the 1840s the old oil lamps in the streets were replaced by gas lamps which continued to give light until 1895 when they were disconnected. This plunged the streets into darkness for about a year until the electric light was switched on on 22 August, 1896.

The oldest road to the south is the one marked Upper Achintore, which climbs up the hill from the roundabout at the end of the dual-carriageway at the south end of the town (0998737), where there is another large car park. This steep road was built in 1751 by Major Caulfeild's men as part of his military road from Fort William to Stirling, but it proved to be too steep for even military use and was soon replaced by the lower road, now the A82. At about the edge of the houses is the beginning of the Peat Road that leads across to Glen Nevis (see p.135).

At Blarmachfoldach until 1950, when the last of the old families left, New Year's Day was kept on what is for everyone else 12 January. The road is passable by cars as far as Loch Lun da Bhra (pool of the two querns) (090660). Before this loch is reached, there is a Forest Walk marked on the map at 100666, where Caulfeild's road bears to the left from the metalled road. The track is now part of the West Highland Way, which carries on, climbing to about 1000 feet at Tigh-na-sleubhaich (136644) before going down to sea level at Kinlochleven.

It is said that Lulach, stepson of Macbeth, stayed on the island in Loch Lun da Bhra about 1050, before he became, briefly, King of Scots after Macbeth's death in 1057. Whether the tarbh-uisge (water-bull) lived in the loch at the same time is not said. This creature would emerge from the loch and graze among the cows to lure one of them to its home under the water.

The A82 runs south along the east side of Loch Linnhe, with views across the loch to the hills above Cona Glen, Glen Scaddle and Ardgour, all in Argyll. It is a busy road in summer, full of cars, caravans and lorries, and it is best to relax and not to try to overtake. At Corriechurrachan (045663) a postman on his rounds once saw two troops of fairies dancing on the grass. At 039657 there is a pleasant picnic place between the road and the water, and about a mile further on is the road that runs down to the right/west to the Ferry across the Corran Narrows to Ardgour and all the wilds of Morvern and Ardnamurchan, the most westerly point on the British mainland, though the weather maps on television sets would not make one think so.

About half a mile further on, there is a Forest Trail up Glen Righ, where there are eight successive waterfalls, well worth seeing after rain. It is unlikely that this is a king's glen, but rather that the word should be Righe, or Ruighe, which means a glen through the lower slope of a hill, a good description. Round the curve in the road is Onich, which lies tucked under the shelter of the hills. The ships carrying kings and highland chiefs on their way to burial at Iona would put in here to wait for a good wind.

The house just beyond the Parish Church (by Alexander Ross 1875), is one of the forty-three manses built in the 1820s by Act of Parliament, along with some thirty churches, one of which stood next door until it was replaced by the present building. There were two different designs of manse, single-storeyed and two-storeyed. This one is single-storeyed, as is the one at Rothiemurchus (see p.75), but it has been much altered. This was the home of Dr Alexander Stewart, who wrote as Nether Lochaber. There is a standing stone, Clach a' Charra, in a field by the shore at 026613, with views out to sea, which is said to date from about 1500 B.C.

Beyond Onich is North Ballachulish, an old crofting area, as can still be seen by the houses and fields beside the road. This was a centre of Episcopalians, and their latest church stands on a bank above the corner of the road. Its dedication to St Bride is a reminder of its builder, Lady Alice Ewing, widow of a Bishop of Argyll and the Isles and daughter of an Earl of Morton, a Douglas, whose family patron saint is St Bride. Two prominent Celtic crosses in the graveyard commemorate Alexander Mackonochie (see below) and Bishop Chinnery Haldane.

The A82 runs out of North Ballachulish and over the bridge that has replaced the ferry and disappears from Inverness-shire on its way to Glencoe and Glasgow.

A short distance before the bridge the B863 to Kinlochleven turns away to the left/east. In November, 1880, some men digging at the cairn at 051601, between the road and the water, unearthed a carved female nude, about 4 foot 9 inches tall, with eyes of white quartz, which is thought to have been linked with the inhabitants of these parts in 'the early centuries A.D.', but later maps show it as 'Iron Age'. Bishop Chinnery Haldane gave it to the Society of Antiquaries of Scotland and it is now in the Royal Museum of Scotland in Edinburgh.

Take the B863 to Kinlochleven. There are some islets in the loch, the largest being Eilean Munde (St Munde's Isle) (084592) where the Camerons of Callart were buried on one side, the other sides of the holy island being reserved for the Macdonalds of Glencoe and the Stewarts of both Ardsheal and Ballachulish. There are parking places along this road, by the water, with views of the hills, including the Pap of Glencoe.

At 092603, behind a wall and difficult to see, is Callart, the home of Cameron families from about the fifteenth century. In the seventeenth century a daughter of the house, Mary Cameron, had offended her father by being too friendly with his tenants and so he locked her into her room as a punishment. He would not let her out, even when a Spanish ship arrived in Loch Leven and everyone else went down and looked at her cargo of silks and damasks. Some were bought and brought home. Mary heard through her door of one particular dress which everyone tried on.

The next day, and the next, the house was silent. Mary was hungry but could not open her door and was considering the window when she heard voices outside. One of the speakers was a friendly tenant, a Donald Cameron from Ballachulish. He told her that he had orders to burn the house with everything in it, because it was thought that everyone had died of the plague brought by the Spanish ship. He agreed, however, to delay the burning until he had sent a message to Diarmaid Campbell, the heir of Inverawe, Mary's betrothed. Diarmaid came at once, bringing a change of clothes for Mary, who climbed out of the window and washed herself thoroughly in the burn before she dressed herself in them. As soon as she was safely away, Callart, with everything that was in it, was burned to the ground.

When they got to Inverawe (021314), Diarmaid's father refused to allow them into the house. He made them take solemn vows of matrimony and said that they must stay in a bothy for a month before they could be considered free from infection. All was well, but Diarmaid died of wounds received at Inverlochy in 1645 and is buried at Ardchattan (981351).

When the old family left the district at the end of the eighteenth century, Callart was bought by the father of Colonel John Cameron of the 92nd regiment (see p.215), Ewen

Cameron of Fassfern, who built the present house. Ewen's grand-daughter married Mr Campbell of Monzie in Perthshire (see p.137). One day, when they were at Callart, Monzie thought he would dig in the grassy mound, which was all that remained of the old house. Workmen dug a large trench, but found nothing. When they returned the next day, Monzie told them to fill it in again. No one knows what made him change his mind overnight.

The Spanish ship just mentioned may be the same as the 'Foreign Ship' that brought the 'plague' to Skye at about the same time. Among the victims there were seven of the eight sons of Padruig Mor MacCruimen, perhaps the finest piper of all that family. To mark his loss, he composed his masterpiece, the most heartbreaking of all pipe music, his 'Cumha na Cloinne' (Lament for the Children).

From Callart the road runs to the head of Loch Leven. Kinlochleven is a divided village: the river Leven, flowing from the dammed Blackwater Loch, leaves the northern part, once Kinlochmore, in Inverness-shire, and the southern part, Kinlochbeg, in Argyll. It was the setting up of the British Aluminium works here, powered by the water from the loch above, that enlarged Kinlochleven from the three houses in each to the present village. The works were built between 1904 and 1907 and were opened in 1909. The enlarged Blackwater Loch holds no less than 4,000 million cubic feet of water. This was the second large water-powered scheme in Scotland, the first being the same firm's works at Foyers (see p.93), and was followed by the large works at Fort William. From Foyers and Kinlochleven came the vast Alcan company with branches all over the world. The works may be visited if permission is sought from the Management, British Alcan, Kinlochleven. The road that continues round the loch, from here to Glencoe, was built during the 1914-18 war by German prisoners-of-war.

At 264613, two miles north-east of the western end of the dam is a memorial cross which marks the spot where the body of the Reverend Alexander Heriot Mackonochie was found in December, 1887. It was guarded for two days by the two dogs of his host, Bishop Chinnery Haldane. Father Mackonochie, a Scot, was the first vicar of the famous London slum parish of St Alban's, Holborn. For decades he was persecuted by the

Glencoe and the Ballachulish Bridge. Before the bridge was built, the crossing by ferry was an exciting event. This is an aerial view looking up Loch Leven towards the hills of Glencoe on the right. Ballachulish lies on the side of the loch in the middle distance. The fields running down to the water on the left of the picture show signs of the earlier crofting system of farming.

Church Authorities for his High Church views, which led many people to think of his death as a sort of martyrdom. There are still pilgrimages to the site.

Returning to the bridge, which replaced the ferry in 1975, the A82 crosses the narrows at Ballachulish (Baile a'chaolais, township of the narrows). On the right/west at the south end of the bridge is the memorial to James Stewart of the Glen, who was executed there for the murder of Colin Campbell of Glenure in Appin in 1752. Although the monument can be reached from the bridge, by leaving the car at the south end of the bus stance, it may be best to follow the Oban road from the roundabout a little further on and to leave the car just before the Ballachulish Hotel. From here there are stairs to the monument. The curious white stone on the top of the monument is said to have been the favourite seat of James Stewart, though not on this spot.

The estates of the Jacobite chiefs which were forfeited to the Crown after the various Risings, particularly in 1746, were known as Forfeited Estates. The tenants paid their rents to appointed factors who sent them on to the Board of Commissioners. Some of the money thus acquired was used to improve roads and bridges (see p.146). Many of the tenants also paid a second rent to their landlords, and this money was sent out of Scotland and helped to support Jacobite exiles. The Forfeited Estates were returned to their owners, or their heirs, in 1784, on payment of a fine. The fine on the Lochiel Estates, which was paid by the grandson of 'The Gentle Lochiel', was £3,432.

Colin Campbell of Glenure was a Government factor on the Forfeited Estates, with a salary of ten guineas a year. His mother was a daughter of Sir Ewen Cameron of Lochiel, so his position must have been very difficult, for it is said that he was an easy going man, who was being pressed by his superiors to be less friendly to his neighbours. Among the estates he managed was that of Stewart of Ardsheal, whose natural brother was James Stewart of the Glen, whose then home was Acharn (997549) in Glen Duror. The two men were neighbours and friends.

On 14 May, 1752 Glenure with his nephew and another man was riding into Appin, either to evict a Jacobite family or possibly on his way home to Glenure (045482). The road ran higher up the hill than it does now, and as the party rode along there were two shots and Glenure was mortally wounded. There is a cairn at 032595, reached by a turning from the A828 just over a mile from the hotel, with a signpost To The Monument. This is seen only when driving towards Oban. It is a pleasant walk – good for dogs once they are over the stile – up the track into the hills. The access to the Cairn is a narrow, obviously artificial, gravelled path to the left, about 1000 yards from the road. The car can be taken a yard or two off the road at the turning.

The murderer was only glimpsed as he ran, but suspicion fell on James Stewart, since it was said that the two men had disagreed. Stewart was arrested and, after being confined in the Fort at Fort William, he was taken to Inveraray and tried for being 'art and part' of the murder. It was a show trial, designed to stall any surviving Jacobite sentiment. The advocate for the Government was Simon Fraser of Lovat (see p.171), whose father had been executed only a few years before, and who, like many others, was coming to terms with the present. Since many families who had lingering Jacobite sympathies were unwilling to serve on the jury, it was composed of Campbells. Argyll himself was Justice General. Stewart steadily protested his innocence, but he must have known that he had no hope of acquittal. If he had lent the murderer some clothes, as was said, then he was guilty of 'art and part'.

He was brought back to Fort William and thence, on a wild day in November, he crossed the ferry for the last time and was hanged at the spot now marked by the memorial. Before he died, he recited Psalm 35, 'Plead thou my cause, O Lord, with them that stand against me . . . False witnesses did rise up, that laid to my charge things that I knew not . . .' This has ever since been known as Salm Sheumais a' Ghline (The Psalm of James of the Glens). His body hung there in chains, saluted by all the neighbourhood, until, as some say, the seven Livingstone brothers, who had rescued the Stewart banner after Culloden and brought it back to Castle Stalker, removed his remains and gave them Christian burial. Others are also given the credit for this act of charity.

No one now, and few even then, thought that James Stewart was guilty of the death of Glenure. It is said that the name of the man who fired the fatal shots has been passed down by word of mouth. It is also said that the murderer was locked up by his friends to keep him safe, and that he was driven mad by the knowledge that an innocent man had died in his place, and this could be true if, as some say, the murderer was Stewart's son. Many people agree with Robert Louis Stevenson's verdict in *Kidnapped* that the murderer was Allan Breck Stewart.

In the loch are two islands connected with the saints who brought Christianity to these parts. Eilean Choinnich (St Kenneth's Island) recalls Kenneth (see p.208), who came from Derry in Ireland in 562, a year before St Columba crossed to

Iona. Kenneth went back to Ireland and died at Achadh nam bo, where he received the last rites from Fintan-Munde, just before the latter crossed to Scotland in 597, the year of Columba's death (and the year in which St Augustine arrived in England). St Munde, as he is known, eventually settled on his island, Eilean Munde, having left his name in the various Kilmuns. Here the local families were buried, each having their own landing place.

The opinions of the ministers who wrote the Statistical Accounts for the parish of Appin, which contains Glencoe are interesting. In 1791 there were 'four or five Papists in the parish. Great numbers of Episcopalians, with four places of worship in the parish, viz. Lismore and Appin, Glenco and Kingerloch'. Fifty years later, the Reverend Gregor McGregor wrote, 'The majority of the heritors are of this persuasion and I am glad to have this opportunity of bearing testimony to their good wishes to the Establishment, as well as their kindness to its ministers. I do not think that there is a parish in Scotland in which the Episcopalian heritors deserve at the hands of the Establishment more honourable mention to be made of their name'. The enormous graveyard, with its 'exceptional collection of 19th century finely inscribed and carved Ballachulish slate tombstones', round St John's Episcopal church by the road near Ballachulish, bears witness to the numbers of Episcopalians who were, and are, in the district.

By then there were fifteen Roman Catholic families in the large parish, but the only other dissenters were three or four Anabaptists in Lismore. Mr McGregor cannot have cared for the Roman Catholic church. Of the parish church at Ballachulish, he wrote, 'It is not impossible that, after the Reformation, the people who disclaimed everything Popish, would pull down the Popish church of St Munde and build on its ruins the plain fabrick whose remains are now to be seen, there to meet the minister, when he visited them once a quarter'.

The Commissioners of the Forfeited Estates were encouraged to build a new road. The fifteen miles were estimated to cost £1000 and would join Loch Leven to the military road at the King's House (259546). The old road, the military road, now part of the West Highland Way, ran over 'high, almost perpendicular hills, often impassable, even on horse, in winter'. In 1791 the minister wrote, 'there is an excellent line of road carried through Glenco, from whence these romantic stupendous hills, when contrasted with the delightful valley below, appear uncommon objects to strangers and never fail to attract attention.'

The inn at Clachaig was built in 1839 and the regular coach from Inverness to Glasgow started in 1843. The present road through Glencoe was built, amid a fury of protests, in 1933. Since 1975 the road from Ballachulish Bridge to Glencoe has been much improved, the heaps of discarded slates have been removed and some excellent landscaping work has been done.

The first slate quarry was opened by Stewart of Ballachulish in 1761 on his farm at Larach, behind the present village of Ballachulish. A hundred years later there were three levels, all starting from the north end and running at an angle of 80°. The top level was 216 feet above the lowest and they were about 536 feet long. The works went on until about 1955. Some of the handsome slate gravestones in Lochaber and Appin came from here. The railway from Connel, which was closed as a result of the Beeching cuts in the 1960s, had its terminus at Ballachulish.

After Ballachulish and before Glencoe, a house (103595) which is now a hospital, on the west side of Sgurr na Ciche (the Pap of Glencoe), can be easily seen. This was once the home of Donald Smith, whose father was a small shopkeeper in Forres in Moray. He died in 1914 as Lord Strathcona and Mountroyal, K.C.V.O., K.C.M.G., High Commissioner for Canada, Governor of the Hudson Bay Company. He was the man who suppressed the Red River Rebellion, raised a regiment, Strathcona's Horse, and was one of the creators of the Canadian Pacific Railway (see p.77). At his house here, he carried on his work. He had six telephones in Glencoe when the Duke of Argyll had only one at Inveraray Castle. But he never tried to push himself into 'society'. He encouraged emigration from Glencoe to Canada, paying the passage out and helping the emigrants until they found work; but if they wished to return, they had to pay their own way.

At 097587 the road from Kinlochleven joins the A82 (see p.142) and the old road runs into the village of Glencoe, through it and across the river Coe. Leave the car just before the stone bridge over the river and walk up the road towards Upper Carnach for a short distance to see the fine Celtic Cross which is the memorial to MacIan of Glencoe. It was put up in 1883 by one of his descendants and is approached through a wooden gate up some steps. From the bridge the road turns south-east and runs up the right bank of the river, passing the Youth Hostel and through the woods until it joins the A82 at 137566.

Most people will continue along the main road. At 128564 is the National Trust for Scotland (N.T.S.) Visitors' Centre, with a car park on the left/north of the road. Here there is a good deal of information about the hills, the flora and fauna, and, of course, about the Massacre which took place on 13 February, 1692.

That great fictional Cockney, Mr John Jorrocks, once commented that he had seen a yard and a half of books on the subject of foxhunting. He could have said the same of the books that mention the Massacre of Glencoe.

In 1691 William of Orange was ruling the United Kingdom in right of his wife, Mary, the elder daughter of James VIII (II of England), whose throne she and her husband had usurped in 1688. This state of affairs was not universally popular, particuarly among those who had earlier sworn allegiance to the House of Stuart. Many held out for some time – the Bishops of the Episcopal Church in Scotland did not abandon their allegiance until the death of Prince Charles in January, 1788 – but to most it became clear that they had to live with the world as it was. Orders came that the Highland chiefs must take the Oath of Allegiance to the Crown by 1 January, 1692, or else they must face the wrath of William. This order went on to France, so that the Jacobite chiefs might get permission from King James to swear allegiance to his son-in-law.

Not until 29 December did the news come from King James that Alasdair Macdonald, chief of the Macdonalds of Glencoe, better known as MacIain, 'a person of great integrity, honour, good nature and courage', might take the oath. He was the last of the chiefs to receive notification of this permission, and the others, Lochiel, Keppoch and Clanranald among them, had only just had time to take the oath. MacIain went to Fort

William, arriving there on 29 December, 1691, only to hear from Colonel Hill that the rules had been changed and that he must swear before the Sheriff at Inveraray. He had sixty miles to go and the weather was bad, but Hill gave him a letter of protection and MacIain hurried along as best he might. Unfortunately Captain Drummond arrested him in Appin and kept him overnight. The next night he spent at Taynuilt, and he reached Inveraray on 2 January, which was good going.

The Sheriff, Campbell of Ardkinglass, was not there – he had gone home for the holiday and did not return until the 5th. He explained to MacIain that he was too late, but having read Hill's letter and thought things over, he administered the oath on 6 January and sent the document off to Edinburgh at once, together with Hill's letter and his own notes. Among those who saw it there was Lord Stair, father of the Master of Stair, and the collection of papers, explaining all the difficulties of MacIain, was never presented to the Privy Council. So all was done in vain, the oath was null and void and the plans of the Master of Stair, made long before, were ready. MacIain was to be the victim. 'Argyll tells me that Glencoe hath not taken the oath, at which I rejoice,' wrote the Master.

The orders to Hill from the King were dated 16 January, and William signed them both at the top and the bottom, so there is no doubt that he read them. The final paragraph reads, 'If M'Ean of Glenco and that tribe can well be separated from the rest, it will be a proper vindication of public Justice to extirpate that sect of thieves'.

It was not unusual for troops to be billeted in villages, and the company of Argyll's Regiment which arrived on 1 February in Glencoe was commanded by Robert Campbell of Glenlyon, the uncle of Alasdair Og Macdonald's wife. The three officers said the Fort was too full, so that they, with others, were moved out into the villages round about; they gave their oath that they came with no hostile intentions. So, however uncomfortably, the soldiers were put into the crowded houses, for most people were down from the remoter farms at this season.

On 12 February the orders were sent to Glenlyon. 'You are ordered to fall upon the rebells the Macdonalds of Glencoe and put all to the sword under seventy. You are to have special care that the old fox and his sons do not escape your hands; you are to secure all avenues, that no man escape. This you are to put in execution at five of the clock precisely; and by that time, or very shortly after it, I will strive to be at you with a stronger party. If I do not come to you at five, you are not to tarry for me, but to fall on. This is by the King's special commands, for the good and safety of the Countrey, that these miscreants be cut off root and branch. See that this be put in execution without fear or favour, or you may expect to be dealt with as one not true to King or Government, nor a man fit to carry a commission in the King's service. Expecting you will not fail in the fulfilling hereof, as you love yourself, I subscribe this at Ballychyllis, the 12 Feby. 1692. Robert Duncanson.'

The orders arrived by seven that evening when Glenlyon was playing cards with Young MacIain and his brother Alasdair Og, but it would seem that the soldiers at any rate had some knowledge of what was afoot, for there is a stone near Inverigan, now known as MacEanruig's Stone (The Son of red John's stone), and it was here that the boy heard a soldier say to the stone, 'Ah! Great stone of the Glen. If you knew what is to happen tonight, you would not be lying so peaceful there!' The boy took these words to Alasdair Og, who had always had his doubts about the visit of his wife's uncle and his men. No doubt other warnings were given by soldiers to their hosts, or the massacre would have been much greater.

Alasdair's wife made ready for flight even though Glenlyon had told her husband that the orders were merely for a move to Glengarry. So they were not surprised when news came that soldiers were approaching the house and they got safely away. His father and mother were not so fortunate. The sound of gunfire and the light from the blazing houses must have aroused the other people and many fled into the hills before the reinforcements arrived under Duncanson and Drummond.

'It were to be wished that a veil could be thrown over this part of our history, as it was the most barbarous transaction of modern times sanctioned by any regular authority from government. The massacre of Glenco happened in King William's reign, and is a circumstance well known. As it does not add much lustre to the humanity of the times, it may suffice to observe, that all the inhabitants who could be seized were indiscriminately butchered in cold blood, mostly in their beds, by the soldiers and officers who were their guests and hospitably entertained for ten days before. The officers were playing cards with Glenco and Mrs Macdonald the early part of the night: Before day, Glenco was murdered in his wife's arms. Mr McDonald of Achtriachatain shared the same fate'. So wrote an eighteenth-century reporter.

As early as 28 March, Hill was writing to Lord Tweeddale asking that the survivors might be allowed to return to the glen. Stories were flying round Edinburgh and London; on 12 April the account was printed in the Paris *Gazette*. In May the MacIains were given 'a protection' by the Privy Council.

In 1985 in the Kingshouse on the Moor of Rannoch Dr Paul Hopkins read to the Inverness Field Club a paper which was later published by the Field Club and later still developed into a book. He opened by saying, 'My position in presenting this paper is a delicate one – an Englishman, with few Scottish connections, with little personal knowledge, unable to speak Gaelic, discussing an episode of Highland history still of strong emotional as well as historical interest. It is particularly delicate because the Massacre of Glencoe, carried out by one group of Scottish Highlanders upon another group of Scottish Highlanders, upon orders issued by a Scottish Secretary of State and countersigned by a Dutch king, is something for which, naturally, no true Scottish nationalist will ever forgive the English'.

The real villains were perhaps Major General Thomas Livingstone, who was commanding the troops in Scotland, Dalrymple and the Master of Stair, all of whom came to no harm as a result of their work. But no one will ever agree the details. As the old lady said about the Gowrie Conspiracy, 'We shall know at the Day of Judgement, but not before'.

The actual number of those killed on 13 February, 1692, is said to be thirty-eight, but the systematic destruction of the houses and steadings, so that there was little shelter to be had from the bitter weather, may have doubled the number who lost their lives.

Thanks to the work of Colonel John Hill at Fort William, who 'persistently solicited those in authority', the Macdonalds were allowed to return and settle peaceably in Glencoe in August, 1692, trying to make their destroyed homes habitable for the winter. Their livestock had been taken, they had not been able to have a harvest, but their neighbours helped them and at least they were home again. So well did they settle that, despite the losses of 1692, 1715 and 1746, towards the end of the eighteenth century the glen was over-populated. Then the introduction of sheep drove them to emigrate and all the land on which they had grown corn for centuries was abandoned to the sheep.

It is worth recording that, in the 1715 Rising, the hundred Glencoe men whom MacIan brought to the Jacobite standard were brigaded with the Glenlyon men, while the Mackintoshes marched with the Macdonalds of Keppoch.

Calum Maclean wrote, 'I first saw Glencoe on a darkening November evening some years ago. Even if I had not known that it was Glencoe, I would have been awe-stricken, for under such conditions it was exactly the place where terrible things could happen'.

CHAPTER 8

Drumnadrochit to Beauly by Cannich

The A831 leaves the A82 just north of the bridge at Drumnadrochit to run all the rest of the way up Glen Urquhart, over the top to Cannich and round towards Beauly (see p.237).

John Bright, the nineteenth-century Radical statesman, stayed at the Drumnadrochit Hotel and wrote in the Visitors' Book on 21 June, 1856,

> In Highland glen 'tis far too oft observed
> That man is chased away, and game preserved.
> Glen Urquhart is to me a lovelier glen,
> Here deer and grouse have not supplanted men.

Today, despite early planting by the Forestry Commission along the south side of the Glen, Mr Bright could repeat those lines at the end of the twentieth century, though as late as 1987 the Glen people fought against another would-be planter.

On the right/north of the road is Kilmichael Church. There is early mention of a Kilmichael hereabout, but this one was built about 1910-12 as a United Free Church, with its manse alongside. In 1929 the United Free Church amalgamated with the established Church of Scotland and the services have been held alternately in Kilmore (see p.113) and Kilmichael, but now are held in Kilmore only. The minister also has Glenmoriston in his care, the name of the parish being Urquhart and Glenmoriston.

High on the hill above Kilmichael is Achmony, where Mackays lived from Whitsunday 1554, when they had a lease of these Church lands from Patrick Hepburn, the Bishop of Moray. Within three years they had paid 'a certain great sum of money in advance' and acquired the freehold and were there until Alexander of Achmony, who was 'out' in the '45, sold the estate to Sir James Grant of Grant in December, 1779. Of this family was Dr William Mackay, the author of *Urquhart and Glenmoriston*, 1893, and many other useful works of local

F

history. Patrick Mackay, brother of Alexander of Achmony, emigrated in 1770 to Pictou, Nova Scotia, and was followed by many others from the Glen.

Almost opposite is a two-storeyed building. What is seen is a house that has been building for many years, while the builder and his family live in their old home. This is not unusual, but for the fact that the old house stands inside the newer one. This is also the site of one of the carding mills, though there was a linen 'Manufactory' at Kilmichael which was 'on the decay' in 1763. It was here that a weaver saw an old woman doodling in the dust with a stick, and from her design made the famous Glen Urquhart tweed.

The village of Milton was by-passed when the road was improved. Sir James Grant, *The Good Sir James*, decided to enlarge Milton to be a centre for weaving, to discourage people from emigrating. The plans were drawn by George Brown, one of Telford's surveyors, in 1808, but the village was not completed until after 1820. The water power was carefully channelled so as to drive about five mills, the first being the sawmill. The last mills finally closed in the 1930s.

The rebuilt Free Church (491304) is on the right, and behind it is the hollow field where the congregation would sit during the services leading up to the Sacrament Sunday. Just beyond it is the turning, A833, to the right/north to Beauly.

The A833 leaves the A831 by a hairpin bend and then climbs very steeply to open moorland. A short way up the hill is a side road to Gartally, where there were limekilns to burn the lime from the hills on the north side of this end of the Glen. It is to this lime that much of the fertility of the Glen is due.

Just where the moor opens out, a turning on the right/east leads to the farm of Garbeg, where a cairn cemetery at 511319 was excavated in 1974. One of the graves was of an unusual design, being roughly square with a pile of stones in the middle, the whole surrounded by straight ditches which were not connected at the corners, at each of which was a single stone – a sort of 'four poster bed' dating from the first millenium B.C. Fragments of a Pictish symbol stone from one of the other cairns, though it must have arrived later than the cairn burial, are now in the Inverness Museum. Recently a great deal of careful planting of trees and digging of pools to

Glencoe. This is an autumnal view from the Moor of Rannoch. The glen drops down through the gap seen through the leafless tree. The Glencoe hills are a challenge to climbers all through the year.

encourage wildlife have won Mr Younie and his family public acclaim at the Royal Highland Show. Further up the hill, to the east of the road at 5032 and also at 5131, are settlements and field systems.

The road drops down through a small but attractive gorge into Glen Convinth. At 512375, to the west of the road, is the ancient site of Convinth Church, which was 75 feet long by 25 feet across, a large building for its time. There is a tradition of a monastery here (see p.172) but no evidence remains. There were said to have been some Pictish stones here in the nineteenth century, but they have vanished. Since there was a Coan's Fair held here in the seventeenth century, it seems likely that the dedication was to St Comghan, who lived in the eighth century. The first husband of Gruoch (whose second husband was Macbeth) was Gillechomgain (pronounced Gilcoan), meaning 'the servant of Comghan'. The mound to the west of

the wall round the burial ground has two names, Angels'
Hillock, or Maclean's Mound, the latter recalling that Farquhar
Maclean lived here in the fifteenth century.

In the Privy Council papers there is an account of an action
by Lovat against one Doughal Mor Mackintosh, who was
accused of taking rents that were due to Lovat. This Doughal
Mor denied, though he admitted having taken 'ane Unicorn'
from Farquhar MacEachan (Hector's son) Maclean, who was a
cousin of Doughal Mor. Although 'ane Unicorn' was a coin
worth 18 shillings, in this beautiful glen it is easy to imagine a
herd of unicorns grazing peacefully.

By turning right at the next turning and taking every right
turn thereafter, Loch Laide and Abriachan are reached (see p.
108), though by keeping left at 529378 and running through
the Caiplich and South Clunes, Moniack Castle (552436) is
reached (see p.110).

A833 continues north. At 516413 a turning to the left/west
leads to the present Kiltarlity church, dating from 1763 and
1829. The stone over the door, with M.W.F. and 1626 cut on it,
came from the older church (see p.162). In the burying ground
is a mound, some ten feet high, known as Tom-na-Croiche, the
Gallows Hill. No doubt the Frasers used it as such after they
acquired Dounie (now Beaufort) in 1511, but it probably
started as the base of a timber motte-hill fort. Outer rings of
defensive earthworks can be seen, which enclosed the whole
area of the present graveyard.

The A833 runs along the wall of the lands of Beaufort Castle
(457430) (not open), which dates from c. 1880 with later
rebuilding after a fire, the current successor to Dounie, the
castle of the Fentons in the thirteenth and fourteenth
centuries, when it was probably a simple affair, to control the
Stockford of Ross. This seems to have been the name of the
crossing of the river Beauly wherever the ford might be at any
moment. Dounie passed by marriage to the Frasers, and was
burned by Cumberland in 1746. The A833 joins the A862
(once the A9) at 528440. Return now to Glen Urquhart.

There was a house at Polmaily (476306) about 1500. There is
little or nothing left of it in the present house, which is now a
hotel with a curling pond as well as a swimming pool. About
1540 the Big Smith of Polmaily, one of the armourers of the

Glen, was known to be friendly with the fairies of Tor-na-Sithe (see below). They gave him a little filly, who could plough tirelessly and so was of great use to the smith and his neighbours, but she was never to be yoked to anything but a plough. Needless to say, one day she was harnessed to a cart – and her power departed from her. The Big Smith is said to be linked with the Great Raid of 1544, when Macdonald of Clanranald and his allies raided the Glen, seizing the Castle and killing the Smith's sons, among others, before taking south 1500 cattle, over 300 horses, 2000 sheep, 1000 lambs and nearly 1500 goats, besides quantities of oats and barley. A raid today could not provide such booty, but the Glen was always known to be rich in such things and was therefore raided frequently. This particular raid was completed by the Battle of Blar na Leine, further south (see p.130).

Below the road, at 452296, is the Mill of Tore, which hopes to be open from June to September from 2-5pm, but not on Sundays. This is an old meal mill, powered by water coming by a long lade from the River Enrick to drive the big wheel. Until quite recently it was grinding oats as it had done for centuries. There is a good car park by the road and entrance is free, though the guides on duty will show where the donation box stands, for the mill relies on these chance donations to keep itself in order. It was restored in 1976 in memory of Alastair Mackell, O.B.E., once Head Master of Glen Urquhart Secondary School, the author of *The Glen Urquhart Story*, which was originally written for his pupils. The old road that runs between the mill and the miller's house, where the Macdonald family of millers lived for some 400 years, was upgraded by Telford early in the nineteenth century, but has now been bypassed by the present road. The small house further along, on the old road, was built as the Poor House, but more recently was the Post Office for Balnain. On the other side of the A831, high on the rock of Tor-na-Sithe (Hill of the Fairies) (452299) is a hill fort, now very overgrown, about 150 by 100 feet. The road takes a sharp bend round the foot of the rock.

Just round this bend is a wide space on the left/west where cars can be left and the passengers may walk up the forestry roads to the top of the hills, or through the now largely felled forest, along the south side of Loch Meiklie, and their dogs can have a good run. This is one of the old roads or tracks which ran near Lochletter and on to Shewglie and Corrimony (see below). The other track is now the A831.

Above Loch Meiklie, on the left of the road at 432304 is St Ninian's Episcopal Church, a listed building, and the work of Dr Alexander Ross (see p.18). It is plain outside, with corbie-stepped gables, but interesting inside. Built into the altar is a stone carved with a simple cross which was once part of the church at Temple, (see p.112). Unfortunately, when it was set in place it was enclosed within a sentence linking it with the Knights Templar, who were never known in these parts. The name of Temple had confused a non-Gaelic speaking donor. The carpets in the chancel were designed in the 1930s by George Bain, who taught art. Recently the east windows have been filled with modern glass panels. In the graveyard is a mort-safe, to deter grave-robbers.

> St Ninian's church is half-way up the Glen,
> Some seven miles from where our patron saint
> Set up his base, to bring to Pictish men
> The good news of the living Christ we love.
> Our church, surrounded by God's Acre, stands
> Beside Loch Meiklie, the great hills above,
> A Highland Galilee, where seasons paint
> The trees, the sparkling flowers, with lavish hands.
>
> We are surrounded by our many friends,
> Some in the pews, the others, now at rest
> Outside, will join us as we come to share
> With them again God's own familiar feast.
> In this dear place we'll wait for Gabriel's call.
> God's Acre here is Eden's grove writ small.

South of the road, at 416296, is Shewglie, once the home of a Grant family. Though most of the house is dated 1762, some of it survived the destruction of 1746, after Ludovick (Lewis) Grant of Grant had betrayed the men of Glen Urquhart to the Duke of Cumberland. Old Shewglie died in London, having been released from Tilbury Fort shortly before his death, but his son, who was with him, and the Reverend John Grant, the parish minister, did return to the Glen. But of the sixty-eight men from Glen Moriston and the sixteen from Glen Urquhart whom their Chief had handed over to Cumberland, only

Glen Urquhart. This picture is of the village of Milton before the new road was made in the 1960s to the right of the trees below the road. In the foreground is a small stack of hay, rarely seen now that most hay is baled, or silage is made instead. In the background lies Drumnadrochit with Loch Ness beyond it. The view is to the east.

eighteen were still alive in 1749, as prisoners in Barbados. The descendants of one who returned still live in Inverness.

Beyond Glen Urquhart Post Office and Restaurant a narrow road to the right/north goes to Buntait. Just before the wooden garage on the right at the top of the hill there is a field gate also on the right. Just over the horizon from the gate is Char's Stone (398311). The stone has fallen and is presently propped up against a heap of smaller stones. The whole group stands on a circular mound, with wonderful views of the surrounding hills. There are three round cairns to the east. North-east of Upperton at 395313 is a large hut settlement with the remains of thirteen stone-walled houses, averaging thirty-three feet in diameter.

Returning to the A831, at 394302 there is a turning to the left/south to Corrimony, crossing the hump-backed bridge, which has a plaque saying 'Built by Alec Grant of Corriemony with the aid of a generous country, 1790'.

There is an Ancient Monuments sign for the chambered cairn, which is on the right of the road nearly a mile from the turning (373300), a few yards beyond the car parking space on the left. The stone circle is seventy-seven feet in diameter around a fifty-foot diameter cairn. The chamber inside the thick corbelled walls is thirteen feet across and the large stone lying on the top must once have been the cap-stone to close the cairn. When Professor Stewart Piggot worked here in 1952, he found on the ground a stain, almost a shadow, of a crouched burial, but nothing solid, not even a tooth, had survived.

It was at Corrimony in 1797 that woods were felled, by men from the south, to make one of the first Highland sheep-farms; it was soon followed at Knockfin (299268) in Strath Glass. Rather earlier, Monie, a Norse raider, was defeated at Drumnadrochit, near Craig Monie (see p.113). He fled up the Glen and was killed at Coire Mhonaidh, which has become Corriemony, where Monie's Stone (3374300), a standing stone, is said to mark the spot. To find the stone, drive past the houses and cross a concrete bridge over the burn towards a fine row of Wellingtonias and beeches. The standing stone is a few yards over the bridge, on the left of the drive that once led to the Victorian house at Corriemony, which was demolished after a fire in 1951. It is said that Temple Pier could be seen from the top of the tower, and that the front doorstep was on a level with the roof-ridge of the Drumnadrochit Hotel.

The old house (376303) (not open) of 1740 survives with an armorial and marriage stone 1730 A.G. and J.O. In July, 1746, many houses were burned and a party of soldiers were sent to Corriemony to burn it also. Alexander Grant of Corriemony had raised his men for Prince Charles, and was not at home when the Government troops came. His wife, Jane Ogilvy, faced them, and found that the officer was also an Ogilvy and so the house was spared. Corriemony himself came to no harm and, after the 1748 Act of Indemnity, was able to live openly at home.

Beyond the house is Cladh Churadain (377300), St Curadan's burying ground. The wall dates from 1890, but the hollow stone set in the east side is Clach-an-Tullan, the font from the church that must once have stood here. In early spring the walls enclose a sheet of snow-drops.

One of the farm buildings reached by crossing the bridge by the House is a scheduled Ancient Monument, a large barn of five bays, built with couples (called crucks in England). The couples (large timbers), not the stone walls, take the weight of the roof. The barn is sideways on from the farm road, to the left of the other buildings. The roof is corrugated iron and the entry is on the left as it is approached. It dates from the late seventeenth century and is the 'finest cruck building in Scotland' according to the experts, and may have been the home of the Grants before they built the white house in 1740.

Beyond the Corriemony turning the A831 continues up Kerrow Brae, with a splendid view of the Affric and Cannich hills from the top of the pass.

At the bottom of the hill beyond Kerrow Brae, a narrow turning to the right/north to Eskadale, one of the few Norse names in the district, runs north along the east bank of the river Glass (which later changes its name to the Beauly after the Farrar joins it at Struy (see p.170). This apparently little used road is part of St Duthac's Road which led pilgrims from the west coast, following in the footsteps of St Duthac to the great shrine of that saint at Tain in Easter Ross (see p.164). Just before Struy Bridge (405396), on the left is a white house that was once a school, and in its grounds, but visible from the road, is a seven-foot-tall stone, inscribed W.C. and C.F. and dated 1746. It commemorates the death at Culloden of William Chisholm, standard-bearer to his clan. His widow, Christina Fraser, composed in his memory the famous poem, 'Mo run geal og', 'My fair young love'.

About four miles further on at Eskadale is St Mary's Roman Catholic church (454399), which was built in 1826 by Thomas Fraser of Strichen, who was created Baron Lovat in 1837. Many of that family are buried there, as are the Sobieski-Stuarts.

A narrow road on the left before Hughton Post Office leads to Eilean Aigas House (469418) (not open) on the island of the same name. Built in 1839 by the same Thomas Fraser as a shooting lodge, it became the home of the Sobieski-Stuarts. They were two brothers who claimed, probably wrongly, to be descended from Prince Charles Edward Stuart, but they harmed no one by this claim. What they did achieve was the writing of the *Vestiarum Scoticum* about tartans; there is a copy in the Public Library in Farraline Park in Inverness. It is by no means a book to be relied on, but nonetheless it is one of the great nineteenth-century tartan publications and, if time allows, it is one to look at.

The road divides at Hughton, the left road running on to join the A831 at 497444 (see p.175). Just before crossing the river Beauly on the right/east of the road are the remains of the ancient church of Kiltarlity in its burying ground. The ruins date from 1626 (see p.156), but the site is much older, the dedication being to St Talorgan, who lived c.720. No doubt it was a resting place for the pilgrims as they walked to Tain, or home, their pious duty done.

Instead of crossing the bridge at 345314 and going straight into Cannich, keep straight on into the narrow road for Tomich.

About a mile on, at 335306, is Clachan Comar, with the remains of the sixteenth-century church on the site of an ancient church dedicated to St Beathan. It is the scene of part of a fine story from the eighteenth century.

At that time some of the Macraes from Kintail had grazing rights in Strathglass. One of them was Muireach Fial MacRath, Generous Maurice Macrae. He and his wife used to sell their produce in Inverness, Kintail not being far through by Glen Affric, but many miles round by the modern road. One day, on the way home, some men persuaded Muireach to stop at the inn at Struy, but Mrs Macrae went on, expecting him to catch her up on the way. When she got home and he had not done so, she sent out a search party, but Muireach could not be found and all but one of the party returned home.

The man who stayed on in the Strath pretended to be simple-minded and wandered about, begging. One night he heard a conversation which referred to a white-bellied salmon tied to a bush and hidden in a certain pool in the river. He went to look and found the body of Muireach Fial, which he removed and hid before heading for Kintail. He returned with a strong party to bring the body back for burial. On their way west they passed a funeral at Clachan Comar and, hoping for a fight, the Macraes took the stone which the mourners had intended to set up in Clachan Comar. The Strathglass people did not object, so the Macraes went on, taking the stone as well as Muireach's body. They buried him at Clachan Duich (946210) (Duthac's

Corriemony Cairn, Glen Urquhart. This is a fine example of a Clava-type cairn, complete with its ring of standing stones. The large stone on the top is the cap-stone, which has been moved at some distant period. It is possible to crawl into the burial chamber in the middle of the cairn.

place) where they set the stone above him. It is still there at the south gable of the ruined church and is known as An Leac Chuileanach, the Puppy Stone, because it was broken on the way and is now in two pieces, one larger than the other, like a bitch and her puppy (see p.00).

Beyond Clachan Comar, drive slowly because of hens and geese and ponies all over the road at Kerrow Farm. Between 1977 and her capture on 29 October, 1980 a puma, later called Felicity, was often seen round Kerrow. After her capture, she was taken to the Highland Wild Life Park (see p.71), where she eventually died. Her stuffed body can be seen in the Museum in Inverness. Other pumas were seen in Glen Urquhart, but they are better at concealing themselves now. At the next bridge, keep straight on again for Tomich (306273). This is a planned estate village, the work of the first Lord Tweedmouth, who built Guiseachan House (now a ruin) c. 1850, and also bred here the first Golden Retrievers.

Although Guiseachan House is a ruin, the farm is still very much alive. Take the turning in Tomich that says Guiseachan Chalets and at the top is a very fine farm steading, complete with a turret whose clock is working. To the left of the steading is the Guiseachan Dairy, a listed building, and rightly so, for it is a splendid example of an expensive Victorian working dairy. Scattered through the estate, and visible on the way to the Plodda Falls (see below) are more handsome examples of Lord Tweedmouth's buildings.

Tomich is a much older place than would be guessed by a quick look at it. Its origins lie in the fact that it was the centre of a number of tracks in the Middle Ages, principally those used by pilgrims on their way to and from the shrine of St Duthac at Tain, which was a favourite place of prayer of King James IV, who came regularly and frequently between 1496 and 1513, and where the king worshipped was a good place to be seen, even if there were no better reason for being there. Since Tain is outside the borders of this book, it is sufficient to say that St Duthac seems to have been born in Tain c.1000 and died at Armagh in Ireland in 1067; his remains were translated to Tain on 19 June c.1253. Because of Duthac's sanctity, King Malcolm III obtained for his birthplace the special 'protection of the Apostolic See.' King Robert I's wife and daughter fled here from Edward I of England, only to be betrayed to that invader by the Earl of Ross.

The oldest route to the west from Tomich lay across the water to Knockfin and then along the south side of Loch Affric, and so over the pass to Loch Duich and the church where Muireach Fial is buried. That way is now a forestry road which can be walked over (see p.166). A later track by Glen Cannich led further north (see p.167). It is still possible to walk along the old way through to the south-west from Tomich which became the drove road through the hills to Glen Moriston (319140) (see p.121). Follow the road marked to the Plodda Falls passing the ruins of Guiseachan House at 277238 to a car park. The way up to the Falls, a steep climbing track, is clearly marked. There is a viewing point, and the track goes right on to the Falls. Yet another track leads up the Amhuinn Deabhag (shrunken river) from Tomich past Cougie (242212), where only a couple of houses stand today. In 1746 there was a big enough population for fifty men to have gone to Culloden. This track comes down into Glen Moriston by Glen Doe.

Returning from Tomich, keep left/west over the Fasnakyle Bridge and join the road from Cannich to Glen Affric by the North of Scotland Hydro Electric Board's turbine house at 318296. It is open to visitors, and has a 66 megawatt capacity. Even if not going in, look up at the fine reproductions of Pictish carved animals high on the walls. Turning past the power house, the road runs to Cannich past Comar (see p.166), but keeping round to the left/south it runs to Glen Affric, said to be the second most beautiful glen in Scotland – the most beautiful being one's own.

Guides to the walks, which also give details of the animals and plants that can be seen, and advising the visitor to bring binoculars to help to identify the more distant birds or beasts, can be bought from the Forestry Commission Office in Church Street, Inverness. There are two way-marked walks, one longer and one shorter, that can be taken from the car park beyond the Dog Falls, next to the bridge at 284283.

The dam at Loch Benevean (properly Beinn a'Mheadain, Hill in the middle), which raised the level of the water a good deal, is part of the North of Scotland Hydro Electric Board's works. The road goes on through the country in which the TV film of *The Last of the Mohicans* was made – through clouds of midges! At 215243, just before the bridge, there is a monument on the left to Clan Chisholm. Continue to the picnic place at the end of the public road at 201233. From here there are two short walks. One leads from the south side of the car park by a well-worn track. Across the river to the south, the woods are fenced against sheep and deer to allow the natural regeneration of the remnants of the old Caledonian Forest, which once covered much of Scotland. The difference that the fencing makes is noticeable at once. The other walk starts from the north side of the road and climbs to a seat at the viewpoint (208238).

Beyond the picnic place is Affric Lodge (not open). The drive is private, except for walkers. Sir Edwin Landseer stayed here in a wet season and filled his time by painting sporting scenes on the dining room walls. Sir Winston Churchill, at a later date, preferred bridge-building.

Walkers may go through the hills from here to Loch Duich
in Kintail in Ross-shire. This is the way that the Macraes came
and went (see p.162). With careful arrangement, two parties
can walk the twelve miles through from either end, one walking
east and the other west. Car keys are exchanged when they
meet on the way. If this is done, always start from the other
party's car. It is easier and safer to drive one's own car when
tired.

Returning to the fork for Tomich, the A831 bears to the
right at the bottom of the hill and on, over the River Glass and
past St Mary's Roman Catholic Church, to Cannich. This is a
small village, which probably developed as an adjunct to the
ancient home of the Chisholms, at Comar (334312). There is a
hotel, from which fishing permits can be had; a shop; the
Roman Catholic church of St Mary and St Bean; and a Church
of Scotland church, which was built and presented to the
congregation in 1866 by Mr Robertson, who was then living at
Comar. A turning almost opposite St Mary's church leads to a
Youth Hostel.

Turn left/south at the cross-roads by the bridge, a short
distance beyond the houses, and Comar (334312) (not open)
can be seen. This was for many years the home of the chiefs of
the Chisholms. Although they also owned Erchless Castle (see
p.171), they were known as the Chisholms of Comar, never of
Erchless. The house looks plain and like many lairds' houses in
the Highlands, but it probably dates from the seventeenth
century. In an upstairs room there is a lintel stone over the
fireplace dated 1740, with the initials R.C. They are those of
Roderick Chisholm (1697-1767) who was 'out' in 1715, when
his lands were forfeited, but, by passing through a succession
of friendly hands, were restored to his eldest son. It is said that
Roderick bought Glasleitir from Mackenzie of Gairloch and
that he tried to drain Loch Mullardoch. Those who have seen
this loch at the end of Glen Cannich will 'gasp and stretch their
eyes', but the water level is far higher than in his day. His
younger son, Ruari Og (Young Roderick), led the Chisholms at
Culloden, where he was mortally wounded.

Roderick's grandson, Alexander, An Siosal Ban (the fair
Chisholm), died in 1793 and was succeeded by his half-brother,
William. William had married Elizabeth Macdonald of

'The Glorious Twelfth'. The twelfth of August is the day when the grouse-shooting season begins. It ends on 6 December. The party complete with guns, dogs, beaters and lookers-on, is well wrapped up against the Highland midges, whose attacks can seem as painful as if they were the size of the grouse.

Glengarry, a sister of Alastair Glengarry (see p.127), and together they 'cleared' Strathglass in 1801, 1810, and finally in 1831. They were helped by Thomas Gillespie, who had earlier approached Alexander, when, whatever may have been the Chief's intentions, the appearance of a thousand tenants round Comar House made him send Gillespie away. William welcomed him. Bishop Angus Chisholm wrote to Alexander's widow, 'Oh, madam, you would really feel if you only heard the pangs and saw the oozing tears by which I am surrounded in this once happy but now desolated valley of Strathglass'.

It is pleasant to record that Thomas Fraser, Lord Lovat, allowed some of the evicted people to move into Strathfarrar after the final eviction, where they proudly and regularly paid their rent. Perhaps the ruins of a group of houses in Strathfarrar were their homes. But, after fourteen years, they were again evicted – when Glen Strathfarrar was turned into a deer forest.

Going straight across the cross-roads at Cannich (337317), a narrow road, signposted for Mullardoch, climbs sharply to the west and leads for nine miles through Glen Cannich (cotton sedge) to the end of the road at the large hydro-electric dam at Loch Mullardoch (221316). This glen is not visited as much as Glen Affric, but it is as beautiful in its own way, and the shooting lodge at Cozac (231317) is now a hotel.

From Loch Mullardoch a four-mile-long tunnel leads through the hills to Benevean (see p.165), which was not drowned as deeply as was Mullardoch.

This is a glen in which deer may be seen quite close to the road. They are often indifferent to the presence of motor cars and can be watched from inside, though they will bolt if people get out. *Quiet* winding down of the window will often allow a photograph to be taken at quite close range, but some luck is needed for this. At 311331 was Tombuie (yellow mound) where there was once the 'Holy Stone', now said to be at Glassburn House (see below). There is no way through beyond the dam, but the glen looks very different on the way back.

In 1878 Mr Chisholm wrote, 'In Glencannich even within my own recollection, there were a number of people comfortably located. Of the descendants of Glen Cannich men, there lived in my own time one Bishop and fifteen priests; 3 colonels, 1 major, 3 captains, 3 lieutenants and 7 ensigns. Such was the class of men who had their early education in the glen or in Strathglass, and now there are 8 shepherds, 7 gamekeepers and one farmer in Glen Cannich'. Today there are even fewer people living in this glen.

Turning to the right/north at the bridge in Cannich, the A831 heads for Beauly. At Upper Glassburn (not open), once the home of Captain William Mackay (d. 1976), a son of Dr William (see p.153), there is said to be a so-called Mass Stone in the garden, but this may be the remains of a standing stone; next door, at Glassburn House (369344) (not open), once the home of Captain Archie Chisholm, who did so much to revive shinty in this part of the Highlands, is said to be the 'Holy Stone' of Tombuie in Glen Cannich (311331). This hollow stone was used as a font by Father Farquharson when times were bad for Roman Catholics and he was hiding in Glen Cannich. Most of the people in this part of Strathglass were strongly Roman Catholic and they still have two churches, one in Cannich (342317) and one at Eskadale (454399).

Dam Building. This is the Mullardoch Dam, at the head of Glen Cannich, in its early days. It was started about 1947 and completed by 1951. The two men in the foreground give an idea of the size of the work. The dam is part of the North of Scotland Hydro-Electric system.

At 371346 is 'St Ignatius' Well' on the left/west of the road. It has no antiquity, having been built in 1880; it was tidied to commemorate the coronation of Queen Elizabeth in 1953. It was supposed to encourage the passing traveller to refresh himself from the spring, but today it is not advisable to drink the water. At the turn of the century it was recorded that 'one gentleman, who frequently drives that way, cannot pass the well without stopping for a drink – of whisky from his flask!'

Shortly before reaching Struy (stream) there are two duns on the left/west of the road, Dun Coille Struy (Fort of the wood and stream) (396396) and Dun Struy Beg (397392), both reached by steep, though short, climbs. The first is oval, thirty-six feet by twenty-three, and is a strongly defensible site. The other is circular, sixty feet in diameter, with the foundations of three rectangular buildings inside it.

Just before the Struy Inn a road turns right/east to join the Eskadale road on the other side of the bridge, An Drochaid Dhu (the Black Bridge) or the Bridge of Mauld, over the river Glass, above its confluence with the Farrar.

Beyond the Inn is Struy Bridge, built by Telford's men between 1809 and 1817 of stones that used to be studded with tiny garnets, most of which have been picked out by now. It crosses the Farrar, which may be the 'Varrar' mentioned by Ptolemy of Alexandria (c.90-168 A.D.).

The narrow turning to the left/west immediately north of the bridge leads up Strathfarrar, which is a National Nature Reserve as far as Deanie (320398). Here there are many fine Scots Pines. Permission to drive the seventeen miles up the glen can be got by asking at the gate house, except on Tuesdays and on Sunday mornings. There is a limit to the number of cars allowed through, but none for walkers or cyclists. When the stalking season is on, August to late October, visitors are asked to keep to the road, which is no serious limit to seeing the views.

A passing merchant was killed in the glen by Government troops and was buried there; he is now remembered by the naming of a newly-made pool as The Merchant's Pool, for his grave, now washed away, was near it. There are dams for hydro-electric power at Lochs Beannacharn and Monar, and power stations at Culligran and Deanie. Well up the glen, beyond Loch Beannacharn, is Loch a'Mhuillidh. In it, at 277382, is the tree-covered Eilean a'Mhuillidh, one of the hiding places of Simon Fraser, Lord Lovat, in 1746.

At Broulin (233386) General Monk camped with his army in 1654. He marched with a considerable force from Perth by Aberfeldy, Loch Laggan and Loch Lochy to Loch Quoich and

Kintail. Then he went north and on 29 July he camped 'at Glen-teuch in the Shields of Kintail, the night was very tempestuous and blew down most of the tents. In all this march we saw only two women of the inhabitants and one man. The 30th – The Army march't from Glen-teuch to Brouling. The way for neere 5 miles soe boggie that about 100 baggage horses were left behinde and many other horses bogg'd or tir'd. Never any horse men (much less an armie) were observed to march that way'. Among the troops were the beginnings of the Coldstream Guards. Monk's own regiment. If they saw so few people, they could not have done much 'overawing', which was their intention. A shilling of the reign of Charles I (1625-49) was found here in 1940.

Many of the men of Fraser's Highlanders, raised by General Simon Fraser (see p.145), son of the Lord Lovat who hid on the island, came from Strathfarrar and climbed the Heights of Abraham to take Quebec, and Canada, from the French. Even further on, Loch Monar, now dammed, is an ice cauldron. When a geologist was asked for the reason, the answer was, 'What else could you call it?'

To the right/south of the A831 at 410408 is Erchless Castle (not open). The tower house was probably built by John Chisholm of Comar about 1610. This family descends from Sir Robert Chisholm, who was Governor of Urquhart Castle in 1359. His second son, Alexander, married Margaret del Ard, Lady of Erchless, in 1368, and they probably lived on the motte-hill at Cnoc an Tighe Mor (Hill of the Great House), which stands on the other side of the road at 411411. It became the burial place of the Chisholms during the last and present centuries.

The del Ard family (of the Aird – this part of the county is known as The Aird) is recorded in 1296. Their timber castle measured seventy-five feet in diameter and was defended by the Erchless Burn to the north and west and a ditch to the east. It is easy to reach by walking up the path through the rhododendrons and, now that the other rhododendrons that recently clothed the sides of the motte-hill have been cleared away, the strength of the position is obvious to every eye. In 1902 the Sacrificial Stone of Erchless had just been 'found', though its existence was remembered in the district. It then lay

'200 yards above the road where it crosses the Erchless Burn by
the stone bridge'. It has a hollow in the middle and stands
'outside the wall that once surrounded the buildings', traces of
which could then be seen. To find it today, go through the gate
near the entry to the motte hill and follow the track up through
the field until it divides. Take the right fork and turn right
under the electric pylon and downhill for a few yards. The
mossy stone is held in the trunks of several silver birch trees. It
is large, about five feet by three, and about a couple of feet in
height. In the middle of the flat top is the hole, quite small in
proportion to the surface. Its purpose is not known.

By the way, it was always considered that there were ever
only three in the world with 'The' in front of their name, An
Siosalach, Am Papa agus an Diabhal (The Chisholm, the Pope
and the Devil). Today, 'The' is inaccurately applied to various
Clan Chiefs, but the more knowledgeable would not say 'The
Mac-whatever' or 'The Fraser'.

After passing through some woodland the road widens, and
just before this, at 431405, on the left/north of the road is
Crunaglack (not open). The original name was Craobh na clag
(Tree of the bell), as it is on the map, and it dates from a very
long time ago. Erchard, or Merchard (Mo Erchard, my Erchard,
mo being often prefixed to the name of a saintly person), was a
disciple of St Ternan, who had been taught by St Ninian, who
flourished at the end of the fourth century (see p.112).

Erchard was working in Strathglass with two companions
when he noticed a white cow which did not graze, as did her
companions, but stood and gazed at a certain tree, yet in the
evening she would go home as well fed as the rest of the herd.
When he had seen this strange occurrence for some days,
Erchard decided to dig up the grass at the foot of the tree and
there he found three bells 'new and burnished as if fresh from
the maker's hands'.

He took one himself and gave the others to his companions
and told them to go off, each by himself, and to build a church
at the place where his bell should ring for the third time of its
own accord. One man went to the east, and not very far, for he
settled and founded his church in Glen Convinth (513375)
(see p.155). The second went west and his bell rang for the third
time when he reached Broadford in Skye. Erchard went south

Pony Express. Postie is on his way, bringing news and gossip and some letters and parcels, too. Although he is later in date than the group at Drumnadrochit, page 104, he is not as speedy as the air mail on page 29 though some of his letters may have come by that means of transport to the sorting office.

over the hills to Glenmoriston (see p.122) and settled there.

Aigas House (458414), a large Victorian mansion, is now a Field Centre where people come to study the surrounding countryside. There are excursions into the hills, and evening lectures, and accommodation. For several years, starting in August and lasting for about six weeks, there has been an exhibition of Scottish paintings at Aigas, some of which are for sale. To the north of the house, at 459434, a chambered cairn of the Clava-type (see p.42) has recently been found in a wood. To the south-east of the house are hut circles and another fort, Craig Dubh (Black Crag) (449408).

North of Aigas the road runs above the river as it passes through the gorge, in the middle of which is Eilean Aigas (see p.161). There are four parking places along this part of the A831, and from the large one just north of Crask of Aigas, where there is a picnic place, Dun Fionn on Eilean Aigas can be seen across the river. This stretch of the river is still wild, but used to be much wilder, before the dams were built. Mr Carruthers, in his *Highland Notebook,* says that the road leads 'through superb mountain scenery. The high banks are covered with birch trees ascending to a great height, with occasionally rocks, fir plantations and mountain paths to vary the scene; and the river foaming and breaking into numerous falls below. The rocks sometimes project into the bed of the stream, forming sphinx-like and fantastic figures'.

To reach Dun Mor Tighnaleac (Big Fort of the House of the slabs), turn left at 475438, to the Cluanie Deer Farm. Ask permission and advice about going on from here; the way is private and, more to the point, both bulls and stags are bred there. It is unmarked and tends to be boggy. Both stout shoes and a compass are necessary to find the Dun. From Tighnaleac itself the climb is steady to 600 feet, where Dun Mor Tighnaleac stands, protected by a gorge on the north-west, north and north-east sides. Across the gorge are settlement sites and a cairn, but it is difficult to get to them.

If a more energetic tour of the Farley Forts is wanted, ask at the Lovat Estates Office in Beauly for permission, because they are in a deer-stalking area, and it might not be wise to go there on a particular day. Assuming that all is well, turn right at the turn for Torgormack. Keep left at the T-junction, then right when through Torgormack to the end of the road at Cnoc na moine. From here there is a fairly easy walk, first to Dun a'Chliabhain (Fort of the Creels) (477460) by the track that goes north and then west. The Fort, on a rock 900 feet high, is seventy-seven feet by thirty-six inside its twelve-foot-thick walls, which can be made out. The next fort, Dun Garbhlaich (Rugged Fort) (466466), is beyond Dun a'Chliabhain and is reached by passing through a gate in the deer fence and following the 'peat' road to climb up to it, but the view is worth the climb. The walls are a mere 8½ feet thick. Returning through the gate in the fence, the track leads on towards the south end of Loch nam Bonnach (Loch of the Bannock) and then east, through the plantation and so up to Dun Fhamhair (Fort of the Giant) (484471) at 1000 feet, with views east over the firth, if the trees are not too high.

On the north of the road at 495444 is Kilmorack Church, dating from 1786 and now disused, standing in its burying ground, which is still used. In 1902 there were regular Gaelic services here. Opposite is the site of the earlier churches in the older graveyard above the River Beauly. The earliest dedication was to St Moroc – hence Kilmorack (Moroc's church). Possibly the same dedication was turned into 'St Maurice' (see p.236), which is also the anglicisation of Muireach (see p.162). It was surprisingly close to the next parish church, just across the river by a modern bridge. This was the site of the parish church of Kiltarlity, the first of which was dedicated to St Talorgan, who lived c.720; a later building on this site was built by John Bisset, Lord of the Aird, about 1220, when he founded a Priory on the 'lands of Ess'.

Presumably 'the lands of Ess' refers to the waterfall (Eas in Gaelic) which is now swallowed up in the Hydro-Board's dam at 495443. Before the dam was built the fall was a great attraction to visitors and a little handsome summerhouse was built on the north side of the narrows 'from which an advantageous view of this romantic scene can be obtained'. One of the attractions was watching the salmon leaping up the falls, at which they were not always successful. Lord Lovat would tell his guests that the fresh salmon that they were eating had cooked themselves and, to prove this statement, he would lead the party to the falls, 'where a fire was placed on one of the rocks and a pot with water placed upon it, when a salmon of good size, mistaking its direction in attempting to ascend the fall, soon leaped into the pot!' The salmon can still be seen, by visiting the dam at times that can be obtained from the Tourist Office in Inverness.

At 514449 the A831 joins the A862 below the steep hill on which stands the War Memorial.

CHAPTER 9

Glengarry, Loch Hourn and Glenelg

At 308012 the A87 leaves the A82 for Skye. This route up Glen Garry is used more by drivers coming north from Spean Bridge, although those going to Skye, but also wishing to visit Tobar nan Ceann (305992) (see p.128), which is south of this turning, could drive back the mile or so to Invergarry and turn west on the A87.

Because of the remorseless clearing of the Glengarry estates by the Macdonalds over the seventy years between 1772 and 1853, there is little of interest to be seen along this road. Invergarry is spread out along the north side of it for about half a mile. The church at 304013 was built as a *quoad sacra* chapel in 1867 by Mrs Eliza Ellice. At 297013 the road crosses the Aldernaig burn that flows from Loch Lundie (see p.116), and it is here that the Coffin Road from Achlain reaches the road, having climbed over 2000 feet to the cairns at Ceann a' Mhaim, presumably on the way to Kilfinnan or Munerigie, since there is a burying ground almost opposite Achlain at Dalchreicart (see p.122).

In 1727 Glengarry leased some land to an English company of iron-founders, the Invergarry Company, who used the local hardwoods to work the ore in small bloomeries in this glen. To the manager, Thomas Rawlinson, is often given the credit for seeing that the belted plaid (an feildeadh mor, the great kilt) could be divided to make approximately the kilt that we know today, an feileadh beag (the little kilt). Rawlinson repaired the Castle to some degree of comfort, which cost him £100. It had been a ruin since 1716 (see p.127). On one occasion he was entertaining his neighbours to dinner and after the usual toasts he said, doubtless not thinking that he was giving offence, 'Be welcome, gentlemen, to anything that is in my house'. The response was speedy. Up got a Macdonald, 'Damn you, sir! – Your house? I thought it had been Glengarry's house!' Not surprisingly, the enterprise did not last long. Rawlinson left the Castle in 1731 and the Invergarry Company left the district in 1736. Some of their work survives at Gairlochy (176841) (see

176

Cattle Droving. A herd of Highland cattle moves slowly through the pass to reach southern pastures. There are only about twenty head of cattle here, but at the end of the eighteenth and beginning of the nineteenth centuries, at the height of the droving days, one man, John Cameron, Corriechoille, used to send 20,000 sheep and 2,000 cattle yearly from the Highlands to Falkirk Tryst. They moved about ten or twelve miles a day and, given a chance, the cattle preferred to walk in single file along the verge of the stony tracks as they are doing here. Often they would go to East Anglia to fatten on the pastures there, before reaching the London markets. At the end of the journey the dogs would be sent off to make their way home. Various farms along their way would feed them when they arrived, and this continued into this century after local markets, when the men would go home by train.

p.187) where some of the 'headstones' are 'pigs' of iron from the works in and around Glengarry.

At 266027, about 1½ miles from the turning at Invergarry, on the north side of the road, behind a safety rail, is the circular burying ground of Cill Donnain, just up the turning to Munerigie Farm. The car can be left in the wide space in front of the entry to the Forest Gates, and a few steps up the little farm road and then down to the right gives access to the overgrown burying ground. Here can be seen the graves of the Gillies family. Hugh MacGillies, of this family, was an early member of the North West Company of Canada.

After passing through the woods, a turning at 244028 to the left/south leads to Tomdoun (157012) which is little more than a hotel and a church above the river Garry (Garbh, rough). This is a narrow, but attractive, road, though it comes to an end at Kinloch Hourn, yet the hills and Loch Quoich (cuaich, a cup) look very different either way.

Before reaching Tomdoun, a narrow road to the left/south over a bridge across the Garry leads to Greenfield (not open) and another burying place at 202005, where are buried the Macmhuicgens, who had this part of the glen before the Macdonalds. This must have been disused for many years, for on some occasion a funeral party set off, shouldering the coffin the seven or eight miles, up to 1027 feet, at 255984, over the shoulder of Ben Tee (2957 feet) and on to the funeral at Kilfinnan (276967), where their burden was duly interred. On the way home they stopped at Loch Diota (loch of the dinner, or snack) (268985) for a break in their journey. They ate and drank and quarrelled and one man was killed. They carried him back to Ladaidh (231003) and on the way they met his grandmother, who greeted them: 'My blessing on the Glengarry men, who will take one corpse out and bring another one home!' When the Forestry Commission was planting east of Greenfield in 1953, they unearthed another bloomery.

West of the bridge over the Garry is Eilean na Cloinne (186015) (Island of the Children). This recalls the story of a picnic that turned to tragedy. Eight children were playing on the island when a water-bull came wandering along and stood by them. All but one child climbed on to its back, but the eldest was doubtful and put his finger on the beast's hide. It stuck. To free himself, he cut off his finger and the beast galloped into the river. The children were not seen again, though their seven hearts were later found floating on the water.

At 134011 is the dam across the river Garry, built by the North of Scotland Hydro Electric Board, which has turned the river into a loch.

At about 039021 the road runs through rhododendrons which must have escaped from the house that has been drowned by the Hydro Board. They are an amazing sight in May. After this, the road crosses a modern bridge (016036)

Hinds Boxing. This is a winter scene, when the Red Deer come down from the hills to be nearer the food provided for them in the glens. This is a mixed group of stags and hinds, which may account for the quarrel between the hinds.

over the river Quoich. The way up Glen Quoich is a 'coffin road' to Glen Shiel via the Bealach Dubh (Black Pass) where there is a wide gap in the county stone dyke to let funeral parties and droves of cattle through.

The road carries on for nearly two miles to Bunachoille, where it keeps to the right and winds its way between the hills to the sea at Kinloch Hourn jetty (944069). Coming down the hill at about 964044, it is surprising to see some Monkey Puzzle trees (*Araucaria*) by the lochan on the right. They may have escaped from a semi-tropical garden that was planted at Kinloch Hourn. What can be the story behind Loch Corrie na Cnamh (Loch of the Corrie of the Bone)? The car should be left in the car parking space at Kinloch Hourn, to enjoy a walk along the south side of the loch. It is extremely difficult to turn at the end of the road, which is only just round the corner, anyway.

If the driver is not used to mountain roads, it is best not to attempt the whole distance, but to turn at the bridge (016036)

or above the Monkey Puzzles, turning there at one of the larger
Passing Places, but DO NOT cross the Cattle Grid.

In Loch Quoich, near the south side in a sheltered bay at
013021, is Eilean MhicPhi (Macphee's Island). Here lived for
some years in the middle of last century Macphee the Outlaw.
Once a soldier, he deserted and returned to Glengarry, where
he lived with his sister at Feddan. He was arrested as a deserter
on the instigation of Glengarry, but broke his handcuffs and
escaped and fled to the island, where he built himself a bothy,
and carried off a girl from Glen an dubh lochan (of the little
black loch) in Knoydart (820002), whom he duly married. He
was noted as a seer and a weaver of charms. On one occasion
he wandered into Glen Quoich Lodge (028028) (now
vanished), and Mr Ellice, who owned the land, asked him by
what right he lived on the island. Macphee, who always wore
Highland dress, drew his dirk and plunged it into the table, 'By
this right I have kept it and by this right I will hold it!'

He was said to be 'upwards of 60' in 1841, and Robert
Carruthers, writing in *The Inverness Courier,* said that he
supposed that the old man would be allowed to live in peace
henceforward. In the following year the famous drover, John
Cameron, Corriechoille (see p.199), drove off Macphee's goats,
partly as 'grass-mail', partly to compensate himself for
Macphee's harrying of Corriechoille's sheep. Mrs Macphee
chased the men with a gun, and they were so scared of her that
they enclosed the goats in Inverlochy Castle. Macphee vowed
vengeance, and eventually he was paid the value of his goats.
But a time came when his sheep-stealing was more than his
neighbours could stand and Sheriff-officers came from
Inverness to take him. He was not at home, but his wife was,
and she again fired on the intruders, who sensibly fled. But
they came back, properly armed, the next week and took him.
When they searched his bothy they found that it was full of
bales of skins and tallow. He died in prison (see p.138).

Edward Ellice had bought Glen Quoich and other parts of
the Glengarry estates in 1839 and spent most of the summer
and autumn months there until his death. He was at the
opening of the Highland Railway at Inverness on 2 September,
1868, and at the dinner which followed. After dinner he drove
back the forty-seven miles to Ardochy (210024), went to bed

and died in his sleep.

To the south of Loch Hourn lies Barrisdale, a vast area with no public road, running on to Knoydart, which is in much the same condition. To the north are the hills that run to Glenelg (see p.189).

Returning to the A87 at 244028, turn left and, after passing through the trees, the road climbs to a viewpoint on the left/ west of the road. Here there are fine views of the western hills. From here the road runs between the shoulders of the hills and Loch Loyne before crossing the river Loyne at 2112085 to absorb the A887 at 211100. The dam at the north-east end of Loch Loyne raised the level of the water and so closed the drove road that ran between Kintail and Tomdoun. By turning left/west here the road goes to Kyle of Lochalsh, about forty miles, or right/east, it goes to Invermoriston, about fifteen miles.

The only way to get to Glenelg, which is in Inverness-shire, is through part of Ross-shire. Within a couple of miles of the junction is the great Cluanie Dam at 184100. The work of the North of Scotland Hydro Electric Board has greatly altered the face of the Highlands, sometimes to the distress of visitors, but certainly to the increased comfort of those who live here permanently, and we do, winter and summer, spring and autumn!

The A87 runs along the north side of Loch Cluanie, crossing into Ross-shire at 130099. The military road, which has been met from time to time and along which Boswell and Johnson rode in 1773, is sometimes above and sometimes below the modern road. From the west end of the loch the National Trust for Scotland has acquired patches of land, gradually growing larger until the whole range of the Kintail hills, the Five Sisters of Kintail, are now in the Trust's care. Only about four miles, as the eagle flies, from the head of Loch Cluanie are the headwaters of Glen Affric (see p.166). The names of the peaks are, approaching from the east, Sgurr na Ciste Dubh (3370 feet) (high pointed hill of the black chest); Sgurr na Carnach (3000 feet) (of the stony place); Sgurr Fhuaran (3505 feet) (of the spring); Sgurr nan Saighead (2800 feet) (of the arrow) and Sgurr na Morachd (2870 feet) (of Majesty).

The ridge to the east of Sgurr na Ciste Dubh is Coirean nan

Spainteach (3129 feet) (little hollows of the Spaniards), and below, at 991134, north of the road before the bridge, is the site of the battle of Glen Shiel, which started at 5 p.m. on 10 June, 1719 and lasted for three hours. There is a notice near the long parking place on the right/north of the road at 994133, directing people to the plan and explanation of the battle, which is just a minute's walk away. Here was the final battle of that largely forgotten rising. The Duke of Argyll, after 1715, said that north of the Tay nine people out of ten were Jacobites, and the Tay was no barrier to this feeling. There was even a rising in the north of England in 1715, and feelings would not have changed much in the three years since 1716.

Some think that this, as part of a plan by some of the European powers to invade England, had the best chance of all the anti-Union risings, but an event completely outwith any Scottish power to prevent was to make the invasion impossible. Charles XII of Sweden, who was to have brought his men to Scotland, was shot and killed by a silver button, possibly aimed by one of his own men. 'The death of the heroic Charles XII of Sweden was about the greatest tragedy that ever befell the Gaels of Alba ... Had the heroic Charles lived to lead his expedition and make contact with the loyal clans, thousands of Highland hearts might have been spared the anguish of *Lochaber no more*.' Despite this blow, 300 Spanish troops were landed from frigates in Loch Duich to join the Earl of Seaforth's men, with Rob Roy and some Macgregors. The combined force got no further than Glen Shiel, where they came up against Government troops, Munros, Sutherlands and Hanoverians under General Wightman. Curiously, it was the great heat of that day in the glen that killed as well as the bullets, and the poets left no songs of this campaign.

Just beyond the Information Office, and before the bridge at Shiel Bridge, take the well-marked road to the left/south-west for Glenelg and, in about half a mile keep left again, away from the water, for the road climbs to 1116 feet to Mam Ratachan, where it returns to Inverness-shire at 902197. The climb is steep, one in six, and has hairpin bends, but, although trees have been planted, the passengers, if not the driver, can enjoy the views. That to Loch Duich and Kintail is said to be 'one of the grandest in Scotland'. At 905198 there is a car park off the

Glenelg Broch. This picture shows the curious but effective way in which these strong circular defensive structures were built. There were probably huts against the inner walls when the broch was in use. The interesting thing about the word Glenelg is that it is a palindrome.

road to the right/west of the road, and an indicator across the road from it. It is not surprising that Dr Johnson's horse, 'weary of the rise, staggered a little', and on the way down the other side, which is not so steep, 'as Dr Johnson was a great weight, the two guides agreed that he should ride the horses alternatively'.

The ferry to Skye still runs in the summer months and is reached by turning at 821198 just before Glenelg. It is well marked and at the end of the road there is a large turning place for cars that do not wish to cross. In the days of the great cattle droves, this was a major crossing, with an average of 2000 head a year. The cattle swam across the narrows and then walked on south.

The village of Glenelg lies along a sheltered bay, looking across to Skye. At 815197 are the ruins of the eighteenth-century Bernera Barracks, easily seen on the right as the road approaches Glenelg. Designed to hold 200 men, they were occupied from 1722 until after 1790. A stone dated 1730 in the churchyard is that of one of the officers. The reason for the Barracks is that they lay at the end of the military road and controlled the crossing to Kylerhea on Skye. The Highland Society of London suggested that they might be used as an Academy of Piping, but the military authorities would not support the Society and nothing came of it.

The old Inn has now been refurbished. Between the road and the sea is a fine bronze War Memorial. The list of names shows the large number of men from here who were lost, particularly in the 1914-18 war.

Continuing along the shore, do not cross the bridge at 806180, but turn into Glen Beag (small glen), signposted to the brochs, and keep to the north of the river to reach Dun Telve, the first of the three brochs, at 829172, the second, Dun Troddan, being a short distance further on, on the north of the road at 833172. These, though ruined now, date from the late 1st millennium B.C. to the early 1st millennium A.D. and are considered to be the finest on the mainland, Dun Telve's walls rising to about thirty-three feet. The road ends at Balvraid (846167) but a walk along the old, closed, road, with dogs on leads, reaches, at 852158, Dun Grugaig, near a waterfall, on a high rock above the river. This is an unusual broch, if it is one, in that it is semi-circular, the steep drop being enough defence on that side, but the footings of a circular building have been found within the outer wall.

Brochs are mostly found in Scotland, generally in the Highlands, although there are outliers further south. They are circular and double-skinned, with passages and stairs between the inner and outer walls, and are built without the use of mortar. The double walls, tied together with rows of horizontal slabs, were probably so built to save weight. It is supposed that there was a wooden floor at about ten feet, supported by the specially provided ledge at that height, perhaps by some form of cantilever with posts on the ground beneath. There may well have been a roof over the exposed central courtyard, with some form of vent for the smoke from the fires to escape. They must have been defensive structures and were mostly occupied in the first centuries B.C. and A.D. Presumably the cattle and sheep could be herded into the central area at the last moment before an attack came.

Returning to the bridge and crossing it, the road wanders on along the hills above Loch Hourn to Arnisdale, with wonderful views from the higher parts of it over the Sound of Sleat (pronounced Slate) towards Skye and the peaks of Rum. Tom Weir wrote, 'From Glenelg to Arnisdale by ten miles of winding switchback road is a must for any collector of difficult roads. It is without doubt the loneliest approach to any village in Scotland'. But this is a much easier road than that down to Kinloch Hourn (see p.179).

Three miles from the bridge, at 784146 there is a house on the right of the road, lying between the present road and a bit of the older one. Leave the car here and find a track which goes down the hill through the trees to Sandaig (773147). This was where Gavin Maxwell lived at 'Camus Fearna' (an invented name, meaning the Bay of the Alders) and wrote his *Ring of Bright Water*. You will come to the site, but nothing of the burned-out house remains. Gavin Maxwell's ashes are buried under the slab of pink rock at its site. Edal, the otter, is buried under the rowan tree. A mile further on along the road is a picnic place with a table.

Arnisdale must have been the home of a Norse settler, Arne. The road goes on as far as Corran (sickle) at the foot of Glen

G

Arnisdale where there is a notice saying that the public road ends at a turning place. From here there are tracks along the coast, further into the wilds of Loch Hourn, and a short distance before the turning place is one that runs up the glen, past Dubh Lochan and on to 915098 where it bears south-east through the pass, emerging eventually at Kinloch Hourn (950071) (see p.179). From there, too, there are tracks along the coast, further into the wilds of Barrisdale and Knoydart. But these walks call for maps and proper clothing.

CHAPTER 10

Gairlochy, Loch Arkaig and Banavie

At 207823, just south of the Commando Memorial, the B8004 turns sharply to the right/north-west down to the Caledonian Canal at Gairlochy.

At 197833 this road crosses the line of the old military road which is on its way south to cross the river Spean at High Bridge (see p.133), and a little further on it crosses the line of the old railway between Fort Augustus and Fort William. The cutting at Mucomir Bridge was made originally by Telford's men, when they took over the river's outlet from Loch Lochy to be part of the canal. It was cut in dry ground, but the water of the loch was raised by the canal works so that it ran down the new cutting. In 1962 the Hydro-Board's work diverted the river once again and now its waters flow through a turbine house before reaching the Spean.

On the left/west of the road is the old burying ground of Gairlochy, where some of the 'pigs' of iron from the smelters at Invergarry were used as gravemarkers, though few, if any, remain there now (see p.177). A story is told of a traveller reaching Gairlochy late on a stormy night when all were in bed. In vain he hammered on the doors, and at last he cried out 'Are there no Christians in the place?' Back came the answer, 'No, we are all Camerons here!' Yet it is possible that the original parish church of Kilmonivaig was in this burying ground.

It is possible that there may be a delay in crossing the canal, if the waterway is open to allow boats, whether working fishing boats or pleasure craft, to pass through the locks. Once across the canal, take the turning to the right/north on the B8005 for a pleasant run of a few miles up the west side of Loch Lochy. In less than two miles, at 184872, is the turning to Achnacarry. A Clan Museum has just been built, which will be of great interest for its collection of treasures.

Achnacarry House (176839) (not open) is the home of the Chief of Clan Cameron, at present Sir Donald Cameron of Lochiel, K.T. (Knight of the Thistle), generally referred to as

Lochiel. The present house dates only from the last century, having been started in 1802 and finished, after a considerable gap in operations, in 1837. It replaced the house which was destroyed on 28 May, 1746 by men under the command of Captain George Munro of Culcairn (see p.191). This house was wooden, with a stone chimney, like many houses of the same date in New England. The chimney stack survived the burning of 1746.

The Chiefs did not live at Achnacarry until Sir Ewen Cameron (1629-1719) built himself a house here after the settlement with Mackintosh which granted him legally the lands of Glenlui (Glen Loy) and Loch Arkaig, which the clan had occupied for centuries. Before this house was built, Lochiel stayed at Tor Castle (see p.195). Of Sir Ewen pages might be written, and the following lines, from beneath a print of him, sum him up:

> The honest man whom virtue sways,
> His King adores, his God obeys;
> Does factious men's rebellious pride
> And threatening tyrant's rage deride;
> Honour's his wealth, his rule, his aim,
> Unshaken, fixed and still the same.

Near the House is the beech avenue which was planted by Sir Ewen's grandson Donald, 'The Gentle Lochiel', named for his true gentleness, not for any meekness. He was planting the avenue when the news came of Prince Charles' arrival on the west coast. Part was completed, the trees being well spaced, but he hurriedly heeled the rest into the ground to keep them in good order until his return. Lochiel never did return for long enough to go gardening and so the avenue is how he left it. It was his arrival at Glenfinnan (see p.222) that really made the Rising possible, though he knew that it was a very chancy affair indeed, but the Camerons were natural supporters of the Royal House, so he saw it as his duty, whatever his misgivings. After his death in France in 1748, a Whig admirer sent a poem to the *Scots Magazine* about him:

The River Spean, Lochaber. Behind rise the hills that run up, further to the right, to Ben Nevis, 4406 feet. The site of General Wade's High Bridge is out of sight behind the trees. The view is to the south-east.

Mistaken as he was, the man was just,
Firm to his word and faithful to his trust;
He bade not others go, himself to stay,
As is the petty, prudent, modern way;
But like a warrior bravely drew his sword,
And reared his target for his native lord.
Humane he was, protected countries tell,
So rude a host was never ruled so well;
Fatal to him, and to the cause he loved,
Was the rash tumult that his folly moved;
Compelled by hard necessity to bear
In Gallia's band a mercenary spear,
But Heaven, in pity to his honest heart
Resolved to snatch him from so poor a part;
The mighty mandate unto death was given
And good Lochiel is now a Whig in heaven.

In February 1942 Achnacarry became the Commando Basic Training Centre. Over 25,000 Commandos trained here and in the surrounding hills, including British, American, Belgian, Dutch, French, Norwegian and Polish soldiers. So lifelike was the training that, when the Commandos landed in France on D-day in 1944 against the German guns, they were of the opinion that things were 'getting as bad as Achnacarry'.

About half a mile further on, the road crosses the river Arkaig on its short dash from Loch Arkaig to Loch Lochy. A little further on, on the left of the road, is Clunes (200885) (not open) (cluain – a meadow), the former home of the Camerons of Clunes. It was here that the treaty between Lochiel and Mackintosh was finally signed in September, 1665. The road turns westward and runs through the Dark Mile, which is not as dark as it once was. It was in the woods to the right/north of this part of the road that Clunes lived after Culloden and where he sheltered Prince Charles, Dr Archibald Cameron (Lochiel's brother, who was executed at Tyburn in 1753) and the Reverend John Cameron from Fort William.

The road that crosses the river at 172886 where it leaves the loch, runs along the south side of the water and up into the hills of Glen Mallie, passing first on the left, a burying ground, and on the right, in the loch, a small island (159887), which was the burial place of the Macphees and where there are still the remains of a chapel. This is a road better walked than driven. There is a fish farm in Loch Arkaig.

The road along the north side of Loch Arkaig reaches Achnasaul (Achadh nan sabhail, field of the barn) (154894), which is where the Seven Men of Glenmoriston (see p.120) handed on Prince Charles to the care of Clunes and the Camerons on 21 August, 1746. The Reverend John Cameron described him: 'He was then barefooted, had an old black kilt-coat on, a plaid, philibeg, and waistcoat, a dirty shirt and a long red beard, a gun in his hand, a pistol and dirk by his side. He was very cheerful and in good health'.

About halfway along the loch is a length of road known as The Straight Mile, though it is neither straight nor a mile long. It starts about a mile west of Rudha Cheanna Mhuir (promontory of Mary's head) (103913). The slope above the Straight Mile is known as Culcairn's Brae. During the ravaging of the glens, a party of troops commanded by a Captain Grant set out from Achnacarry along this road, where they met young Alexander Cameron carrying a gun. Grant asked why he had not surrendered it and Cameron said that he lived in a remote place, had only just heard of the order and was now on his way to hand it in. This did not satisfy Grant, who had him tied to a tree and then shot him. Cameron's father vowed vengeance.

Some time later, when Grant was returning from another such excursion near the head of Loch Arkaig, he met a similar party commanded by Captain George Munro of Culcairn. The two officers exchanged mounts and rode on at the head of their men. Grant was known to ride a grey and so, when Cameron killed the grey 's rider, it was Culcairn who died. Since he was the man who had burned Achnacarry, perhaps his death was seen as the choice of the Almighty.

From the head of Loch Arkaig an old track leads through Glen Dessary (glen deas airidh, glen of the south sheiling) to Loch Nevis at Soulics (869952) and thence over the hills to Inverie in Knoydart (766999). This was the way that the cattle from Knoydart (see p.230) walked out on their way to the southern trysts. Miss Jenny Cameron of Glen Dessary, her brother being away from home, raised his men and led them to Glen Finnan on 19 August, 1745. She was not the Jenny Cameron who was a camp follower and who was taken prisoner at Falkirk.

In June 1864 Dr Archibald Clerk, minister of Kilmallie, recorded in his Notebook: 'Today I baptized a child of Thomas Aitchison – Shepherd in Glendassarie. He and his wife left their home at 1 p.m. today and were here at 8 p.m. – a wonderful walk for a women carrying a heavy child. She tells me there are 21 regular shepherds on these farms which Cunningham had – No School among them, or those on the Fassiefern Farm – I must try what can be done to get an itinerating Teacher among them'.

Returning to the canal at Gairlochy Locks, take the left fork at 175843 to run along the west side of the canal to Banavie (111770). If returning from Achnacarry, keep right at the fork above the canal. If walkers are among the party, they can walk along the east side of the canal and rejoin the road near Banavie.

In the fifteenth century there lived at Moy (magh, a plain) (164829) a wise women named Gormshuil (blue-eyed) Cameron, who married one of the Mackinnons of Moy, and was known as Gormshuil Mhor na Maighe (Great Gormshuil of Moy). She met Lochiel one day when he was about to meet the Earl of Atholl to settle a boundary dispute at Lochan a'Claidheimh (little loch of the sword) (408602) on the Moor of Rannoch where the counties of Inverness, Argyll and Perth meet. The arrangement was that each would bring a small number of men, so that the meeting should be peaceful. She said that Lochiel should be very careful and take certain precautions. He did so. When he met Atholl tempers became heated, Atholl made a gesture and from behind him rose a large number of armed men. 'Who are they?' asked Lochiel. 'Just a few of my sheep,' said Atholl. Lochiel took his cloak off and put it on with the lining outside. At once his armed men rose from the heather. 'Just my dogs to chase off your sheep,' he explained politely. The problem was solved, and a sword was thrown into the loch. Some years ago someone fishing there drew up an old sword but his gillie made him put it back, for fear that Lochiel and Atholl might fall out again.

Between the farm house of Moy (the old house was burned out some years ago) and the canal is a small burying ground, known as the Mackinnon burying ground. Those stones that are still legible have this name on them and the family is supposed to have come from Skye when a Lochiel took a bride from that island. It is said that, a few days before the battle of Culloden, Lochiel took a blind piper with him and together they buried seven jars of the French gold in this ground.

Some years later, a man digging here, perhaps to open a new grave, found a jar full of gold, which he gave to Henry Butter, the factor for the Forfeited Estates of Lochiel. There is no story of the other six jars, but Dr Clerk notes a story of one being found some eighty years before 1858 in a potato field by a woman who tried to give it to her husband, but he turned her off rudely and so she went straight to Mr Butter. The swing bridge over the canal here is the only surviving original bridge and it is still worked by its original mechanism.

At 149820 there is a rough turning to the right/north-west which runs into the mouth of Glen Loy (laoigh, a calf) and to

White Rose Necklace. This necklace of white roses, the emblem of the Jacobites in 1745, supports a miniature of Prince Charles Edward Stuart. In the middle, the heart has cut into it, *I live and dy in loyalty, 1648,* and doubtless commemorates an earlier supporter of the House of Stuart. It is to be seen in the Inverness Museum.

Erracht House (not open), standing in its grove of tall trees. This was the home of the Camerons of Erracht, who descended from Ewen Cameron of Lochiel (c.1480-1546, the first to be styled 'of Lochiel') by his second wife, Marjory, the daughter of Lachlan Mackintosh and sister of William Mackintosh of

Mackintosh. Because Donald, the eldest son by the first wife, had to be legitimated, and Ewen of Erracht had no such need, a feud raged between the two families for some 450 years, but all is now friendly: Donald's heirs are at Achnacarry, and Ewen's are extinct in the male line. But the quarrel left is mark not only on Lochaber, but also on the British Army, for when in 1793 Alan Cameron of Erracht (1750-1828) raised the 79th Regiment of Foot, later the Cameron Highlanders, later still the Queen's Own Cameron Highlanders, and now part of the Queen's Own Highlanders (Seaforth and Camerons), he not only had no help from the Lochiel family, but had to raise the regiment in the teeth of their opposition.

Alan's father, Ewen, was not 'out' in the '45 – he does not seem to have had good health – but it is likely that the Prince, who came over the hills from Fassfern (see p.218), up the west side of the Allt Dogha, down Glen Laragain, and past Erracht's road end, would have stopped for some refreshment. The occupying troops were still billeting themselves at Erracht as late as 1753. Alan's mother, Marsaili Maclean of Drimnin, daughter of Charles Maclean of Drimnin (554551) who was leading Clan Maclean at Culloden when he was killed, married Ewen Cameron of Erracht in the late 1740s, after her home had been destroyed by the men from the well-named H.M.S. *Terror*. It was she who, in 1793, designed the tartan for her son's regiment, the famous Erracht Cameron set.

Just beyond the Bridge of Loy, a turning to the right/north leads up in to Glen Loy. It is a good place to go for a picnic and to give the dog a run, but there is no way out at the end. Soon after this turning, on the left/east of the B8004, is Strone (147814). This was the home of the Macgillony (pronounced Maclony) family, one of those absorbed into Clan Cameron. Above the canal on a mound shaded by a few trees is a little burying ground where are buried, among others, the bones from the old burying ground at Bunloy (mouth of the Loy). This was at 152815, on the north side of the mouth of the Loy, until the river moved and destroyed it. After much pressure from the local people, for bones and coffins were appearing on the banks of the Lochy, the parish council in 1927 exhumed the remaining relics and moved them to Strone, together with the iron pigs from the Glengarry smelting works (see p.176) which had been used as gravemarkers.

At 131794, where the Allt Shenagain, flowing down Glen Laragain, crosses the road by a public telephone, there is a track down to the left/south which passes under the canal by a tunnel and leads after a few hundred yards, to the site of the ancient Tor Castle and the ruins of the nineteenth-century Torcastle, which was built early in that century for the factor. In 1947 Torcastle was opened as a hotel, but it was destroyed by fire in 1950 and not rebuilt.

The foundations of Tor Castle are on a very ancient and strongly defensible site, which can be reached by a green track just beyond and to the right of the cottages. 'There was ane ancient castle builded whaire this Torcastle is which was called Beragonium and this Torcastle was builded last by ane which is called Ewen MacAllane the Chief of Clan Cameron', wrote an anonymous author about 1630. Not long after, in Timothy Pont's notes is, '. . . the Castell of Torriechastell upon the west bank of the River Lochy. Sum suppose this to have been the place of Berigonium so much spoken of in our old monuments, how trulie or upon what grounds I cannot judge'. Hector Boece, in his *Scotorum Historiae* in 1527, gave this name to a vitrified fort in Benderloch, but, said Timothy Pont, perhaps, 'upon what grounds I cannot judge'.

Possibly the word should be Torc Castle, and perhaps this is the site of the capital of the Dalriadic Scots. Banquo is said to have lived here in the 1030s. Angus, chief of Clan Mackintosh, who married Eva, the heiress of Clan Chattan in 1291, lived here with Eva until about 1308, when they moved to Badenoch (see p.48). The Camerons then took it over, on the grounds that Mackintosh had left it, but they allowed it to decay. When the Lord of the Isles granted the lands of Glen Spean and Mamore to his youngest son, 'the illustrious man and potent Alexander of the Isles, Lord of Lochaber' (1361-1440), the progenitor of the Macdonalds of Keppoch (see p.201), Alastair either repaired the old castle or built a more up-to-date one on the site. He and his family lived here from about 1380 until 1440. The Camerons then got it back and Ewen, the first to be styled 'of Lochiel', rebuilt the castle about 1530 and it remained the home of the Cameron chiefs until after 1665.

About a quarter of a mile north of the site of the castle, hidden in the trees, is Banquo's Walk. To reach it, leave the car near the forestry gate to the left of the cottages and go through the gate into the forest. After a few hundred yards the tracks divide, and the right fork leads down towards the river and, without warning, Banquo's Walk begins. It is an avenue about twenty feet wide, with moss-covered banks on either side, and is a good quarter of a mile long, close to the river, which is largely hidden from view. It had this name in 1793, when the old *Statistical Account of Scotland* was printed, and it probably once led all the way to Tor Castle, the intervening part being destroyed when Torcastle House with all its gardens and outbuildings was built early last century. It is a fine place for exercising dogs, but it is distinctly damp, and wellies are advised.

At Banavie (115773) is the series of eight locks on the canal which lower ships seventy-two feet to the level from which, about half a mile to the west, at 099766, the last three locks let them into the sea water of Loch Linnhe. Thomas Telford, who designed the canal, called them *Neptune's Staircase,* and the name has stuck.

Banavie, according to a small book published in 1948 by the Reverend Father P.J. O'Regan, of Glenfinnan, was the birthplace and boyhood home of St Patrick (c.385-461). He was quoting a tenth-century writer who says, 'St Patrick belonged to the village of Bannavie, not far from the western sea'. In 1461 'Banvy' is mentioned in a grant of lands, but it really came to life when the Caledonian Canal was being built. Houses were needed for the workers, some of whom were crofters evicted from Glendessary and Loch Arkaigside on the Lochiel estates.

One of the lock houses was turned into an inn by the Canal Commissioners in 1824 for the benefit of their passengers, and two years later Lochiel built an inn. Another building, three storeys high and seven bedrooms long, was completed in 1849 and enlarged in the early '80s when it was called a hotel. It was lit by electricity about 1900. It became a convalescent home in 1914 and was burned out in 1924.

In the days when the passenger steamers and fishing boats were keeping Neptune's Staircase busy, the hotel was a lively place, complete with a ballroom. It was sometimes so-crowded

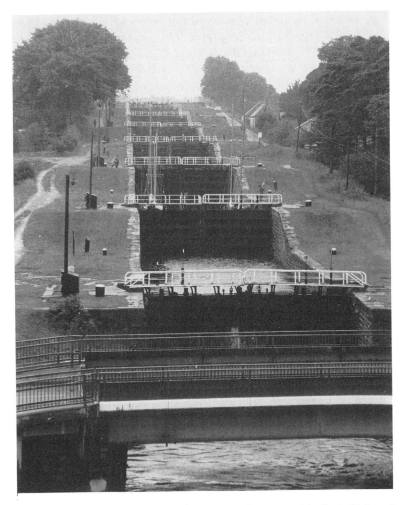

Neptune's Staircase, Banavie. The name given to this fine flight of locks by its builder, Thomas Telford, has stuck. They raise the ships going east from almost sea level to the canal above. Two vessels, lying in one of the locks, are making the passage.

that would-be visitors were boarded out in the village, though they dined in the hotel. In the 1890s a chatty American visitor asked one of the porters, 'Are there any of the old cattle-thieves or brigands left in Lochaber?' The porter said, 'No,

they were all banished overseas long ago'. 'What for?' said the
American. The porter answered, 'For picking the locks of the
canal'.

The road runs past the present hotel and joins the A830 at
112769.

CHAPTER 11

Spean Bridge to Newtonmore

Just before reaching the bridge at Spean Bridge (223816) the A86 leaves the A82 to run through Glen Spean and on to join the A9 at Newtonmore (713988) or, further south, through Dalwhinnie, at 639828. Most of the road is the work of Telford in the early nineteenth century, though there was a route through the glen before then.

This lower part of the glen is known as Brae Lochaber. To the left/north of the road is Tirnadrish (not open) (234822), the home in 1746 of the Macdonald who, with eleven men and a piper, routed two companies of the Royal Scots at High Bridge (see p.133). That house was burned in 1746. An earlier, gruesome, event happened here about 1611, when five men begged for shelter, the leader saying 'Mention of my name is forbidden', implying that he was a Macgregor. Unfortunately for him, Tirnadrish's fiancée, Miss Colquhoun of Luss, had died of grief after the murder of her father and brothers by a gang of Macgregors. So no shelter was given and, as he was supposed to, Tirnadrish sent a message to Alasdair of Keppoch to say that these outlaws were on his land. As was *his* duty, Keppoch hunted them down and, since they would not surrender, killed them all. Their heads were sent to Edinburgh and their bodies buried near Tirnadrish House. For this, Keppoch was given £100 by the Privy Council, but his brother, Ranald of Inch, who disapproved of the action, was prosecuted by the same Council for not having helped Alasdair.

Opposite Inverroy (the signpost points away from the river), on the other side of the Spean is Corriechoille (corrie of the woods) where lived John Cameron, the King of the Drovers. At one time he was tenant of eleven farms and sold annually about 20,000 sheep and 2,000 cattle. His droves, when moving south, stretched for several miles. He said that, for fifty years, he had never missed a Falkirk Tryst and that in one year he clipped 'upwards of thirty-seven thousand sheep'. Corrie, as he was known, died on 16 February, 1856, aged 75, and is buried in

Cill Choirill (see p.204).

At Roy Bridge there is a turning at 270814 to the left/north into Glen Roy. The road up into Glen Roy is steep and no caravan should attempt it, but it is not difficult. The first small community is Bohuntine. Donald Donn (Brown Donald) of Bohuntine loved Mary Grant of Glen Urquhart, but, since he was a notorious cattle-thief, her father did not approve. After one of his raids, Donald stopped to see Mary and the herd was recovered by its owners, though Donald Donn escaped. He hid in a cave above Loch Ness, but was tricked into coming out, and was taken and condemned to death. He asked to be beheaded, not hanged, 'The Devil will take the Laird of Grant out of his shoes, and Donald Donn shall not be hanged'. When his head was severed, it said, 'Mary, lift my head'. His body was taken home to Bohuntine for burial. He was a poet and one of his last poems ends, in translation:

> Tomorrow I shall be on a hill, without a head.
> Have you no compassion for my sorrowful maiden,
> My Mary, the fair and tender-eyed?

At 296846, on the right of the road, just before a comfortably enlarged passing place, is a square stone with a chalice and host cut into it by D.C. Macpherson, who died in 1880. It is a reminder of the days when the Penal Laws lay heavily on Lochaber and the Episcopalians and Roman Catholics were not allowed to practise their faith. Another such stone, with a cross on it, is on the top of Maol Doire (291814). Brae Lochaber still has many Roman Catholics in it.

At 297854 is a parking place with a view point. Beyond this, at 297867, is Achavady (Achadh a' Mhadaidh, field of the wolf) where Montrose's troops rested (see p.126). This is the Glen Roy National Nature Reserve, and by this time the famous Parallel Roads are clearly seen on either side of the glen, high above the river. They are about thirty feet wide and run round every curve, but disappear at the head of the glen. There are other such 'roads' in the neighbouring glens, as the map shows. It was Dr John MacCulloch, in 1817, who realised that they were formed as freshwater beaches. Charles Darwin preferred the theory that they were sea beaches. They were formed

The Lairig Leacach. A walker has reached the Lairig Leacach from Roy Bridge. On the right is Coire na Ceannain, tucked into the hills. This is the route that some writers think was taken by Montrose's men before the battle of Inverlochy in 1645, though others disagree.

because the melting glaciers, after the Ice Age, were held up by a glacial dam made by a later glacier from Glen Spean that blocked the mouth of Glen Roy, probably at more or less the spot where Roy Bridge is now. As the dam melted slowly, and then stayed at its new level for years before being reduced again, the 'roads' were formed.

Some two miles further on, across the river at 318897, is Brunachan, where there is an old quarry from which the finest quernstones, for hand-grinding, were cut. They were known as Lochaber Stones and were famous all over the West Highlands; some have been found in the Outer Isles.

At Roy Bridge a road leads down the west side of the Roy, under the railway, to Keppoch House (not open) (268809). Beyond it, at the junction of the Roy and the Spean, is the motte on which stood the former little castle of the Macdonalds of Keppoch. This was demolished after the Keppoch Murders (see p.128). The chief's next home was burned in 1746 and the present house was built about 1760 by Ranald of Keppoch. This branch of Clan Donald usually spell their name Macdonell, with the accent on the 'don', not the 'ell'.

Alasdair nan Cleas (of the tricks), who died in 1635, was the Chief who hunted down the Macgregors. He was chief for over forty years and died in peace. He is said to have been the hero of *The Chieftain's Candlesticks*. On one occasion when he was in England, his host was boasting of his handsome candlesticks:

> Say now, Macdonald, in your home
> Beyond the mountain ranges lone,
> If aught like this you own?
> The stems are richly crusted o'er
> With strange device from foreign shore.
> I'd give their value, yea, and more
> Were I their equal shown.

Keppoch said, 'I will pay you three times their value if I cannot produce candlesticks in my own house which far surpass these in both design and intrinsic value'. Some time later, the Englishman came to stay at Keppoch, in the old home on the motte. When they went to dine, the room was lit by tall Highlanders holding flaming pine-torches:

> The tartan draped in many a fold
> With war-like trophies decked the hold
> And here within the hall
> Six stalwart men the entrance line
> Whose flaming torch of resinous pine
> In ruddy shadows fall.

So wrote Alice C. Macdonell of Keppoch. Sir Walter Scott fitted the story into *A Legend of Montrose* and wrote, 'behind every seat stood a gigantic Highlander, completely dressed and armed after the fashion of his country, holding in his right hand his drawn sword, with the point turned downwards, and in his left hand a blazing torch made of bog-pine'.

'These,' said Keppoch, 'are my candlesticks, which all the wealth of England could not buy.'

Keppoch is one of the houses that had a charm-stone which cured illness. This one was 'an oval of rock crystal, about the size of a pigeon's egg, fixed in a bird's claw of silver and with a silver chain attached'. By this chain it was suspended when being dipped in water drawn from a well near Keppoch, Tobar Bhride (St Bride's Well), while a Gaelic rune was recited over it. This charm-stone is said to have been taken to Australia when the owner emigrated in 1854.

North of the A86 at 272827 is Meall Ruadh (red round hill), which is better known as Mulroy, the site on 4 August, 1688 of the last inter-clan battle and the last in which bows and arrows were used. The men of Brae Lochaber were famous archers. The reason for the battle goes back nearly 300 years, to about 1390, when Alasdair, the youngest son of the Good Lord John , Lord of the Isles, and Princess Margaret of Scotland, was given Glen Spean and Glen Roy. After the first battle of Inverlochy, in 1431, Alasdair's lands were forfeit and were granted to Malcolm Mackintosh, Captain of Clan Chattan, in 1433. From then on there was constant friction between Keppoch, who held the land, and Mackintosh, who held the charter.

When Coll of Keppoch inherited at the age of 18, in 1682, he was at St Andrews University. He was 'of low stature, but full of craft and enterprise', and also well educated. He decided to see whether he could come to some agreement with Mackintosh, who had been negotiating with his father, Archibald of Keppoch, when the latter died. So in 1683 Coll went to Inverness and suggested that there should be an arbitration. Lachlan Mackintosh's answer was to have Coll arrested and locked up in the Tolbooth in Inverness. Coll himself immediately wrote to the Privy Council and he was released. This behaviour of Mackintosh was described by a Mackintosh historian as 'ungenerous and unfeeling in the extreme. To take advantage of an hereditary foe, and that foe a mere boy, on such an occasion and in such a manner, might have passed without censure a few centuries earlier, but was scarcely worth the enlightenment and politeness of a more civilised time'. From then on, Coll began to earn his by-name of *Coll of the Cows*, and his principal targets were Mackintosh's lands and cattle.

In March, 1688, Mackintosh obtained a Commission of Fire and Sword against Keppoch, this time with Government backing. The Macphersons refused to go with him, to show that they were not his vassals, but, with most of Clan Chattan and Kenneth Mackenzie of Suddie and his Government troops, Lachlan had about 1000 men. He surprised the Braes. Coll was from home and Mackintosh moved into Keppoch House.

Coll was furious and gathered about 700 of his friends and relations, including Glengarry, Glencoe and the Macmartins from Letterfinlay, and took up his position in a hollow on the north side of the hill. Mackintosh was too old to take part and stayed on at Keppoch, sending his men up the hill in the night, but before they reached the top, they found that Coll held the high ground. One of the Government soldiers, Donald Macbain, said: 'the Macdonalds came down the hill upon us without either shoe, stocking or bonnet on their heads; they gave a shout and then the fire began on both sides and continued a hot dispute for an hour'. Mackintosh was taken prisoner in the house, but when a party of Macphersons turned up late, for their share of the spoils, Coll released the old chief and the other prisoners into their hands. It was as a reprisal for this occupation of Keppoch that in 1689, Coll ravaged Mackintosh's land and burned Dunachton (see p.55) before, under Dundee's command, he took and burned Ruthven Castle (see p.80). Later, Mackintosh assessed the damage done by Coll of Keppoch in this raid at the large sum of 40,000 merks.

At 303810 a turning to the left/north of the A86 winds up the side of the hill between cairns. One commemorates Ewen Macdonald of Inch (264803) who distinguished himself in the Indian Mutiny, 1856-7, one is to his son, Alasdair, the third was built in 1891 to D.P. Macdonald, son of 'Long John' Macdonald, of whisky fame. Long John, who died in 1856, is buried in the churchyard.

Before driving up the hill, stop to get the church key from the cottage opposite the turning. At the top is Cill Choirill (church of St Coirell). The highest point of the churchyard is Tom Aingeal. Coirell was an Irish missionary c.600 and he returned to Ireland, where he is buried at Clonkeen-Kerril, but he left behind a handful of place names, including Pitkerrald in Drumnadrochit. His name has been 'translated' to 'Cyril', so that he is confused with Cyril of Alexandria. He may have been the founder of the church at Kilmonivaig (Cill-mo-naoimh-bhig, church of my little saint).

A Clipping Day. Everyone turns out to help when the sheep are brought together to be clipped. The fleeces are packed into the long sacks, which hang from the gallows-like wooden frames, before they are loaded into lorries and taken away.

Cill Choirill was restored by Ewen Allanson of Lochiel (see p.195). In course of time it fell into disrepair, but was rebuilt by descendants of Brae Lochaber emigrants to Nova Scotia. It was re-opened in July 1932 by Bishop Alexander Macdonald, of Victoria, B.C., whose family emigrated from Glen Roy.

Here is buried Iain Lom Macdonald (Bare, or Satirical, John), the Keppoch Bard (see p.129). The monument to him, which was put up by Charles Fraser Mackintosh, M.P., is in a different spot from his grave, which is by the door of the church. On it there is a verse which Dr Alexander Stewart, minister of Onich, whose pen name was 'Nether Lochaber', has translated as:

> Here in Dun-Aingeal, in the Braes of Lochaber
> The Bard of Keppoch is very sound asleep;
> His name was John Macdonald, John the Bare –
> John the *Bare* and *Biting!* but by some called
> John the Stammerer.

It is now thought that this stone stands near the grave of another poet. Domhnall MacFinlay, who wrote *The Song of the Owl*. Domhnall asked to be buried outside the door of the church, his face towards his home at Fersit (353782), and, instead of a shroud, to be wrapped in the skin of the deer he had shot from his deathbed. There he lies under the stone that, when younger, he had carried up to mark the spot. Someone has driven a fence straining post through it.

At 342809 a road to the right/south crosses the railway to Inverlair (339799), the home of the Macdonalds of Inverlair who murdered Keppoch and his brother (see p.129). The house now on the site was built by a Lord Abinger. During the 1939-45 War, it was occupied by the Commandos and at one time Rudolf Hess, the Deputy Nazi Leader, was interned here after his flight from Germany to Scotland in May, 1941. The road goes on to Fersit, which is east of the river Treig, the natural outlet from Loch Treig. The road ends some 2½ miles from the A86 at a wide turning place.

Loch Treig is a narrow slash, some six or seven miles long, almost north to south, in hills that rise to over 3000 feet. There is no road round it, but the Fort William to Glasgow railway runs along its eastern side. The water from the loch mostly flows through a fifteen-mile tunnel through the hills to the 'enormous drains' (see p.134) and so to the British Alcan works at Inverlochy. It is supplemented by the water from Loch Laggan (lagan, hollow) which arrives by another tunnel, three miles long.

At 412822 the A86 leaves Lochaber for Badenoch. To the south of the road is the drowned valley of the river Spean, now controlled by the great Laggan Dam at 432826, and to the north are the tangled high hills of Moy Forest, which rise to 3700 feet at Creag Meaghaidh (4418876), the highest of a group of hills about ten miles long that seldom fall below 3000 feet. Most of this area is a National Nature Reserve, and at Aberarder (478876) there is a car park with a map and there are walks in the hills. It was at Aberarder that Prince Charles Edward was given a 'short brown coat', after walking down through the hills from the north. One of the first farms of Blackfaced sheep in the Highlands was here.

Loch Laggan's water level was raised considerably by the

building of the dam, but while the work was being done in 1933-4 the level of the water was lowered. It was then that six canoes were found, varying in length from thirteen to thirty-seven feet; the largest had traces of a figurehead and a steering socket. There were wooden drinking vessels, some shoes and a building on a crannog.

The islands in Loch Laggan are Eilean na Righ (of the King) (498875) and Eilean nan Con (of the hounds) (502875). There are traces of buildings on the first and of kennels on the second. They are said to have been the hunting lodge of King Fergus, but who he was, no one can tell; perhaps he was the one who drove the Lochaber men into Glen Nevis (see p.1). One day he was tired by hunting and fell asleep. A boar attacked him, but his hounds defended him until he woke and killed it. He called seven of his daughters and sent them to look for a certain herb to heal his favourite hound, which had been wounded. Six came back with the herb, but the seventh had forgotten to ask what it looked like. They were all too late and the dog was dead. Fergus therefore placed his dog in the sky, as the Dog Star, and his daughters, too, because they were so slow. They are the Pleiades, the seventh being the last daughter, who was always a bit dim.

The Feinne (the prehistoric Celtic heroes) are also said to have kept their hounds, including Bran, on Dog Island. Bran had yellow paws, two black flanks and a white belly, a green back under which game would lie and two sharply erect scarlet ears. Not one to meet on a dark night. Perhaps the large boat belonged to them.

At 508875, on the south side of the loch is Ardverikie (not open). It is a splendid sight from the road, a Victorian pile, but behind it and part of it is the small house where Queen Victoria and Prince Albert stayed in August and September, 1847. The Queen described the scenery as 'splendid; high bold hills with a good deal of wood; glens with the Pattack and a small waterfall; the meadows here and there, with people making hay, and cottages sprinkled sparingly about ... We were delighted with the scenery, which is singularly beautiful; wild and romantic – with so much fine wood about it, which greatly enhances the beauty of a landscape'. They were looking for a Highland home, but something prevented their buying this estate. Some say that the owner was unwilling to sell to them. Others say that their physician thought that it would be better to buy a more eastern property, which would be drier and better for the children's chests. It is often said that it rained for every day of their visit, but the Queen's description does not support this: no one makes hay in the rain. They visited Balmoral the next year, and Prince Albert bought it in 1852. In 1869 Sir John Ramsden, who already owned Alvie (see p.69), bought Ardverikie from Cluny Macpherson.

At the north-east end of Loch Laggan was the church of St Kenneth (see p.145), who died on 11 October in 599 or 600. He was a friend of St Columba and one day he interrupted his service in his monastery in Ireland, saying that he saw that St Columba was in danger from a storm at sea and that they must pray for his safety. An hour later, Kenneth told the monks that all was well. Later it was learned that Columba was indeed in danger when he was seen by Kenneth. From him the parish of Laggan used to be known as Laggan Choinnich (hollow of Kenneth).

The site is reached by going up the drive on the left/north of the road just west of the attractive lodge over the river Pattack. Macnab of Dalchully was a factor who was brutal to the tenants and when he drove an old woman from his land for grazing her cow there she cursed him, prophesying that 'no grass would ever grow on either that field or his grave that would be covered only with weeds'. He died and was buried here and the prediction was fulfilled, for it has always been covered by nettles and thistles. There was once a boy and a girl who were in love, but both sets of parents were against any marriage. In time they both died, and were buried on either side of the church. Rose trees sprang from the graves and met and were there for many years until they were cut down in the grounds that they encouraged superstition.

Just beyond the church is the lodge by the entrance to Adverikie. The bridge crosses the River Pattack, which rises far to the south at 3214 feet at 484726 on the north side of Ben Alder (497718) and in Loch a' Bhealaiche Bheithe (of the pass of the birch trees) (512720) on Ben Alder's shoulder. At 566903 the river turns from flowing north-east to run westward, with a final waterfall at the end of the gorge. There

Pony Trekking, Newtonmore, Badenoch. This popular way of seeing the countryside started in Kingussie. Today there are many places where sturdy ponies will carry even inexperienced riders to otherwise inaccessible places. At Borlum, Drumnadrochit, handicapped riders and drivers are specially catered for, and all riders there, whether handicapped or not, wear hard riding hats.

are several falls along its length, and it is a fast and dangerous little river. To the east of it, the col which separates its west-flowing water from the eastward flow of the Mashie is 848 feet above sea level. At 588910 there is a dam on the Mashie and much of its water is carried by a pipe which runs just south of the road to empty into the Pattack near the waterfall by the road and so, eventually, to the Alcan works. Even the headwaters of the Spey are diverted to Loch Laggan, where the salmon are said to run up to 12lb.

At 582929 is Dun-da-Lamh, a large fort, 500 x 250 feet and some 500 feet above the surrounding ground. If walkers leave the car at 601934, there is a pleasant walk for them and their dogs which reaches the military road (see below) at Spey Dam (584936).

The A86 comes to a fork at Drumgask at 614937, where the A889, part of Wade's military road, keeps to the right, past the gutted church which is where Dr Grant once housed her collection (see p.72), to pass Catlodge and join the A9 near Dalwhinnie (see p.59). The fork to the left at Catlodge passes Breacachy (see p.58) and a stone by the side of the road which is said to mark the geographical centre of Scotland.

Returning to the fork at Drumgask, the A85 runs across the river flats to Laggan, where it joins the military road from Fort Augustus to Ruthven by the Corrieyarick Pass, and turns right/ east to run along the north side of the Spey to Newtonmore (see p.72). At 645944 is Cluny Castle, built in 1805 to replace the previous building, which was barely finished when it was destroyed in 1746. This was the ancient home of the Chiefs of Clan Macpherson.

Ewen Macpherson of Cluny was hiding in his 'cage' on Ben Alder when Prince Charles stayed with him for nine days in 1746. It is said to have been built of logs for the floor, with stakes driven into them and interwoven with ropes of heather and birch twigs for the walls and roof. It was oval and moss-covered, with a large birch tree lying along its length, and it seemed to hang from this tree, which gave it the name of 'The Cage'. Some say that it was two-storeyed and could hold six or seven people. Robert Louis Stevenson, in *Kidnapped*, described it as 'hanging like a wasp's nest in a green hawthorn tree'. Nothing marks the spot, though it was known to an old shepherd who was willing to show it to visitors, but, as he grew older, it is said that the site moved to a more easily visited spot.

Cluny had another hiding place. At 674961 on the north side of Craig Dhu (which is also the rallying cry of the Macphersons) is Uamh Cluanaidh (Cluny's Cave). It was probably here that he was hidden when the soldiers came to look for him. A game of shinty was taking place close by, and for that reason the soldiers passed by, thinking that the men would not have been playing a game if their fugitive chief were close by. Between these refuges Cluny stayed hidden for some ten years 'in a seclusion partly savage, partly animated by the manners of a polite and hereditarily aristocratic society'.

On the opposite side of the road from Cluny's Cave is a house called Craig Dhu Lodge. This was the home of Robert Fitzroy, R.N., who was Captain of H.M.S. *Beagle*, in 1831 when Charles Darwin made his voyage in that ship. A meteorologist, he was Governor of New Zealand from 1843-5 and died as a Vice Admiral in 1865. His wife was a daughter of Cluny Macpherson and they are buried just east of their home.

The A86 crosses the Calder by a modern bridge and reaches Newtonmore by the Clan Macpherson Museum (see p.73).

Returning to Laggan, at 615945 take the road to the west. This is the military road, built by soldiers originally under the command of General George Wade, but, after 1732, under Major Caulfeild. The work took from 1731 to 1734 to complete and it joined Dalwhinnie on the Stirling to Inverness Line of Communication, as it was then called, to Fort Augustus in the Great Glen. It also carried, from Laggan, the road from the garrison at Ruthven to Fort Augustus. From 1750-84 this road was extended to Bernera Barracks at Glenelg on the west coast opposite Skye (see p.184).

It is a magnificent piece of civil engineering, working its way to the summit of 2,507 at 418987 by elegantly designed traverses which made the road easier for marching men. Each traverse was buttressed on the outside by a stone wall ten to fifteen feet high and flanked on the inside by a drain. From this eastern end there were originally seventeen traverses, but they were later reduced to thirteen. The road ran more steeply down to the west above the narrow gorge of the Tarff to Cullachy (376066) and so to Fort Augustus. From Dalwhinnie to Fort Augustus is thirty miles, with fourteen bridges of more than a three-foot arch.

At Blargie (600945) the farmer in the second half of the eighteenth century was Serjeant John Macpherson. It was in his arms that General James Wolfe died on the Heights of

Abraham on 13 September, 1759. Across the Spey, when the Government troops were hunting the Jacobites in 1746, they came to Dalchully (not open) (575936). A rather grubby young man with a dirty face obligingly held the officer's horse and was given a tip for doing so. His name was Ewen Macpherson of Cluny.

Near the Garva Bridge is the site of the Battle of Mamgarve, where William the Lion in 1187 defeated and killed Donald Ban MacWilliam, one of the northern claimants to the crown of Scotland.

Today it is possible to drive about seven miles along the road from Laggan to Garva Bridge (522947), which crosses the Spey. It is a two-arched bridge and was completed in 1732. This is just beyond Garvamore, where there was a King's House (528943), which was the base for the work on the road from this end. It is possible to walk through the pass to Fort Augustus, but if this is attempted, it is better to walk in two parties, exchanging keys as they meet on their way to their own cars.

A traveller saw six oxen being roasted as a treat for the 500 men who had completed 'the great road for wheeled carriages between Fort Augustus and Ruthven, it being 30th October, His Majesty's [George II] birthday'.

It was, as is well known, the Jacobite army that was the first to use the fine new road intent on warfare. Before this, in August, 1745, there was a rumour that three companies of Government troops were to march from Ruthven Barracks (see p.79) to Fort Augustus. So Donald Macdonald of Lochgarry and his men guarded the pass for three days, but the troops never came. Lochgarry wrote: 'While I lay in ambush on Corrierick there passed a Captain Switman [Swetenham] who was going to Fort William as he was reckoned a very good ingeneer. I detached four of the Glengarry Kennedys to apprehend him, which they did effectually, horses, baggage and servants. I delivered him to General Gordon [of Glenbucket] who delivered him to H.R.H. [Prince Charles Edward]'.

CHAPTER 12

Fort William to Mallaig

At 125757, north of Fort William, the A830 to Mallaig leaves
the A82. Before 1849 there was no bridge over the Lochy, the
charge for crossing by the boat in 1835 being 'one half penny'.
The first bridge was a suspension bridge, which was
demolished in 1929, when a new one was built, to be replaced
by the present bridge in 1965. Telford built the road west of
the crossing and his road has been altered over the years, being
widened and the line changed at the canal in 1965.

If the turning to the left/south, just after the bridge, is taken,
the best view of Inverlochy Castle (see p.134) can be seen
before the road reaches the railway. This road runs on through
the new town of Caol (narrows) and back to the A830 just
before the canal.

Across the canal (the bridge may be closed to let a ship
through) the B8004 turns right/north to Gairlochy (see p.187).
The township that the road goes through is now known as
Corpach (corp, a body, –ach, a place) all the way, but it used to
be a string of small groups of houses, each with a different
name. Although Corpach is mentioned in a grant of 1461, it
was then applied to the land where Caol is today. The present
Corpach was built to house the canal builders and workers and
it gradually absorbed the western houses, which were called
Kilmallie, where the church stands.

The first Corpach was on the curving bay and here the
bodies of Scottish Kings, and Norwegian Kings, too, would wait
for good weather before setting out for burial at Iona. The
Scottish Kings who died in the north and are buried at Iona
include Duncan, Macbeth and Lulach. The Norse Kings could
have come down the Great Glen, and perhaps they waited
across the water at Camusnangall (bay of the strangers). The
Ordnance Survey calls it Camusnagaul. It was from
Camusnagall that Argyll on his galley watched the second battle
of Inverlochy, 1642, (see p.126). Others who rested at Corpach
would include those to be buried on Eilean Fhiannan in Loch
Shiel (see p.224) or on one of the islands in Loch Eil itself, as a

protection from the wolves. The Gaels believed that to reach Tir-nan-Og (land of the young, the Celtic heaven) the dead body should cross water before burial.

At one time the chiefs of the Camerons lived on one of the islands in the mouth of Loch Eil, Eilean nan Craobh, Tree Island. A good, but confused, story says that when Alan became chief as a child in 1569, he lived there with his mother, who, according to this tale, was a Mackintosh and hated all Camerons. On one occasion, the Mackintoshes raided the head of Loch Eil, but were wiped out by the Camerons who were led by Domhnall, an Taillear Dubh na Tuaighe (Donald, the Black Tailor of the axe). It was therefore his duty to tell the result to the chief's mother, who had a fierce temper and kept a large stick behind the door. Donald asked for admittance, but refused to leave his axe outside. He was scarcely tactful. His hostess being a member of Clan Chattan, whose badge is a cat, he said 'Cats' skins were going cheap today'. She picked up her child and threw him on to the fire, cursing all Camerons. Before she could reach her stick, An Taillear Dubh raised his axe and threatened to use it if she did not lift the child at once. She did, and Alan was soon taken from her and put to foster parents, as was the custom.

On a small mound on the north of the road is the parish church of Kimallie. The parish is one of the largest in Scotland: it takes seven 1″ O.S. maps to trace its boundaries, reaching from Loch Leven to Glen Garry and out to Loch Quoich. The modern maps do not give this useful information. Since 1860 Fort William has had its own parish church, but it was formerly part of Kilmallie. The Reformation was fairly peaceful here, and there are still many Episcopalians and Roman Catholics in these parts:

> The Reformation came and went
> With fighting and with storming;
> The Highland clans paid little heed,
> For they were past reforming.

In the old part of the burial ground is a small unroofed building which the Reverend Dr Archibald Clerk (who was parish minister from 1844 to 1887) said was 'a ruinous aisle of

Inverlochy Castle. This great castle, largely built by the Comyns, held the southern end of the Great Glen, as Inverness Castle held the northern end. It is not surprising, therefore, that the first two artillery forts built in the mid-seventeenth century in the Highlands, with earth-backed ramparts and projecting corner bastions, were Inverlochy and Cromwell's Fort at Inverness. Two battles were fought for Inverlochy, in 1431 and 1643.

the old church'. A detailed map shows that this part of the burying ground is circular, or near enough for it to be a Celtic foundation. This was for many years the burying place of the Camerons of Lochiel. Among others here is Colonel John Cameron, younger of Fassfern, who was killed at Quatre Bras on 16 June, 1815, when commanding the 92nd, Gordon Highlanders. His father, Sir Ewen, who was given a baronetcy after his son's death, and his grandfather, John of Fassfern, brother of the Lochiel of the '45, are also buried here. Buried here, too, is Ewen Macmillan, foster-brother of Colonel John, who carried him from the battle and in whose arms he died. Ewen died in 1840. But, to find any particular grave among the brambles and nettles, wellies and a machete are necessary.

It is to Colonel John that the sixty-foot obelisk was raised, and the long epitaph is said to have been composed by Sir Walter Scott. The body was brought back to Scotland and the funeral was attended by three thousand people. There is a cairn to Colonel John's memory, on Tor Alvie in Badenoch (see p.66).

In 1963 the Government lent £10,000,000, half the cost, to the building of the pulp and paper mill at Annat, to help the people of Lochaber. Unfortunately, the business did not prosper and some of it is now closed.

Opposite the entrance to the paper mill, on the north side of the road a little west of the church, is a little wooded hill (086768), which is probably the scene of a story which was first written down in 1630. '. . . Ancient men doeth say that there was a battell foughten on ane little hill not the tenth part of a myle from this church, be certaine men which they did not know what they were. And long tyme thereafter certaine herds of that toune, and of the next toune, called Unnatt, both wenches and youthes, did on a tyme conveen with others on that hill; and the day being somewhat cold, did gather the bones of the dead men that were slayne long tyme before in that place, and did make a fire to warm them. At last they did all remove from the fire, except one maid or wench, which was verie cold, and she did remaine there for a space. She being quyetlie her alone, without anie other companie, took up her cloathes above her knees, or thereby, to warm her; a wind did come and caste the ashes upon her, and she was conceived of a man chyld. Several tymes thereafter she was verie sick, and at last was knowne to be with chyld. And then her parents did ask her the matter heiroff, which the wench could not well answer which way to satisfie them. At last she resolved them with an answer. As fortune fell upon her concerning this marvellous miracle, the chyld being borne, his name was called Gille dubh mac na'n cnaimh, that is to say, the Black Child, son to the Bones. So called, his grandfather sent him to school, and so he was a good scholar and godlie. He did built this church which doeth now stand in Lochyeld, called Kilmalee'.

But which of the layers of church buildings at Kimallie was the work of the Black Child, son to the Bones, history does not say, nor is any date given. The old name of the little hill was Cnoc nam Faobh (hillock of the spoil).

West of Annat (annaid, this is usually where an early 'mother church' stood) is the Allt Dogha. The bridge has motorway-

Ben Nevis from Corpach. The snow lies for most of the year on the 4406-foot summit of Ben Nevis, but this clear view of it is unusual, for it is normally clouded. The buildings on the left are those at the southern end of the Caledonian Canal, those in the background are Fort William. Loch Linnhe runs away to the west past the Fort, and Loch Eil comes down to the foreground.

type metal rails, but is otherwise not easily recognised. Part of the Jacobite army turned aside here to avoid any danger from the Government troops at Fort William. They crossed the saddle at about 500 feet and came down Glen Laragain by the side of the Allt Sheangain, and so up the glen to Moy, where they spent the night (see p.192).

Achdalieu (057784), now the Loch Eil Centre, was the scene of an event in the long life of Sir Ewen Cameron of Lochiel (c.1637-1719). In July 1654, soldiers from the garrison at Fort William had sailed across and were busy cutting down the trees, without permission. Lochiel, with thirty-seven clansmen, attacked the 150 soldiers and took them by surprise. Ewen tackled the sergeant, who was a good swordsman and knocked the sword out of the young man's hand. Lochiel flung his arms round the sergeant, who had also dropped his sword, and in the course of the struggle they fell and rolled into a dry burn, with the sergeant on top. He saw his sword within reach and raised himself to get it. As he lifted his head, his throat was exposed and Lochiel reached up and bit through it, saying afterwards that it was the sweetest morsel he ever tasted. But this is not the end.

Years later, Lochiel was in London and went to a barber's shop for a shave. The barber said, 'You are from the North, sir?' 'Yes,' said Lochiel, 'do you know it?' 'No, and I do not wish to. Would you believe that one of the savages there tore out my father's throat with his teeth? I wish his throat were as close to me as yours is!'

Just before this scuffle, a Cumming came from Mackenzie with a letter containing a message about Macleod's intended treachery against Charles II. Cumming was one of Macleod's retainers and did not dare to return to Skye, so Mackenzie asked Lochiel to look after him. Having no time to read the letter, Lochiel thrust an axe into Cumming's hand and said if he fought well, he would be rewarded. On three occasions Cumming saved Lochiel's life and when he had read the letter, Lochiel gave Achdalieu to Cumming and his descendants for a nominal rent. The last of this family died in 1863 and, as late as 1971, the axe was preserved. It was about two feet long, with a head measuring eight inches from the cutting edge to the point of the spike at the other end. There was a loop which slipped over the user's wrist. It was a useful weapon and is more likely to have been a Lochaber axe than the halberd which is so called today. There are representations of this short axe on tombstones, and Colonel Gardner was killed at Prestonpans in 1745 by Sorley Cameron from Corpach with a short axe.

At 022787, on the north side of the road, is Fassfern House (fasadh-fearna, house of alder) (not open), almost hidden by the trees in the summer. Here John Cameron, a younger brother of Donald of Lochiel, lived in 1745. He was so strongly against the embryo Rising that he left his house, after advising Lochiel to send a message to the Prince telling him to abandon the attempt. 'No,' said Lochiel, 'although, with neither men nor money nor arms, the campaign is madness, I should at least wait on his Royal Highness'. 'Brother', said John, 'I know you better than you know yourself. If this Prince once set his eyes on you, he will make you do as he pleases.' He was right.

The night of 21 August the Prince spent at Fassfern. The

The Glenfinnan Viaduct, on the West Highland line, carries the trains from Fort William to Mallaig. Here a steam locomotive is hauling a passenger train across it to the west. Steam locomotives run along this line during the summer months. To the right, the land runs down to the place where Prince Charles Edward Stuart raised his standard in 1745.

window of the room in which he slept is the left-hand upstairs window of the central block (or the fourth from the left of the whole of the present front, the western block being later than 1745). The bed is in the West Highland Museum in Fort William, but not on show. It is said that the next morning some of the Highlanders picked the white roses growing at Fassfern, and so the White Rose became the emblem of the Jacobites. But the sweet-scented Jacobite roses could not survive long in anyone's bonnet or plaid pin. That great modern poet, Hugh Macdiarmid, wrote:

> The Rose of all the world is not for me.
> I want for my part
> Only the little white rose of Scotland
> That smells sharp and sweet – and breaks the heart.

After the Rising, John Fassfern was arrested twice. On the second occasion, Cumming of Achdalieu was in Edinburgh on business. He heard that Government officials were on their way to search the house. Riding hard, he got to Fassfern first. Knowing where the box containing the private papers was kept, he took it and buried it in a wood. Although Fassfern was exiled for ten years, had Achdalieu not disposed of the box of papers, his fate might have been worse.

Corriebeg (995788) was the home of Mary Cameron or Mackellar, the well-known nineteenth-century Lochaber poet. Apart from her poetry, she had a wide knowledge of local history. She told a story of the raising of the Cameron Highlanders in the 1790s by Alan Cameron of Erracht. 'He called one day at the house of my mother's grandfather at Druimsallie and asked him to walk the length of Corran Ferry (fourteen miles if they went over the hills, nineteen if they took the easier route by the coast), and it was three years before he returned home again. Ailean an Errachd persuaded him.' Mrs Mackellar was entrusted with the translation into Gaelic of Queen Victoria's *Leaves from our Journal in the Highlands*. She was born in 1836, died in 1890 and is buried at Kilmallie.

At 975794 is Kinlochiel. Prince Charles spent two nights here, after the standard had been raised at Glenfinnan, but where is not known; perhaps he rode on to Fassfern to sleep, returning to his troops by day. It was here that he heard that George II had offered the then enormous sum of £30,000 for his capture, about £30 million in today's money. He retorted by offering a similar sum to whosoever 'shall seize and secure till our further orders the person of the Elector of Hanover'.

The farm of Drimsallie, mentioned above, is on the right/west of the A861, which leaves the A830 for Corran and Salen at 959795. Drimsallie (Druim na Saillie, ridge of the willows) (957788) (not open) takes its name from the ridge that lies to the north of the A830. After passing the farm, the A861 crosses the Dubhlighe (dark flood) and enters Argyll, but it is an attractive drive to the west, if you are not in a hurry.

Although Arisaig and Morar, which lie beyond, were once part of the Lordship of Lochaber, this is about the western edge of Lochaber and the end of the Cameron lands. From here west was the land of Macdonald of Clanranald.

Glenfinnan. On the flat ground here the first supporters of Prince Charles Edward Stuart gathered on 19 August, 1745. The memorial was originally a shooting lodge, but was altered and the statue erected in 1834. On the Saturday nearest to the 19th August the Glenfinnan Games are held just out of this picture. Loch Shiel stretches away behind the tower.

At Glenfinnan there is a National Trust for Scotland Visitors' Centre, where there are displays and commentaries in four languages on the Prince's campaign. To the north is a splendid railway viaduct of twenty-one arches, each fifty-feet wide, the line being a hundred feet above the bed of the Finnan. The cement columns are so large that when they were being filled with rubble, one of the carts, complete with its horse, backed too close to the edge of the hole and fell in. The horse was so injured that it was impossible to retrieve it and it was shot where it lay. The horse and cart are there today, buried in the rubble and cement. The driver did not fall in. The contractor was Robert, later Sir Robert, Macalpine, and it was partly from his work on this line that he acquired the sobriquet 'Cement Bob'.

On 18 August, 1745, Prince Charles Edward Stuart, who had landed on the north side of Loch nan Uamh (of the caves) at Borrowdale (see p.227), was rowed up Loch Shiel from Dalilia (754692) to Glenaladale (824751) where he and his companions spent the night with Alasdair Macdonald. Thus far, the whole expedition, including the rowers, had fitted into three boats. Next day he went on by water, picnicking on the way and landed, probably somewhere near the Games Field, at about 1 p.m.

There were not many to greet him, but gradually about 400 of the Clanranald Macdonalds arrived, and at about 3 p.m. some 600 Lochaber men, with Lochiel at their head, arrived to the relief of everyone. Some more Lochaber men came, probably through Glenfinnan, from Glen Pean, Kinlocharkaig and Glen Dessary, the last group being led by Miss Jenny Cameron because her brother was away from home. Sir John Macdonald, one of the Seven Men of Moidart, the Prince's companions, wrote: 'Never have I seen anything so quaintly pleasing as the march of this troop of Highlanders as they descended a steep mountain by a zigzag path'. This supports the tale that Lochiel came down Glenfinnan, but the two arrivals may have been confused.

The standard was raised by the man who was Duke of Atholl by descent, but known to the Government as the Marquess of Tullibardine, having been attained for his support of the 1715 Rising. The 'official' Duke was his younger brother. It has been well argued by Donald MacCulloch that the standard was raised on a spur below the hillock at 901806, between the road and the railway. It seems a good place for such an event.

It was with this nucleus of an army, or perhaps of a nation, that Prince Charles set off. On his way to Edinburgh he received further reinforcements, and some arms that had been landed at Castle Tioram (see p.227) from *Le du Teillay*, the ship that had brought him from France.

On the flat land formerly called Dalnaomh (holy ground) because there is an ancient burying ground here, between the road and the loch is Prince Charles' Monument. On the eastern inner side of the boundary wall is a marble tablet that used to be over the doorway to the monument. The words are an approximate version of the Gaelic written by Dr Donald Maclean, of Ardnamurchan, and the Latin translation was made by Dr Gregory, of Edinburgh, the man who invented 'Gregory's Powders'.

Castle Tioram, Moidart. This castle was the home of the chiefs of the Macdonalds of Clanranald until Alan of Clanranald, with a presentiment that he would never return from the Rising of 1715, had it burned so that no enemy of his could find shelter there. It is easily reached when the tide is out.

On this spot, where Prince Charles Edward Stuart first raised his standard, on the XIX day of August MDCCXLV, when he made the daring and romantic attempt to recover the throne lost by the imprudence of his ancestors, this column is erected by Alexander Macdonald, Esquire, of Glenaladale, to commemorate the generous zeal, the undaunted bravery, and the inviolable fidelity of his forefathers and the rest of those who fought and bled in that arduous and unfortunate enterprise.

This pillar is now, alas! also become the monument of its amiable and accomplished founder, who, before it was finished, died in Edinburgh on the VI day of January MDCCCXXXV at the early age of XXVIII years.

The tower was originally part of a small shooting-box with several rooms, but in 1834 Glenaladale demolished all but the tower and set the eight-foot-high statue of a Highlander on the top, facing up Glen Finnan. The sculptor was John Greenshields, who went to Lee Castle in Lanarkshire to look at a portrait of the Prince. There were two portraits hanging where he was told to look. One showed a young man in trews, the other a young man wearing a kilt. Greenshields made his notes on the latter and was well on with the work when he was told that the kilted man was George Lockhart of Carnwath. Greenshields simply said, 'It is much more fit than the Prince in pantaloons' and, without telling Glenaladale, he saw to its erection on the top of the tower in 1834.

There is a staircase to the top of the monument and a splendid view from the top of the sixty-three steps. For entrance, apply to the National Trust centre.

It is possible in the summer to take a trip in a boat the length of Loch Shiel to Acharacle· (676682) and back. Dr Bjorn Collinder, Professor of Finno-Ungrian languages in Uppsala, said of this journey, 'I have visited eleven European countries, but this exceeds all I have yet seen. There are places in Làpland and Northern Italy that almost approach it in beauty, but they do not quite equal it'.

A long way down Loch Shiel, at 753684, is Eilean Fhianain (St Finnan's Isle). This was a favoured burial place. John Macdonald of Moidart, who led the victorious allies at Blar na Leine in 1544 (see p.130) and who died at Castle Tioram (662724) (see p.227) in 1584, is one of the many buried here, and there are many cairns on the route between the castle and the island. It was always important to approach the landing place on the island deiseal (sun-wise).

The last Episcopalian minister of Islandfinnan was Alexander Macdonald, better known as Maighstir Alasdair, Maighstir (Master) showing that he had a university degree. He refused to conform to Presbyterianism after 1688 and, though he was formally deposed in 1697, he continued to minister to his people, regularly walking from his home at Dalilia (734694) (Dal an Leigh, the Physician's meadow) to Kilchoan (487638) in Ardnamurchan to take the service and back again, some fifty miles in all. He was the sort of minister who drove a writer in 1750 to say that 'the People of Ardnamurchan and the Stuarts of Appin are the most deeply poisoned with Disaffection to our Happy Constitution in Church and State of any people I ever knew. They Idolize the Non-Juring Clergy and can scarcely keep their temper when speaking of Presbyterians'.

Maighstir Alasdair lived at Dalilia and died in 1724, leaving a large family. One of his sons was Alasdair mac Mhaighstir Alasdair, Alexander the son of Mr Alexander, one of the greatest Gaelic poets. He largely earned his living as a schoolmaster, and published his first book, *A Galick and English Vocabulary*, in 1751, the first Gaelic dictionary to be printed as a separate book. He joined Prince Charles and became a Captain under Alan Macdonald of Morar, who raised Clanranald's tenants in and around Arisaig. This open support of Prince Charles lost Alasdair his job, but the Act of Indemnity in 1748 allowed him to live openly, first on Canna and then in Glen Uig, but he finally settled at Sandaig on the south side of Rudha Arisaig where he died about 1780 and was buried in the now ruined Kilmory, close to the Roman Catholic church in Arisaig, because the weather was too bad for his body to be carried to Eilean Fhianain. He left a legacy to Gaelic literature of poems which ranged from political to martial to licentious. Alasdair's poetry is so rich in language and in classical allusions that 'he was excelled by none in the merit of his war songs'. Gaelic poetry is always difficult to translate, but Professor Blackie's paraphrase of *Birlin Chlann Raonuill* (Clanranald's galley) is described as being as successful 'as a translation of Gaelic poetry ever admits of '.

On the flat land on the west side of the head of the loch, at 901805, the Glenfinnan Games are held on the Saturday nearest to 19th August. Above this flat land is the Roman Catholic church, consecrated in 1873, where the bell hangs on a frame outside.

Loch Eilt (of the hinds) divides the road from the railway, but they come together at the west end of the loch. At 779831 there is a parking place on the south side of the road and, walking back to the bend in the road and under the railway, there is a path through the hills, passing Prince Charles' Cave at 87968549, to Meoble (795877) and the pier at Camas Luinge (bay of the ships) on Loch Morar (784893) which is the only other way to reach Meoble.

It was at Meoble that Simon Fraser, Lord Lovat, surrendered to the Government forces. He was over 80 and very lame and unfit for hiding in the hills. *The Scots Magazine* in 1747 reported that 'Captain Campbell of Achnacrosan found that unhappy

Lord lying on two feather beds, not far from the side of the lake; to whom he surrendered'.

At 767824 the A861, signposted for Ardgour and Strontian, turns south from the A830 to pass Inverailort, where the Special Force, later called the Commandos, trained under Colonel Coates, the Commanding Officer, and Lord Lovat, the chief instructor. This is a new length of road, which was opened in 1966. It runs round by Glen Uig to Acharacle and has magnificent views to the west as it runs along the east side of Loch Ailort. There are fish farms in the sheltered water at the head of the loch and parking places where the views are particularly good. The road turns inland at Glen Uig (of the bay) but a small road turns off here to the west to Salamanan (661775) where there was a Roman Catholic seminary in the early nineteenth century.

The A861 climbs steeply up Glen Uig, the present road running along what was a track when Prince Charles went over it on 11 August, 1745, and down to the sea again at Loch Morar below An Dun (682736). At Kinlochmoidart, where Prince Charles stayed for a week, are what are called The Seven Men of Moidart, consisting once of seven beech trees, each representing one of Prince Charles' original supporters, but now their numbers are diminished. Where the road crosses the river Moidart, the new bridge gives a most attractive view of its predecessor, just upstream. From here the road reverts to being narrow with passing places.

Climbing up again to the next pass, there is a cairn erected to Captain Robertson in 1868 to the west of the road, more or less at the top of the pass. At 719702 a turning to the left/east leads to Dalilia, where Alasdair mac Mhaighstir Alasdair was born and grew up. A track leads on to the pier opposite Eilean Fhiannan (see p.224). A house near the Roman Catholic church at Mingarry (686695) holds Clanranald's banner. It is very old and faded and is sometimes called *The Fairy Flag*.

Just before the road reaches Shiel Bridge, a turning to the right/north at 676693 runs along the right bank of the Shiel, past the site of Dorlin House, to the end of the road. Leave the car here and, if the tide is out, walk across the sand to the ruin of Castle Tioram (dry castle) (663724). It was built by

Amie MacRuarie, who was the first wife of John of Islay, Lord of the Isles. John either divorced or abandoned Amie, 'a good and virtuous gentlewoman', in order to marry Princess Margaret, daughter of Robert II. The castle passed in 1373 to Amie's son by John, Ranald, from whom comes Clanranald.

When Alan Macdonald of Clanranald was killed at the battle of Sheriffmuir on 13 November, 1715, his clansmen hesitated, but continued the fight when Glengarry shouted at them, 'Tomorrow for mourning, today for revenge!' Alan had had a premonition that he might not return and, before he left, he ordered that Castle Tioram should be burned, so that no enemy could ever live in it.

To the south of the A861 before Shiel Bridge lie great flat mosses, and at Shiel Bridge the road runs out of Inverness-shire. If it is followed, a long circuit up Loch Sunart, past Strontian (which gave its name to Strontium 90) and through Glen Tarbert to Inversanda, where the road from Loch Aline joins it, brings us to Loch Linnhe. At Corran Ferry (017636) there is a car ferry to the east side and the A82 (see p.139), but it is a pleasant drive to continue up the west side of Loch Linnhe and then along the south side of Loch Eil to join the A830 at 959795.

Returning to Lochailort, the A830 soon turns into a single-tracked road with passing places as it winds its way between the hills and the sea and over the pass to Loch nan Uamh (of the caves). Just south of the road at 721844 and well signposted is the cairn that marks the place where Prince Charles embarked in 1746. At 696849 is the private road to Borrowdale Farm, and round the next bend is the entry to Arisaig House, now a hotel, and the bay where Prince Charles landed on 25 July, 1745. He stayed at Borrowdale House, or on board *Le du Teillay*, guarded by relays of Macdonalds, until 11 August. The house was burned in 1746.

It was at Borrowdale that Lochiel met the Prince, to try to persuade him that this was not the time for a Rising. Neither side would give way and at last the Prince said, 'In a few days, with the few friends I have, I will raise the Royal Standard, and proclaim to the people of Britain that Charles Stuart is come over to claim the crown of his fathers – to win it or to perish in the attempt. Lochiel, who, my father has often told me, was our firmest friend, may stay at home and learn from the newspapers the fate of his Prince.' This was too much for Lochiel's heart. Forgetting the common sense of his head, he said: 'No, I will share the fate of my Prince and so shall every man over who nature or fortune has given me any power'. Had the Prince's appeal failed, it is unlikely that the Rising, and its aftermath, would have happened.

During the Second World War Arisaig House was a headquarters for training the men and women of the Special Operations Executive (S.O.E.) before they were smuggled into occupied Europe to co-ordinate the resistance movements. They were of different nationalities and each had a separate base along the road, at Traigh, Camusdarach, Swordland and over at Inverie in Knoydart.

From here the road passes through beautiful woodland until it reaches Arisaig (658864) at the head of Loch na Ceall, which is quite a sizeable community, with a hotel and a railway station. Beyond the church the view suddenly opens out. To the north is Skye, the sharp peaks of the Coolins clearly visible on a good day. West are Rum, with its pointed hills, and Eigg, the Sgurr of Eigg being an outstanding feature of the view. The road runs north, past the oddly-named Back of Keppoch, where the crofts can be seen with their long strips of land inland of the caravans. Beyond Traigh (beach) with its creamy sands and the silver sands of Morar (675915) is Camusdarach (bay of the oaks).

A Macdonald, a native of Camusdarach, served in the Napoleonic wars under Colonel Simon Macdonald, whose tenant he was. The wars ended and in course of time the Colonel died and was buried at Arisaig. His successor, one Aeneas Macdonell, began to evict the tenants and on his list was the old soldier who, like so many others, had nowhere to go. Early on the day that he was to leave his home for ever, he went to the burying ground to say farewell to his old Colonel. Later in the day, the bailiff, who was on his way to evict the old man, heard cries from over the wall of the burying ground. 'Arise, arise out of there, Colonel Simon! Arise and help me! Many a day I followed you in Egypt and in Ireland and today I am in dire need! Arise out of thy grave and help me!' The

The Harbour, Mallaig. This was once one of the foremost herring harbours, but is now the busiest prawn port in Europe. The picture, taken in 1983, shows the harbour packed with fishing boats, so it was probably taken on a Saturday or Sunday, when the fishermen would not be at sea.

bailiff was so frightened that he turned back and never disturbed the old soldier.

At 682923 the road and the railway cross the river Morar. A turning to the right, after the road has passed under the railway, leads to Loch Morar and runs along the north side to 726927. From this point a track continues over the hills to Tarbet on Loch Nevis. Loch Morar is seventeen miles long and two miles wide. At its eastern end it is no less than 180 fathoms deep, 1080 feet, the deepest inland water in Britain and, except for one Scandinavian lake, the deepest in western Europe. The sea does not reach that depth until about 200 miles to the west. Like Loch Ness, which is also a deep loch, Morar has a monster. As with Nessie, more people have seen Morag that will admit to it. Returning from the end of the road, keep to the right at the church and rejoin the A830.

From here the road runs on to Mallaig and ends at the harbour. Taking the turning to the right/east in the village,

229

follow it round the south side of the bay, to the very end of the road at Mallaigvaig (little Mallaig), with fine views in all directions.

In 1900 there were only three houses at Mallaig, round-cornered and thatched. In 1901, the railway came and from then Mallaig has flourished in an unplanned way. When the West Highland Line wished to built a pier for the fishing boats to land their catch, they had to negotiate with the Lovat Estates, who made the stipulation that Lord and Lady Lovat, their sons and daughters, their manservants and maidservants, might continue to collect whelks and cockles from the foreshore at low tide. This agreement continues to this day, but it is doubtful whether the Lovats have ever claimed their rights.

Before Mallaig was developed, the fishing boats put into Tarbet on Loch Nevis (791923) where there is a safe harbour. The fish landed there was principally for export to Scandanavia. When the pier was built at Mallaig, with connections to the south, this trade vanished from Tarbet.

Mallaig was once a famous herring port, but in 1976, as so often happens, the herring left. Today it is the busiest prawn port in Europe, exporting its catches to Spain and France. Although it was designed to be a railhead for the fishing, most of the catches now go out by lorry, but the railway is still busy, carrying up to 20,000 passengers a year. Mallaig is a lively place, with the Fishermen's Mission being the centre for all sorts of events. The car ferry runs across the Sound of Sleat (pronounced Slate) to Armadale in the Sleat peninsula of Skye, where there is the Clan Donald Centre, well worth a visit, even by those who are not Macdonalds.

There are passenger ferries to Canna, Eigg and Muck, as well as to Inverie in Knoydart. From there it is possible to get by boat to Tarbet (791923) on the south side of Loch Nevis and on to Camusrory (856957) on the north side, where there is a Mountain Rescue Post. Only by boat is Knoydart easily reached; the alternative entry is by foot from Loch Arkaig or Kinloch Hourn. It is one of the remotest parts of Scotland and was part of the lands of Clan Donald. After a final stormy and difficult time for the Macdonalds in the eighteenth century, 'Knoydart was the last of the broad territories, which once stretched from the Great Glen to the Sound of Sleat, to remain in the hands of the Glengarry family, from whom the MacDonells of Barrisdale sprang'.

Rum is a more private island, being run by the Nature Conservancy Council, largely for the study of deer, though sea eagles, brought from Norway, are being reared there, with the hope that they will settle and nest again in Scotland. It is possible to arrange to go there and it is worth the trouble. Very recently archaeological remains have been found on Rum, dating from about 5000 B.C.

The West Highland Railway runs from Fort William to Mallaig, sometimes with a steam engine to draw the train. It is a beautiful trip, but does not show all that can be seen from a car.

CHAPTER 13

Inverness to Beauly (the old A9)

What was the A9 to the north before the building of the Kessock Bridge is now the A862 going to Beauly and then on into Ross-shire and points north. Either cross the Ness Bridge to the west, continue to the first traffic lights and there turn right/north, or cross the Friars' Bridge and turn right at the roundabout; either way this is the A862.

The Caledonian Canal is crossed at 654457, below the Muirtown Locks, and the road goes on beyond the roundabout to Clachnaharry. The older part of the fishing village lies to the north, between the railway and the Beauly Firth, but before reaching it, notice on the right the large Muirtown Basin and, on the left, a handsome building Clachnaharry House, the headquarters of the Caledonian Canal. On the wall by the road outside the house is a tablet with a poem 'Originally written by Robert Southey to his friend Thomas Telford, at the opening of the Caledonian Canal in October, 1822':

> When these capacious basins by the laws
> Of the subjacent element, receive
> The Ship, descending or upraised eight times
> From stage to stage with unfelt agency
> Translated, fitliest may the marble here
> Record the Architect's immortal name.
> TELFORD it was by whose presiding mind
> The whole great work was plann'd and perfected;
> TELFORD, who o'er the vale of Cambrian Dee
> Aloft in air at giddy height upborne
> Carried his Navigable road; and hung
> High o'er Menai's Strait the bending Bridge:
> Structures of more ambitious enterprise
> Than Minstrels in the age of old Romance
> To their old Merlin's magic lore ascribed.
> Nor hath he for his native land performed
> Less in this proud design; and when his Piers
> Around her coast from many a Fisher's Creek

Unsheltered else, and many an ample Port
Repel the assailing storm: and when his Roads
In beautiful and sinous line far seen
Wind with the vale and win the long ascent,
Now o'er the deep morass sustained, and now
Across ravine or glen or estuary
Opening a passage through the wilds, subdued.

This effusion by the Poet Laureate was erected at the Centenary of the opening of the Canal.

At 647464 is a large conglomerate boulder, the actual Clach-na-fhaire (the stone of watching) from which a look-out could see far along the firth. Just before the bridge over the railway, rather high up on the left/south, is the base of an obelisk put up by Huntly Robert Duff of Muirtown in 1821 to commemorate a battle in 1333, 1378, or perhaps 1454, between the Clan Chattan and the Munros. The latter had raided into Perthshire and had brought their gains past Moy (see p.48), where Mackintosh demanded his *road-collop*, a sort of tax for allowing passengers through his lands. This was agreed, but then Mackintosh asked for more and the Munros refused and set off for home. They were pursued by Mackintosh and Clan Chattan, but managed to send off the cattle by one route over the Ness while they turned to fight near Clachnaharry.

'The conflict was such as might have been expected from men excited to revenge by a long and inveterate enmity. Quarter was neither sought nor granted; after an obstinate struggle, Mackintosh was killed . . . John Munro, tutor of Foulis, was left for dead upon the field: his kinsmen were not long of retaliating. Having collected a sufficent force, they marched, in the dead of the night, for the Isle of Moy, where the chief of the Mackintoshes resided. By the aid of some planks which they had carried with them, and now put together, they crossed to the isle, and glutted their thirst for revenge by the murder or captivity of all the inmates.'

Once over the railway bridge, look carefully on the left/south of the road for the Fuaran Priseag (the Precious Spring) at 645465. It is said to have been blessed by St Cessog, and from his time it was known to be a cure for eye trouble.

Further on, on the right/north is Bunchrew House (621459), now a hotel. It was first a 'castle' built by Simon Fraser, Lord

Lovat, about 1620. There are two armorial marriage stones
dated 1621 with his intials and those of Jean Stewart, his wife.
Little of the old building survived the nineteenth-century
rebuilding, but, since a description in 1847 says, 'A mean
looking building "half barn, half dwelling house", and a
ruinous archway, are all that remains of the ancient manor-
house', some rebuilding was necessary.

Bunchrew was bought by John Forbes in 1670 and there, in
1685, when it was 'a small unpretending, but not
uncomfortable house by the sea-side', John's grandson,
Duncan, later Lord President Forbes, was born. Although he
also owned Culloden House, Bunchrew was always his
favourite home, where he 'delighted to receive and entertain
many of the more highly respectable visitors who came to the
neighbourhood, who were quite enchanted with the President's
affable manners and the decorations of his estate'. Duncan
Forbes did his best to avert the Rising of 1745, and when it was
over, he did all that he could to stop the appalling behaviour of
the Government troops, but 'the fiendish thirst for blood
evinced by the Duke of Cumberland could not be satiated'.
Worn out by his efforts, he died in 1747. 'His name and fame',
wrote John Maclean in 1848, when he was in his 102nd year,
'will live for generations yet to come'.

The pile of stones in the firth between Bunchrew and Coul
Point on the Black Isle, which can be seen at low tide at
618473, is Carn Dubh, one of the five crannogs, or artificial
islands, in the Beauly Firth.

A turning off the A862 at 608457 leads under the railway to
Kirkton, the site of the Parish Church of Fernua, which was
dedicated to St Curadan. It is now part of the parish of Kirkhill
(formerly Wardlaw). There is a walled burying ground by the
farm, and just to the south, at 604449, is Tom a'Chaisteal
(Castle Hill). This is a strongly defended site, with burns on two
sides and boggy ground on the third. Some stone foundations
still survive, but little is known of its history. In the thirteenth
century Thomas, baron of Fernua, was a vassal of the Bisset
Lords of Lovat and the Aird.

To the west, at 597451, is Cnoc a'Chinn (Hill of the Head),
an oval dun 120 feet by 70 feet, with overgrown stone
ramparts. Between the dun and the sea is Phopachy, a farm

Fiddle Making. Mr Donald Riddle, 'Riddle the Fiddle', of Kirkhill, has earned his name not only by making fiddles, but also as a fine fiddle player. The *Inverness Courier* of 14 June, 1988, reporting the Queen's Birthday Honours List, announced the award of the British Empire Medal to 'Mr Donald Riddle of Kirkhill of the Highland Strathspey and Reel Society'.

house and once the home of the Reverend James Fraser, the last Episcopal minister of Kirkhill, or, as it was then called, Wardlaw. He wrote *The Chronicles of the Frasers,* better known as *The Wardlaw Manuscript,* an interesting and informative account of seventeeth-century life, which was published by the Scottish History Society in 1905. At Bogroy, the inn was once said to have been the haunt of smugglers. Almost opposite, the disused church has become Highland Aromatics, a factory, which is open to the public, for the making of good soap. At 557444 a turning to the left/south leads to Moniack Castle (see p.110) and the A862 goes on to the west. At 526440, just beyond a by-road, also from Moniack (these roads were formerly part of the A9 until the road was altered to avoid the right-angled bridge near Reelig), the A833 joins from Kiltarlity.

But, turning right/north along the B9164 to Kirkhill, on the right/north, is the entrance to Newton House. Just inside is a fine circular doocot (562454) dated 1783. Before the wide cultivation of root crops to carry plenty of cattle through the winter, the only fresh meat for many months of the year until the young stock were available, came from the pigeons kept in these doocots. Rabbits, though common in England, were not so in the Highlands. It is said that some of the Highlanders who fought at Culloden in 1746 could have seen a wolf, but could not have seen a rabbit.

Kirkhill today is a village of mostly modern houses, but if we carry on over the cross roads at the top of the hill, the remains of the old church of St Mary, Wardlaw is reached. At the east end of the church is the reroofed mausoleum of the Lovat family (not open). Its curious conical belfry was built by William Ross in 1643.

Returning to the B9164 and travelling west, the first turning to the right/north runs down a narrow road to Wester Lovat, where the steading is on the site of Lovat Castle (539461). After about 1220 the Bisset Lords of Lovat had a timbered earthwork here, which was followed by the sixteenth century stone courtyard fortified house of the Frasers of Lovat. Return to the railway and turn right/west; the ferryman's cottage lies at 528454, and beyond it the side road joins the B9164 at Dunballoch on its way to the A862. Close to Dunballoch, at 524450, is the site of the first church in this parish, referred to as dedicated to St Maurice, but this is probably a rough translation from a Gaelic saint's name, perhaps St Moroc (see p.175). A church was built at Wardlaw as early as 1220, when the old church was abandoned on orders from Rome. Because the new church was built on a hill, it was known as Kirkhill.

Turning right/west on to the A862 for Beauly, the road runs down to the river, at Lovat Bridge, which was built by George Burn, one of Telford's men, about 1813. This is the present-day descendant of the ancient Stock Ford of Ross, the crossing of the River Beauly which seems to have been a moveable site, depending on the state of the river. Just across the bridge the A862 keeps to the right for Beauly, while the A831 goes straight on (see p.175).

The farm on the right/east of the road has the curious name of Teawig, one of the few Norse names in this part of

Inverness-shire. Teawig is a mixture of Gaelic and Norse, Tea, Taigh, a house, and wig, uig, wick, vic, a harbour. The sea must once have come close to the site of the house for its name to be The House by the Harbour. The very flat land between the hills to the west and the firth supports this idea.

The modern building on the left, just over the steep railway bridge, is Highland Craftpoint, where varying exhibitions of crafts are to be seen from the beginning of June to the middle of September, Mondays to Fridays only, from 10.00 to 17.00.

It seems that the Gaelic name for Beauly was Manachain (place of monks), and it was the monks who referred to it as 'Bellus Locus', or Beautiful Place, which, in its turn, was 'frenchified' into Beaulieu, which came to be Beauly. The story linking the name with Mary, Queen of Scots, is likely to be – just a story. As it is seen today, the village is the result of the planning of Thomas Fraser of Strichen, who was created Lord Lovat in 1837. He was a man of ideas and the village was improved and laid out in the 1840s, with a wide rectangular square in the middle, and roads running off at right angles. The monument in the Square recalls the raising in 1900 by Lord Lovat of the Lovat Scouts who served in the South African War.

In the newly laid out area at the north of the Square is the Mercat Cross. This was first set up at Bridgend c.1420 by Hugh Fraser of Lovat. In the 1870s it stood in front of a row of cottages which were destroyed by fire, and for the next fifty years the cross lay broken in a coal yard. Then a journalist, William Ross, managed to get it rebuilt in the 1920s. On a night during the last war some of the Lovat Scouts were in cheerful mood and one decided to climb the old cross. He flung his arms round it and the top stone fell on him and killed him. Later it was rebuilt, but is not as tall as it once was.

Beyond the cross is all that remains of the Valliscaulian Priory. This was built on the site of St Drostan's Church. The order was an unusual one, only two other houses being found in Scotland, at Ardchattan in Argyll (971349), founded by Duncan Macdougal of Lorn, where the ruins and gardens are open to visitors, and at Pluscarden in Moray (142756), which was founded by Alexander II and has been restored by Benedictine monks, who are experts in stained-glass windows,

among other things. Beauly was founded about 1230 by John
Bisset, Lord of the Aird, the same man who built St Maurice's
Church (see p.236) and also Kiltarlity Church (see p.162).
Valliscaulian means 'of the valley of cabbages' and the mother
house in France, from which the name came, lies in *Le Val des
Choux*. The remaining monks of this order merged with the
Cistercians, when that order was revived in 1757. All the
buildings, except the walls of the thirteenth-century church,
have gone, but it is worth going to visit it (guide books
available) to see the monument to Sir Kenneth Mackenzie of
Gairloch, who died in 1591, and a Pictish symbol stone, which
was found at Balblair (511453). Among the many who are
buried here are the Lord Lovat who was killed at Blar na Leine
and his son who was killed with him (see p.130).

There is a tale of a Tailor of Beauly, who, though timid by
nature, was a very brave man when he had taken drink. One
evening he undertook, for a bet, to make a pair of trousers
inside the Priory at night. He provided himself with a candle
and sat down on a gravestone to do his work. All at once a deep
voice from a little distance said 'Behold, Tailor, the hand
without flesh or blood rising up beside you!' 'I see that, but I
must finish my work,' answered the Tailor, sewing on busily.
The hand gradually came nearer, repeating its message, but
still he sewed on. With the last stitch completed, the not so bold
Tailor fled to the door, with the hand so close behind him that,
though it failed to catch him, the marks of the fleshless fingers
can be still seen on the moulding of the door.

The monks made a harbour at Beauly which was used by
ships of up to 150 tons burden until the Great War, carrying in
lime and leaving with farm produce. Only in 1967, when the
houses at Riverside were built, did the old wooden wharf
finally disappear. Another useful thing that has disappeared is
the Spa (523461). This was started by Lord Lovat in 1895 with
the idea of rivalling Strathpeffer, where mineral springs had
been found and where many went on holiday, or for health
reasons. It seems to have been successful in 1902, when Mr
Pollock wrote about the village, but it probably ended in 1914.

The Phipps Public Hall, a handsome red stone building, was
the gift of Mr Phipps from Pittsburgh, who had a lease of
Beaufort Castle around the turn of the century. It was built, at

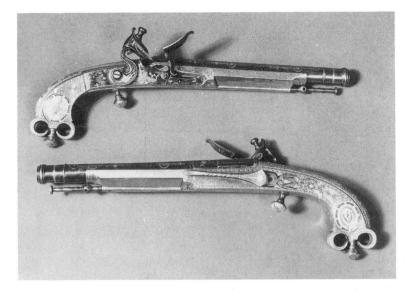

Highland Pistols. These gold pistols, now in the Inverness Museum, were made by Murdoch of Doune, Perthshire, a famous centre for pistol-making, and were given to the Duke of Clarence, later King William IV. Engraved on them is 'To His Royal Highness William Henry, Duke of Clarence, a Prince who, from early youth on various and arduous military service has given signal proofs of inheriting the virtues, the valour and magnanimity which so eminently distinguish his illustrious family. As a testimony of pure respect and gratitude, this piece of Highland armour is humbly presented by Lieutenant Colonel John Small, commander 2nd Battalion of His Majesty's late British Infantry, 1790'.

a cost of £4000, in 1902, and included a library, as did the hall at Kiltarlity, built at a cost of £900, which Mr Phipps gave to that village in 1900.

The A862 runs north past the large Roman Catholic church, dating from 1864, and through large fields of raspberries. The signs go up when the fruit can be bought, either picked by the buyer, or ready picked. Just before the road rises to Wind Hill, it crosses a small burn and leaves the county of Inverness.

Further Reading

Bowman, J.E., *The Highlands and Islands, a 19th Century tour*, 1986.
Boyd, E. Orr, *Cross Country Walks in the West Highlands*, 1952.
Cameron, A.D., *The Caledonian Canal*, 1972.
Close Brooks, Joanna, ed., *Exploring Scotland's Heritage, The Highlands*, 1986.
Drummond-Norie, W., *Loyal Lochaber*, 1898.
Forbes, Robert, *The Lyon in Mourning*, 1895-7.
Fresson, E.E., *Air Road to the Isles*, 1967.
Grant, I.F., *Along a Highland Road*, 1980.
         Everyday Life on an Old Highland Farm, 1981.
Hall, John Inglis, *Fishing a Highland Stream*, 1987.
Henderson, Thomas, *The Findhorn, the River of Beauty*, 1932.
Hopkins, Paul, *Glencoe and the End of the Highland War*, 1986.
Kilgour, W.T., *Lochaber in War and Peace*, 1908.
Lauder, Sir Thomas Dick, *The Morayshire Floods*, 1830.
Lenman, Bruce, *The Jacobite Risings in Britain, 1689-1746*, 1980.
         The Jacobite Families of the Great Glen, 1984.
Lockley, Ronald, *The Lodge above the Waterfall*, 1987.
MacCulloch, Donald, *Romantic Lochaber*, 1939/1948/1971.
Macdonald of Castleton, Donald, *Clan Donald*, 1978.
         Slaughter Under Trust, 1965/1982.
Macgregor, Jimmie, *On the West Highland Way*, 1985.
Maclean, Alasdair, *A Macdonald for the Prince*, 1982.
Maclean, Calum, *The Highlands*, 1959.
Maclean, L.M., ed., *The Hub of the Highlands*, 1975.
         Old Inverness in Pictures, 1978.
         The Middle Ages in the Highlands, 1981.
         The Glen Urquhart Story, by Alastair Mackell, 1982.
         An Inverness Miscellany, Number 1, 1983.
         The Seventeenth Century in the Highlands, 1986.
         An Inverness Miscellany, Number 2, 1987.
Maclean of Dochgarroch, Loraine, *Indomitable Colonel*, 1986.
Macrae, Kenneth, *Highland Ways and Byways*, 1973.
Meldrum, E.A., *From Loch Ness to the Aird*, 1978.
         Inverness, 1982.
         From Nairn to Loch Ness, 1983.
Mitchell, Joseph, *Reminiscences of my Life in the Highlands*, 1883/1971.
Murray, Sarah, *The Beauties of Scotland*, 1799/1982.
Nethersole Thomson, Desmond, and Adam Watson, *The Cairngorms*, 1981.

Pochin Mould, D., *The Roads from the Isles,* 1950.
Prebble, John, *Culloden,* 1961.
             The Highland Clearances, 1963/1971.
             Glencoe, 1966.
Simpson, W. Douglas, *Portrait of the Highlands,* 1965/1979.
The Old Statistical Account of Scotland, Vol. xvii, 1793.
The New Statistical Account of Scotland, Vol. xiv, 1854.
Stevenson, David, *Alasdair MacColla and the Highland Problem,* 1980.
Stewart of Ardvorlich, John, *The Camerons,* 1974.
Stewart, Katharine, *A Croft in the Hills,* 1960.
             Crofts and Crofting, 1980.
Taylor, William, *The Military Roads of Scotland,* 1976.
Transactions of the Gaelic Society of Inverness, 1874 onwards.
Transactions of the Inverness Scientific Society and Field Club, 1875-1925.
Tranter, Nigel, *The Pegasus Book of Scotland,* 1964.
Weir, Tom, *The Scottish Lochs,* 1980.
Youngson, A.J., *Beyond the Highland Line,* 1974.

Fiction

Black, William, The Novels of.
Broster, D.K., *The Flight of the Heron.*
             The Gleam in the North.
             The Dark Mile.
Caird, Janet, *The Loch.*
Gunn, Neil, *The Drinking Well.*
Lauder, Sir Thomas Dick, *The Wolfe of Badenoch.*
Macnicol, Eona, *The Halloween Hero.*
             The Jail Dancing.
Macpherson, Ian, *Land of our Fathers.*
Munro, Neil, *The New Road.*
Scott, Sir Walter, *The Legend of Montrose.*

Index